Current Controversies in Marriage and Family

Current Controversies in Marriage and Family

Edited by
Harold Feldman
Margaret Feldman

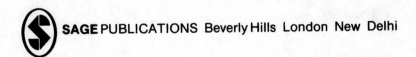
SAGE PUBLICATIONS Beverly Hills London New Delhi

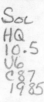

For information address:

SAGE Publications, Inc.
275 South Beverly Drive
Beverly Hills, California 90212

SAGE Publications India Pvt. Ltd.
M-32 Market
Greater Kailash I
New Delhi 110 048 India

SAGE Publications Ltd
28 Banner Street
London EC1Y 8QE
England

Printed in the United States of America

Library of Congress Cataloging in Publication Data

Main entry under title:

Current controversies in marriage and family.

    1. Family life education—United States—Addresses,
essays, lectures. 2. Marriage—United States—Addresses,
essays, lectures. I. Feldman, Harold. II. Feldman,
Margaret.
HQ10.5.U6C87 1985   306.8   85-1934
ISBN 0-8039-2440-2
ISBN 0-8039-2441-0 (pbk.)

FIRST PRINTING

CONTENTS

INTRODUCTION

The chapters in this book have been brought together to illumine current controversies about marriage and family studies by using sets of paired comparisons (or sometimes three or four). Most courses and textbooks on family science do not deal directly with controversy because it is assumed that the value aspects of the course are not appropriate for the academic setting or that research evidence will resolve the issues without requiring explicit discussion of the values involved. It is the thesis of the editors that these value questions should be examined in an explicit manner as a significant function of academia.

We deliberately sought a wide range of styles of presentation and variability in the kinds of evidence presented. Some of the essays in this volume have a religious orientation and have adopted the Bible as their major source, others have taken a journalistic style, but most have used research studies to bolster their points of view. There is a significant relationship between style and substance, and it is the reader's task to evaluate this relationship.

Everyone can learn a good deal by starting with an open mind and by searching for insights from a person with whom one at first disagrees. Those who are trained to look only to research evidence might examine their own perspective and look to the logic of their argument and selectivity of evidence, while those who focus on a biblical or journalistic perspective might look to the research evidence available.

We invite the reader to look for opportunities to change and to attempt to find a new synthesis. This new synthesis does not necessarily mean a need to give up strongly held beliefs without examining their virtue, but to be open enough to make change possible. The moral developmentalist Perry (1968) proposes that there are three levels of moral development. The first is unexamined dualism, where the person has uncritically accepted a set of ideas about what is correct or right without thinking about them. For this person there is only one truth. The second level Perry called relativism. This level implies that there is no single truth but many truths, each equal to the others in value. The third level he called commitment within a framework of relativism. The person has now taken a position and made a commitment but recognizes that there are other valid perspectives, some of which have important points that need to be dealt with. It is the task of the student to find this new synthesis.

Before each section of the book we have suggested a number of questions and activities to facilitate use of the material in the classroom. There is one discussion question and an activity for each article and an integrative question and activity for each topic and each section of the book. One assignment that students should have is to make up a set of questions and activities to aid their and the class's learning. Perhaps a good question is as valuable as a good answer. Also, we have included a few questions at the end that are integrative of the entire set. We are sure that you will find many other ways to use this material in addition to those presented by us, but you may find some of our suggestions useful. We would be interested in hearing how classes have used this book.

We want to thank all of the authors for their part in making the book possible. Although we set the task to take an extreme position, and occasionally offered editorial advice about sharpening a perspective, the major credit and responsibility for each article rests with the author. Bon voyage!

—Harold Feldman
Margaret Feldman

REFERENCE

PERRY, W. G., Jr. (1968) Forms of Intellectual and Ethical Development in the College Years: A Scheme. New York: Holt, Rinehart & Winston.

I. Premarital Relations

This section deals with three controversial premarital issues. One focuses on the use of orthodox or unorthodox means of finding persons to date, the second deals with the value of virginity as opposed to the necessity of premarital sexual relations, and the third concerns the criteria for selection of a marital partner. The lines are quite clearly drawn within each set of chapters: For each topic, one takes a traditional and the other a more liberal viewpoint.

DISCUSSION QUESTIONS

(1) How can the traditional institutions of date selection be made more accessible?

(2) What are some factors that lead persons to use nonconventional means of date selection? Why aren't these methods more frequently used?

(3) How might Dr. Smart respond to Mr. Becker's six criticisms of personal ads?

(4) Dr. Broderick suggests that we are in a postpermissive era. Is there any truth in this assertion? Is virginity functional today?

(5) Why do you think having or not having premarital sex seems to make little difference in terms of later marital relations, as Rubin reports?

(6) Attempt to find a synthesis of the apparently contradictory positions in regard to premarital sex.

(7) What factors keep people from marrying outside of their reference groups?

(8) Is loving different people at different points in one's life healthier than loving only one person throughout life? Discuss.

(9) Make explicit the theoretical bases for the two points of view about mate selection and indicate the relationship of the theories to each other.

(10) Discuss the more traditional-less traditional underpinnings of the three issues. How might the same values be manifested in other behaviors, such as voting behavior and religiosity, and to what extent are they independent?

CLASS ACTIVITIES

(1) Have the class be a meeting of the community youth activities board consisting of school, church, neighborhood, and workplace members called to find ways to help young people get to know each other. Suggest ways to increase the effectiveness of these traditional places.

(2) Do a skit illustrating behavior in a singles bar. Preparation might involve visiting one first. Have the class discuss how typical these behaviors are and evaluate their effects on the persons. What types of behavior seem more effective and why?

(3) Suppose you are a parent and your 25-year-old daughter asks your advice about some of the less traditional ways of getting a date. Enact a skit illustrating what you would tell her based on the material from these two articles.

(4) Have class members draw posters advocating virginity for teenagers and another set advocating it for college students.

(5) A couple is trying to decide whether or not to have premarital sex. They go to some unmarried friends who are currently having sex to ask their advice. Enact a skit illustrating the conversation. Have the class critique the arguments.

(6) Have a debate focusing on the issue, "Resolved: that no one should marry without first having sex with the potential marital partner"; or, "Only virgins should be allowed to marry."

(7) The underlying core of these topics lies in a controversy over a more or less traditional point of view about premarital relations. Analyze your textbook to place it on this continuum.

(8) Analyze current songs as to their advocacy of the attitude that "love conquers all."

(9) Suppose you are considering marrying someone who is very wealthy and physically attractive but of a different race or religion. Ask the class for advice about what to do.

(10) Invite to class a representative of a culture that deals differently with the three issues of date selection, premarital sex, and mate selection. Why are the two cultures different, and what similar functions are performed?

Persons Should Find Dating Partners Only in Traditional Ways— Church Groups, School, Neighborhood, or Workplace

DAVID M. BECKER

The time: approximately 11:00 p.m., Saturday, February 11, 1984.
The place: The Hyatt Arlington Hotel, Arlington, Virginia.
The event: The In Search of Conversational Dance Party.

A fiftyish man who said he worked with computers in Baltimore was interested in the singles scene. "I've thought about writing a book on it myself," he said. He went on to relate his most memorable experience.

"I was standing here with a drink just like I am now, when a woman asked me to dance. So we went out on the floor, and she says to me, 'Haven't I ____ you before?' "

"But she turned out to be a real person," he quickly added.[1]

Welcome to the wild and crazy world of singles in contemporary America. The above-mentioned story may or may not be typical of the atmosphere at modern singles parties. However, few will disagree that earlier conventions of behavior in male-female relations have gone by the board and that dating standards today are more open than ever.

But has this freedom proven to be a boon for the emotional and spiritual well-being of modern adults? Probably not. Turning back the clock is impossible, of course, but Americans were better off when there was more respect and less preoccupation with the physical in the dating relationship.

Dating itself is a relatively modern phenomenon. In many other cultures of the world, parents assume a greater role in arranging dates—and mates, for that matter—than they do in much of current America. This absence of parental authority and involvement is a topic worthy of discussion in and of itself; the apathy of parents could be blamed in part for the epidemic of premarital pregnancy in the 1970s and early 1980s, and for many other ills.

However, for the purposes of this essay we shall assume that a person is alone responsible for the members of the opposite sex with whom he or she chooses to associate, or date, if you will. It is my contention that in most cases prospective daters are well advised to see people with whom they are already acquainted rather than try to advertise to find the right person.

It cannot be denied that the rise of singles parties, computer dating, and advertising has radically affected the way we look at each other; that such trends have occurred in conjunction with the so-called sexual revolution is no coincidence. Many of us seek instant gratification of our passions instead of "One man, one woman for one lifetime," as someone has said.

One aspect of the organized singles scene of which potential participants should be aware at the outset is that involvement is inordinately expensive. Turning Point, a Washington, DC-based group, costs $495 for a one-year membership, in which a person is "guaranteed" one date per month as well as opportunities to gather for other group social events, and travel discounts.[2] One need only check the prices of computer dating and other commercial forms of date-seeking activities to realize that matchmaking organizations are in it for money. One does not have to be cynical to recognize it, when many groups are reluctant to state their fees up front. Clubs exaggerate their successes in bringing young adults into contact with Mr./Ms. Perfect, thus leading the lonely-hearted into perhaps a more advanced state of loneliness. One observer bluntly comments that generally speaking, a lot of lost souls sign up for these services. Despite the claims that 85% of their clients find their mates, I haven't met or even heard of anyone who has done so. Don't allow yourself to be ripped off [Margolies, 1980: 74].

But let use take a closer look at "personals," perhaps the most popular and innovative form of novel date selection. What are personals, after all? Typically, a personal is a classified advertisement of 100 words or less in which the advertiser tells about himself or herself and about what he or she wants in a date. The *Village Voice*, the counterculture weekly of New York City, claims to have been a pacesetter in the personals field. However, sleazy and even pornographic publications have been among those that have pioneered in personals (Kessler, 1984).

Today personals are common, even in respectable high-circulation magazines such as *New York* and the *Washingtonian*. Not only does *Mensa Bulletin,* the regular newsletter for the organization for the highly intellectually gifted, have personals, but so does *Solo,* a magazine for Christian singles. Personals have become a part of the burgeoning evangelical subculture (Morrisroe, 1984: 40).

To be candid, there is an advantage to personals. To the extent that they allow us to evaluate others at our own time and leisure, under no pressure, personals could possibly be helpful. According to John Evans of the *Village Voice,* "It's the antithesis of the bar scene. . . . You have a sober, quiet situation where you sit down and write letters" (Kessler, 1984).

However, the cons to personals far outweigh the pros. The following six points are some of the negatives.

(1) Advertisers Exhibit Preoccupation with the Carnal

Sexual issues are a significant and overriding part of life; and candid inspection of this subject is healthy in many respects. Unfortunately, in personals, people are too often judged on the basis of their physical desirability. Here are just two examples from the "In Search Of" section of the *Washingtonian* (1984: 259), a slick monthly available at most newsstands in the nation's capital.

Successful, secure—DWM (Divorced White Male), 41, 6'—sociable, sensitive, sophisticated, sybaritic, sports-loving, sometimes-silly-Scorpio; seeks singular, sexy, synergetic sylph.

> Beautiful—long-legged, trim/curvaceous WF. Recently "on ice."
> Now: RARIN'-TO-GO! Publicly: elegant/patrician. Privately:
> wenchy/sensuous. Accustomed to finer things. ISO Only highly
> successful WM, 6'+, 46+, explore possibilities. Details, photo.

This cheapens people. Although it would be wrong to accuse all or
even most advertisers of having a motive of fulfillment of lust, one
need only read the advertisements to see what is involved.

We might parenthetically note that even those who have been
active in the sexual revolution in the 1970s have found it necessary
and even refreshing to express some sanity in personal practices.
Feminist Suzanne Fields (1984) properly notes,

> The sexual revolution that pulled aside the cloak of public discretion
> from illicit private intimacy, eliminating the necessity for worrying
> what "others" thought, also erased some of the intimate decencies.

"Commercialization of sex now destroys true feelings as badly as
traditional taboos did," proclaims Peter Marin (1983) in *Psychology
Today*, while *Time* (1984) announces that "in the '80s, caution and
commitment are the watchwords." The well-publicized scare about
herpes has led to the formation of singles clubs for people with
herpes. While perhaps such groups benefit the participants, it is too
bad that they are based on the commonality of an extremely personal
ailment, and remind us of a very private part of us. There is more to
life than that aspect of us.

Indiscriminate sex has been called "the moral equivalent of junk
food" (National Broadcasting Corporation, 1984). Actually, promiscuity is more morally serious than that implies. Many personals, such
as the one by the woman who said she was sponsoring a "Mr. Right"
contest, in which "The prize will be the most rewarding of all, and the
most precious gift on earth" (Kessler, 1984) seem to me to be
excessively reliant on appeal to animal urges.

(2) Adultery Is Sought

Most of the people who advertise in various periodicals are
unquestionably sincere in their search for friends and prospective
spouses. But others—and it seems to be principally men—use the
personals as a means for a fling with a cute young thing. The

following are advertisements from the *Washingtonian* (1984: 259) from married males who want a thrill. Many more examples could be cited.

> I need it bad—ISO an attractive, alarity, risque adventuress for an amatory relationship with a totally discreet MWM with the same quality. Photo appreciated, details.
>
> MWM—30, 5'10", 182. Prof., good looking, very athletic ex-All Am. in great shape. ISO M/D-WF 25-45 in Bethesda, Potomac, Rockville area for discreet relationship.

It may be quaint in many sophisticates' eyes to suggest that such behavior is intrinsically wrong. Nevertheless, it is. Furthermore, it harms society and even the people involved. The idea that there are no victims in extramarital activities is a myth. In *The Romance Factor*, Alan Loy McGinnis (1982: 155) observes,

> For all our so-called sophisticated and permissive society, affairs continue to break up good, functional marriages, damaging children, breaking dreams, and causing permanent damage to people who did nothing to invite injury. In my office, I see these refugees. Children who did their best, who tried to make the right choices. But, because of parents to whom they happened to be born, or because of the mates to whom they happened to be married, they find their lives bombed out. They were not combatants, they did not ask for the artillery; they only happened to be a part of a family in which someone planted an explosive.

(3) Kinkiness Abounds

In conventional periodicals, weird and violent behavior is only hinted at in personals, but strange activities are openly advertised in homosexual publications. However, even in the *Washingtonian* (1984: 259-265) there are references to homosexual acts.

> GWM (Gay White Male)—27, fit, seeks friendship/intimacy with SWM, BI down to earth men, police and public servicemen especially appealing.
>
> GWM—sincere, discreet ISO other male for daytime meetings.
>
> BI MWM—40, bored, adventurous. Seeks novel experiences, either sex.

BIWF—slender, attractive, likes occasional adventure. ISO same to share evening(s) of luxury and pleasure.

BIWM—36, good-looking, trim, athletic build, discreet, seeks like-minded male/female.

BIBF—27, charming, professional, discreet. ISO BISBF to share diverse interests, companionship/possible relationship.

GWM—28, 5'10", 140, attractive, healthy, straight appearing, professional, intelligent, varied interests. ISO similar for friendship/possible relationship.

GWM—25, good-looking ISO same (under-30) for discreet meetings.

In such homosexual tabloids as *New York Native,* "many of the ads are quite graphic, with a heavy emphasis on bondage and sadomasochism," though a growing number of men are said to be also seeking long-term relationships (Morrisroe, 1984: 39). It is impossible—and probably inadvisable—to try to regulate what people do privately (though laws prohibiting sodomy are still on the books in many states and localities). Still, we should encourage healthy treatment of each other. We should not debase one another, or beat and abuse ourselves like brutes. If personals provide an outlet for some of us to do that, then these personals are having a baneful effect. Promotion of wrong and socially undesirable—and, judging from the outbreak of the homosexual-linked ailment, AIDS, grossly unhealthful—actions should be discouraged.

(4) Appearance Is Emphasized

Many advertisers ask for photographs of people who respond. Done with proper motives, this can be justifiable and positive. One woman who advertised in a Christian periodical explained,

> I asked for a photo to accompany letters as I like to "see" who is writing to me. It's always easier to write to friends that you've met personally because you "see" them in your mind's eye as you write. If you can't meet someone personally, a picture is the next best thing. This is the same idea as "Foster Child" type organizations use when they send a photo of your sponsorship child—it adds a more personal touch and helps in further correspondence.[3]

On the other hand, photographs can bring about intense and unnecessary disappointment. One woman tells this frank story about a fellow who responded to her advertisement:

> We had so much in common and he lived nearby and we decided to meet. We exchanged pictures and he wrote that I was pretty. But I think he was disappointed when we met because I had gained weight. I was disappointed because I still looked a lot like my picture and felt, what did looks matter if we had so much in common? But apparently he was a "wife hunter" and had certain qualifications that *had* to be met. This is always a danger in dating.[4]

Some people are not as attractive as others. That is the way it always has been and always will be. Some of the most physically beautiful men and women are also some of the most shallow emotionally and intellectually. And knockout looks can even actually be a hindrance to close friendship and dates, if they intimidate others.

The ideal is that all people should be cherished as creations of God. We should not look down on others no matter who they are. The Bible has something to say, particularly to women, on the "deceitfulness" of outer appearance.

> Wives ... your beauty should not come from outward adornment, such as braided hair and the wearing of gold jewelry and fine clothes. Instead, it should be that of your inner self, the unfading beauty of a gentle and quiet spirit, which is of great worth in God's sight [1 Peter 3:1, 3, 4].
>
> Charm is deceptive, and beauty is fleeting; but a woman who fears the Lord is to be praised [Proverb 31:30].

We should, however, try to make ourselves look as good as possible. McGinnis (1982: 27) notes,

> The trouble with neglecting the body is that we are saying we do not care if our appearance displeases people who look at us every day. It

behooves us to do everything we can with diet, exercise, dress, and the help of professionals to be as attractive as possible. In this case, the motivation is not vanity or exhibitionism, so much as love.

(5) We Exaggerate Our Assets

When we evaluate each other on how appealing we are, how accomplished we are, or how knowledgeable or intelligent we are, then we have a natural tendency to overstate our strong points.

True "openness" and candor, which are a foundation of any serious relationship, are impeded. We find ourselves putting on fronts. We wind up not being ourselves, or at least that can happen.

(6) Relationships Do Not Last

Perhaps most important of all in dating through personals is that the excitement fades, later if not sooner. Many who find themselves resorting to personals are divorced to begin with. It is hard to imagine a liaison resulting from a newspaper contact continuing for decades, although anything is possible.

One reason relationships among singles frequently dissolve is that all too often people are viewed as property. One book (DuBrin, 1973: 199-200) sympathetic to the singles culture relates the tale of a woman who found a husband through singles channels.

> After five months of enjoying a variety of activities together as a family unit, Alan and Sandra were married. One afternoon, about seven months after their wedding date, Sandra was listening to a consumer complaint program on the radio. Under attack that afternoon was computer dating. Sandra phoned in her reaction: "Believe me, I have something to tell your audience. Computer dating was for me a gift from God. I am one of the happiest people in the world today because I met my husband through computer dating. As for the price, I paid more for my stereo set than I did for my husband."

In truth, it is no compliment to say that one's mate has been acquired through shrewd bargain hunting. Romance has ended, replaced by a cold, businesslike approach toward obtaining a partner.

Another single male (a 56-year-old who is separated after 29 years of marriage) talks about his newly unmarried life as "a candy store" (Kessler, 1984). Women should be considered with more honor than that. They are not just some goods through which males extract pleasure.

By this time it should be clear that we are not discussing mere date selection, but also mate selection. As one author (Kirby, 1979: 14) has said, "We usually marry someone we have dated." If we view the dating process as one designed ultimately to provide us with a partner through life, then we have a frank and appropriate understanding of what is happening. Not that the single life is not some people's calling, but men and women are made for each other. The male-female balance has been mysteriously preserved through the centuries.

Dating and marriage relationships demand a consideration of human purpose. What is our purpose? To seek pleasure? To seek knowledge? Do we have a purpose? Do we have a responsibility to a higher power? How does our religion or philosophy of life influence our views on dating?

The book of Genesis indicates that humans are not only created male and female, but are also designed to be fruitful and multiply. Dating and eventual marriage lead to children in most cases; it is not just a case of a man and a woman alone forever. Others enter the scene. And when children are in the picture, it is even more important for a marriage to endure, as divorce has been proven to have a devastating effect on little ones, contrary to the impression portrayed by some popular movies and television programs. In a presentation to the American Psychological Association, Betty Heiman Goren stated,

> Children at various stages of development are affected differently by the trauma of divorce, but all have their energies seriously distracted and diverted from their normal developmental tasks by the profound sense of anxiety, loneliness, confusion and shame the divorce brings. For most children divorce is experienced as a personal, familial and social loss activating the powerful unconscious fear harbored by every child of desertion and abandonment by one or both parents [Family Protection Report, 1983: 14].

It is unlikely that a union based on secular interests such as enjoying tennis or the theater can withstand the pressures suffered by marriages and families. Marriages are having enough trouble surviving these days as it is. Contacts evolving from advertisements for people can foster promiscuity and unhappiness, while sound moral values will encourage marital stability. George Rekers (1984) commented in his testimony before the Senate Subcommittee on Family and Human Services,

> Sex reserved for marriage facilitates an exclusive association of sexual pleasure with the marital relationship and *only* the marital relationship, so a couple can genuinely say, "This is something unique in space and time to our relationship alone. No one else has or will ever share it. It is something of ourselves and for ourselves that is very, very special, for us alone to cherish and enjoy." We question whether something quite precious is not lost when a couple cannot honestly say such things about their relationship. . . . We do not say, "I will hang around as long as you make me feel reasonably happy, after that I might leave." Rather, we say, "I will be here for you, with you regardless of what you may say or do, even if it means you take the opportunity of my vulnerability to exploit me," to loosely paraphrase an old wedding vow expressing enduring commitment "for better or for worse." It is an agreement not to be entered into lightly. But it offers the greatest potential for personal growth and fulfillment of the many alternatives for sexual relationships that are available. Sex is a wonderfully appropriate vehicle for celebrating such an intimate and lasting love relationship, and this kind of marriage is the most desirable environment in which to conceive and nurture children.

So if we disdain the singles and personals scene, where do we go? Religious groups and churches are a most appropriate and logical place to start. Here we have eligible young people at least theoretically seeking to serve a higher purpose. People are exalted in obeying and following God; it is a far cry from mere "relating" to each other in a stilted one-on-one encounter at a local watering hole. Many weddings are even today performed in churches, and that figures to be the case for some time to come. Religion still plays an important part in many people's lives.

School is another obvious place in which dating relationships can be formed and nurtured. There common intellectual interests can be ascertained, as well a commonalities in athletics, or simple fun. For those who do not attend school, a place of employment is somewhere else at which shared ideas and interests can be explored and developed.

At church, school, and work we have the chance to see each other as we really are, in a reasonably relaxed milieu. And, for that matter, one's own neighborhood is another natural area to meet people, particularly when one is pre-adult.

To sum up, perhaps personals can work for some people, in some few-and-far-between instances, but it would be foolhardy to count on it. A safer route to finding dates and ultimate mates is through the more conventional avenues. Leave the classifieds for advertising for things, not people.

NOTES

1. Personal interview by the author, February 11, 1984.
2. Information obtained in personal interview by the author, March 24, 1984.
3. Letter to the author from advertiser in *Solo*, March 14, 1984.
4. Letter to the author from advertiser in *Solo*, March 13, 1984.

REFERENCES

DuBRIN, A. (1973) The Singles Game. Chatsworth, CA: Books for Better Living.
Family Protection Report (1983) "Effects of divorce on children seen to be considerable." (December).
FIELDS, S. (1984) "The sexual revolution has gone too far." Washington Post (January 1): H1.
KESSLER, R. (1984) "Personal ads put new zest in the old dating game." Washington Post (March 5): C1.
KIRBY, S. (1979) Dating: Guidelines from the Bible. Grand Rapids, MI: Baker.
MARGOLIES, M. (1980) Finding Someone to Love. New York: Playboy.
MARIN, P. (1983) "A revolution's broken promises." Psychology Today (July): 51.
McGINNIS, A. L. (1982) The Romance Factor. New York: Harper & Row.
MORRISROE, P. (1984) "Strictly personals." New York (March 19): 40.
National Broadcasting Corporation (1984) "NBC reports: second thoughts on being single." April 25.
REKERS, G. (1984). "Parental involvement with agencies serving adolescents in crisis: adolescent sexuality and family well-being." Testimony before the United States Senate Subcommittee on Family and Human Services, Washington, DC, February 24.
Time (1984) "The revolution is over." April 9: 74.
Washingtonian (1984) "In search of." April: 259.

It Is Equally Acceptable to Meet Others in Less Conventional Ways— Advertising, Computer Dating, Singles Parties, and the Like

LAURA S. SMART

The American mate-selection process is based upon a choice system that is theoretically a free one. People seeking a mate meet others in the same situation, and the selection process begins. But what happens to people who don't seem to meet the right one? Or how about those who don't seem to meet anyone, right or wrong?

Traditionally, persons seeking marriage partners have relied upon their kin, friends, and acquaintances to introduce them to available members of the other sex. However, for persons who live in small towns, or who live in areas with an unfavorable sex ratio, or who have specific (and peculiar) qualities that they find desirable, the traditional means of meeting may not suffice.

An unfavorable sex ratio means that the person in question belongs to the sex that outnumbers the other sex. Glick (1975) calls this situation "the marriage squeeze." In any geographic location, a local marriage squeeze may exist. For example, in Washington, D.C., there are 82 men for every 100 women (Noble, 1983). These figures do not tell us, of course, the sex ratio for singles or a breakdown by age. Furthermore, they do not elucidate the problems of people with special needs or desires in a mate, such as black single professional women, who have a small field of eligibles if they wish to date within their own race. According to Staples (1981), if they wish to marry black men, most single middle-class black women must marry men of a lower socioeconomic status.

In a humorous article, Doudna (1981) asks, "Where are the men for the women at the top?" Interviews with 25 single women aged 29 to 56 revealed that most felt confused by their inability to find partners. All reported difficulty in locating appropriate men; some said that the single men they met were threatened by the women's success and that the most "available" ones were already married.

People who live in small towns may have trouble finding potential partners simply because the field of eligibles is small. And people who live in the city may be hampered by working in sex-segregated occupations that do not provide easy access to potential mates. The bars offer an alternative meeting place to singles whose friends have tired of presenting them with blind dates. However, even the fairly modern singles bar does not meet the needs of all late-twentieth-century single persons.

Newspapers and magazines abound in articles about singles who are trying new ways to meet people (Anderson, 1982; Geist, 1983, Van Gelder, 1983). Newspaper classified advertisements aimed at such singles appear in city and small-town papers alike. Persons with special requirements in a mate may turn to personals sections in magazines such as the *Mother Earth News,* aimed at back-to-the-landers, or *Advocate,* aimed at gays. Singles who want a large number of ads from which to choose may buy local, regional, or national singles magazines.

If reading an ad is not appealing, the prospecting single may turn to computer dating. The client fills out a questionnaire about his or her physical attributes, educational and occupational background, avocations and requirements in a potential date, and for a fee is sent from the computer's files a list of potential dates' names and phone numbers.

For prospectors who prefer an approach that is a bit more similar to a neighborhood cocktail party yet still affords some anonymity, there are singles nights sponsored by churches, personal growth organizations, and common-focus groups. The format of such singles nights varies, but a common one is a lecture followed by a cash-bar happy hour.

The scholarly literature on "new ways of meeting" is sparse. Cameron et al. (1977) did a content analysis of advertisements in a singles magazine. They found that people portrayed themselves in an overwhelmingly positive fashion and that sex-role stereotypes a-bounded. Portraying themselves as successful, men sought attractive women, whereas the women bargained their attractiveness for success in a man. Men sought women an average of seven years younger than themselves. Unfortunately, the average female advertiser was nine years older than the average male advertiser, creating a serious matching problem.

In spite of such problems, Jedlicka (1980, 1981) was enthusiastic about alternatives to face-to-face meeting. Citing a Czechoslovakian study of 20,000 clients of a computer spouse-finding service (Proko-pek, 1974), Jedlicka (1981) noted that the service was able to match 92 percent of the males and 40 percent of the females with potential partners. (Female applicants outnumbered males two to one.) The study apparently did not follow the clients to see how many actually married.

But not all persons who date are immediately in the market for a spouse. An early study on computer dating (Strong et al., 1969) is rare in that it sought to determine the participants' evaluations of the computer matching. A sample of 910 male college students were matched with three dates each. The universe of female dates numbered 620. The men were matched with their dates using three sets of criteria: Date 1 was matched randomly, date 2 was matched with regard to similarity, and date 3 was matched with regard to similarity and also with complementarity on needs, which Winch (1958) had hypothesized to be important to the mate selection process.

Because the majority of subjects did not return the questionnaires, the usable data dwindled to less than 15 percent. (The students, not surprisingly, were more interested in having a date than reporting on it, although a follow-up phone interview of a random sample of nonrespondents revealed that many students had not attempted to make dates with the women whose names had been provided by the researchers.)

Nonetheless, it was found that of those who dated, randomly selected persons were enjoyed less as dates than those who shared similarities. For males, complementarity did not differentiate preference for a date; whether or not a woman was complementary to them (in terms of deference-dominance, deference-aggressiveness, abasement-aggressiveness, or succorance-nurturance) was not a deciding factor. Women, however, preferred men who were low in complementarity but high in similarity on other factors.

Although computer dating and more recently video dating (Jedlicka, 1980) appear to be the most innovative and modern ways of finding a date or mate, advertisements in periodicals have a much larger potential audience. Such advertisements are available to almost any reader of a daily newspaper, and thus afford a way of assesing the availability of potential dates that is low-cost and low-risk. Studies of love in the classifieds have concentrated upon the users of singles magazines (Cameron et al., 1977; Jedlicka, 1978) rather than newspaper classifieds and, as noted earlier, have not dealt with the outcome of such matching.

Nor have magazine articles been much more helpful. An article in *Ms.* (1984) told readers how to place an ad and gave words of encouragement and reassurance that such ads are used by many people who were similar to the reader. Letters from readers of the article reveal enthusiasm. For singles who are having a hard time meeting others, classifieds expand the field of eligibles.

If social scientists have failed to measure the success rates of dating prospectors who use the media, they have not even attempted to examine singles clubs and other methods that rely on old-fashioned face-to-face interaction. An enterprising New Yorker offered a $25 course entitled "Finding a Mate in Bloomingdale's" (Geist, 1983). The instructor took fifteen men and women to the famous department store, having coached them on conversation starters such as "What do you think of this tie?"

Many churches sponsor singles nights that, despite their denominational labels, often cater to singles of various religious persuasions. An alternative for persons living in or near metropolitan areas is the singles night sponsored by personal-growth organizations, such as Chicago's Oasis Center.

The "people sampler" sponsored by Oasis uses standard human-potential exercises as icebreakers. The monthly samplers are attended by between 150 and 200 singles, usually fairly evenly divided by sex. Persons range in age from twenties to fifties; most are probably in their thirties. Participants pay a fee at the door, and are guided to small groups for the opener. They are instructed to discuss something with their group members, such as "what initially attracts me to a person." Soon the groups are disbanded and the prospectors walk around the room, looking over the other participants. Periodically the prospectors are asked to choose a partner for an undescribed exercise. Once they choose, they are given a topic of conversation and ten to fifteen minutes in which to explore it. Then they are instructed to move on to the next person.

Throughout the course of the evening, prospectors are given minilessons on how to get a relationship off the ground in an honest and nonthreatening way. (Recommended are lunch dates, which are relatively free from sexual innuendo and usually have a built-in end point, since the parties have to go back to work.)

At the people sampler the norms are explicit. Prospectors are given blank cards on which to write their addresses and phone numbers, and are told that they may give their cards to people from whom they would welcome a call. It is made clear that being given a card in no way obligates the receiver to reciprocate. Thus, at the end of the night, most prospectors have the cards of persons who would welcome a call.

The people-sampler method has the advantage of providing face-to-face contact with a degree of anonymity. The Oasis Center has not attempted to assess the success rate of their people sampler (Sarantos, 1983). Persons who run singles organizations are reluctant to let social scientists in the door (unless, of course, they are single social scientists looking for a date).

Another method of the 1980s whose success rate is unknown is the health club or the exercise room (Pridmore, 1983). Until this decade solely the province of muscle-building men, weight-training clubs now cater to persons of both sexes. The more socially oriented clubs have sex-integrated weight rooms and aerobics classes, and the trendy ones have juice bars or restaurants attached. One Chicago club even has a laundromat in the basement (Pridmore, 1983).

The health club provides a "closed field" (Murstein, 1976) environment for meeting. In a closed field, potential mates get to know each other in the context of shared or reciprocal roles. Thus, they need not decide to approach each other or whether to accept another's approach strictly on the basis of physical appearance. As fellow fitness devotees, members of a health club can discuss their hamstrings and foot injuries before setting that all-important first date.

Confusion about where to find a mate may be the biggest problem that many prospectors face, but what happens on that date, should it occur, and what should happen later? Changing sexual and sex-role mores have left people confused about more than whether a man should hold a door open for a woman. Although there is a clear need for alternative ways of meeting, some of the old guidelines simply do not apply when two complete strangers try to begin a relationship.

People who meet through friends, work, or a religious organization share common acquaintances. Usually this means that they can get feedback from their mutual acquaintances about their date or potential date. Through such feedback, they can get and give character references, and interpret the behavior of the other person. If their relationship does develop, they have the beginnings of a shared network to provide ongoing feedback and support.

Prospectors have to work harder to build a common network, and may need to work harder at developing a shared understanding and a common language. However, for successful prospectors, this may seem a small price to pay.

Today's courtship customs no longer dictate that potential dates or mates be properly introduced, or that the man pick up the woman at her door and deposit her there at midnight. On the average, first marriages occur later, and higher divorce rates have also meant that more marriages are likely to involve at least one formerly married person. Thus, seeking a mate is not something that is done almost exclusively by very young adults. Greater age and experience means a wider range of needs to be met by a dating relationship, which means that today's prospectors may engage in more role-making than ever before.

However, the wide range of acceptable norms can make prospecting confusing, even for the seasoned seeker. A new etiquette is evolving, although ignorance of the new rules is probably widespread. The anthropologists do not seem to have studied the new tribal customs, but a book editor turned author has. Merser (1983) asserts that etiquette provides necessary boundaries for human behavior, and that the old rules have not simply faded away. Rather, there are new guidelines.

For example, under the old rules it was obligatory that before "getting serious," persons who were becoming involved with each other had to know certain things about each other. They would meet each other's friends and families and know each other's religion, social status, and financial potential before initiating a sexual relationship (Merser, 1983). Under the old rules, a man who had sex with a woman early in the relationship was clearly indicating that he did not think she was the type with whom he could get serious. Now, however, it is more common for couples to have the honeymoon first, before they have any idea whether or not seriousness is on the agenda.

What the long-term effects of the new courtship etiquette will be remains to be seen. The cohabitation literature may provide a clue, however. Two studies have compared persons who married without cohabiting to those who married their former cohabiting partners (Watson, 1983; DeMaris and Leslie, 1984). In very early marriage, persons who cohabited prior to marriage reported somewhat lower levels of marital satisfaction than those who did not cohabit. The authors of these two separate studies concluded that the kind of people who are attracted to cohabitation are probably different from those who do not cohabit. The latter are more conventional, and may therefore be more suited to traditional marriage.

Traditional courtship practices, involving overt male pursuit and female behaviors that at least appear to be responses to the male partner's actions, may be expected to lead to a more traditional type of marriage than would the new etiquette, which gives women a larger share of the responsibility for initiation. A woman who places or answers an ad in a newspaper, or who uses video dating, or goes to a singles night is advertising her availability. By the new rules, she may initiate a relationship with a man that she meets in this way, or even one that she meets under more conventional circumstances.

Relationships that start off on a more equal footing may not follow the same rules as relationships that begin with an assumption of male initiation (and therefore male superiority). Satisfaction levels may be lower, at least in this decade, until the expectations that people bring to marriage change to adjust to the emerging rules for courtship and marital behavior.

The success rate of people who meet by unconventional means has yet to be determined. The definition of "success" is problematic, for not all persons who are seeking a date have marriage on their minds, at least for the near future. For some, success may be a full social calendar, for others it is a "meaningful relationship" carried on from separate addresses or perhaps under the same roof. Some, however, do seek spouses.

Today's less traditional ways of meeting potential dates and mates may be threatening to those who believe only in conventional marriage between a relatively dominant man and a relatively submissive woman, both of correct lineage as determined by their elders. It may be disconcerting for traditional parents or siblings to realize that their unmarried kin are dating (and probably bedding) total strangers who may come from different ethnic, religious, or class backgrounds. Or perhaps the concern is that these relationships are begun without the slightest semblance of having been chaperoned or guided by the older generation.

The complaining relatives, however, are probably the same ones who could not understand why 30-year-old Jane or 28-year-old John had not yet gotten married. For some later marriers, the answer is that career has taken precedence over marriage. For others, it is the marriage squeeze or the inability to find a partner through more conventional means that results in prolonged singlehood.

Conventional means of meeting still appear to be satisfactory for many people. However, to condemn computer and video matching, singles clubs and nights, and the classifieds is to deny access to persons who have not found partners through their established friendship, kin, and other networks. For this reason alone, it is both foolish and unkind to oppose the new alternatives, which meet the needs of persons who may be less conventional, or may simply be less lucky, than the fabled boy who marries the girl next door.

REFERENCES

ANDERSON, J. (1982) "Solos become duos, thanks to Classical Exchange movement." Chicago Tribune, September 19.

CAMERON, C., S. OSKAMP, and W. SPARKS (1977) "Courtship American style: newspaper ads." Family Coordinator 26: 27-30.

DeMARIS, A. and G. R. LESLIE (1984) "Cohabitation with the future spouse: its influence upon marital satisfaction and communication." Journal of Marriage and the Family 46: 77-84.

DOUDNA, C. with F. McBRIDE (1981) "Where are the men for the women at the top?" in P. Stein (ed.) Single Life: Unmarried Adults in Social Context. New York: St. Martin's.

GEIST, W. E. (1983) "New York singles look for romance in a store." New York Times (November 14).

GLICK, P. (1975) "A demographer looks at the American family." Journal of Marriage and the Family 37: 15-26.

JEDLICKA, D. (1981) "Automated go-betweens: mate selection of tomorrow?" Family Relations 30: 373-376.

———(1980) "Formal mate selection networks in the United States." Family Relations 29: 199-203.

———(1978) "Sex inequality, aging, and innovation in preferential mate selection." Family Coordinator 23: 137-140.

MERSER, C. (1983) Honorable intentions: The Manners of Courtship in the '80s. New York: Atheneum.

Ms. (1984) "More who found love in the classifieds." February: 68-70.

MURSTEIN, B. (1976) Who will marry whom?" New York: Springer.

NOBLE, K. B. (1983) "One approach to the shortage of men is sharing." New York Times (September 9).

PRIDMORE, J. (1983) "Of Mr. Jones, hips, and human perfectability." Chicago Tribune (December 16).

PROKOPEK, J. K. (1971) "Nekterym problemum nidani zivotniho partnera pomoci samocinneho pocitace." Demographie 16: 23-31. [Cited in Jedlicka (1981).]

SARANTOS, D. (1983) Personal Communication (December 18).

STAPLES, R. (1981) Black Singles in America. Westport, CT: Greenwood.

STRONG, E., W. WALLACE, and W. WILSON (1969) "Three-filter date selection by computer." Family Coordinator 18: 166-171.

Van GELDER, L. (1983) "Love among the classifieds: a take-charge way to meet new people." Ms. 12, 2: 39-43.

WATSON, R.E.L. (1983) "Premarital cohabitation vs. traditional courtship: their effects on subsequent marital adjustment." Family Relations 32: 139-147.

WINCH, R. F. (1958) Mate Selection: A Study of Complementary Needs. New York: Harper & Brothers. [Cited in Strong et al. (1969).]

PREMARITAL SEX

Both Males and Females
Should Be Virgins
at the Time of Marriage

CARLFRED B. BRODERICK

In the 1960s and 1970s the freedom movement broke upon our society
like a great tidal wave, battering and in many cases sweeping away
traditional values and prejudices like so many beach-front cabanas.
As I write, in the middle of the 1980s, the water has receded in some
measure to its preflood levels, but it has left a greatly changed
landscape behind it. On the positive side there seem to have been
permanent gains in the rights and status of minorities and women.
On the negative side there seem to have been permanent increases in
the availability and acceptability of mind-altering drugs, a lingering
reduction in student discipline and educational achievement, and a
massive erosion of family stability.

Among the changes that are most ambivalently regarded is the
dramatic liberalization of sexual standards and practices. Probably
most applaud certain consequences of the so-called sexual revolution.
Children today are far better informed about their own bodies and

about the sexual and reproductive facts of life. Women are not taking 15 to 20 years after marriage to reach their full orgasmic potential as they were in the days of the Kinsey report (Kinsey et al., 1953) a generation earlier. Married couples successfully negotiated more sexual unions per month than ever before (Westoff, 1976). On the other hand, other developments received more mixed reviews. For example, not everyone was pleased at the increasingly younger ages at which children became sexually active, at the sexualization of college dormitory life and at the explosive increase in the numbers of couples living together without being married. Virtually no one saw anything to hearten them in the rise in venereal disease, teenage pregnancy, abortion, and illegitimacy. Even more negatively viewed were what appeared to be related epidemics of rape, incest, child pornography, and child prostitution.

I am aware that to the true libertarian there is nothing so precious as freedom and the fact that there are casualties is no justification for retreat from a hard-won pinnacle of permissiveness. They reason that the costs of repression are far greater even though they may sometimes be more difficult to tally. My position is that we must not let doctrine blind us to the evidence. It is time to reconsider whether the extreme sexual permissiveness of our society is not costing us more freedom than it is providing us. Freedom to do as we please, is, after all, not the same as freedom from the consequences of our choices.

There is recent evidence that college students, without benefit of any leadership from their elders, have of their own accord begun to return to a more conservative standard. (Laner and Housker, 1980; Robinson and Jedlicka, 1982) My proposal is that those of us in responsible policymaking and opinion-influencing positions consider assuming a belated leadership of that movement. The aim, most simply stated, would be to make it socially acceptable, once more, to choose to abstain from sex until marriage. The means would be to reverse the current officially permissive standard and once again to promote premarital abstinence as the most responsible public policy. Some years ago the public consciousness was raised to the need for more responsible population policy and within a decade America lowered its birthrate to a level consistent with zero population growth. Is it unreasonable to think that the population may respond to an increased awareness of the costs of untrammeled sexual permissiveness and choose to exercise restraint appropriate to the situation?

I should like to argue the case strictly on a cost-benefit basis and leave the more refined aspects of the debate to moral philosophers.

Dr. William Cates of the Department of Health and Human Services Centers for Disease Control states the problem succinctly in a recent article in the *Journal of Reproductive Medicine.*

Human heterosexual behavior is obviously an entity necessary to ensuring both species survival and human happiness. However, sexual intercourse also has some adverse consequences—primarily sexually transmitted diseases (STDs) and unplanned pregnancy. Because both these conditions have been identified by policy-makers as public health priorities, we might expect coordinated efforts to prevent and control STDs and unplanned pregnancies to have evolved. However, such has not been the case [1984: 317].

SEXUALLY TRANSMITTED DISEASES

As to the first point, Dr. Allan Weinstein of the Department of Infectious Diseases, Cleveland Clinic Foundation, writes in a subsequent issue of that same journal:

Sexually transmitted diseases will continue to increase in incidence unless effective control strategies can be applied, and the recent increase in incidence has been due, in part, to increased levels of sexual activity among young people [1984: 412].

He goes on to note that

gonorrhea has dramatically increased in incidence as have non-specific urethritis in men, non-specific genital infection in women and herpes genetalis.

In most clinics 40-50% of the female patients with gonorrhea are under the age of 20. The peak incidence of gonorrhea in women is from 15 to 19 years and for men is 20 to 24 [1984: 412].

The same article points out that new patterns of infection are indicative of more uninhibited sexual practices, namely, pharyngeal and rectal gonorrhea, both in women and in homosexual males.

Perhaps the most alarming datum on the consequences of a more permissive sexual lifestyle, however, is the observation that over 500,000 women in the United States contract pelvic inflammatory disease every year. Literally hundreds of thousands of American women have been permanently sterilized as a result of this epidemic.

The continued epidemic of herpes II has become one of the premier public health problems in America. In addition to its painful effects upon those who contract it, it is also, like syphilis and gonorrhea, highly likely to infect neonates passing through the birth canal. At this writing it is still considered incurable.

In addition to all of these health hazards, young men who are homosexually active are highly vulnerable to that most devastating of all sexually communicable diseases, AIDS (acquired immune deficiency syndrome).

Finally, cancers of the female genital tract are associated with a number of different disease agents and directly correlated to the variety of sexual partners to whom a woman is exposed (Cates, 1984).

PREMARITAL PREGNANCY

The second obvious consequence of increased rates of sexual exposure is pregnancy. Studies have shown that, due to a combination of spontaneous and induced abortions, only about half of all teenage premarital pregnancies end in a live birth. (The abortion rate is substantially higher among women 20 and older.) Of those who do carry their pregnancies to term, 60 percent become single parents and 40 percent get married (O'Connell and Moore, 1980).

It is not necessary to belabor the point that unmarried teenagers make poor mothers. In addition, a number of studies have demonstrated that premarital pregnancy has highly negative consequences for the mother herself, both in terms of her future education and career path and the prognosis for her marriage turning out successfully, should she marry (Christensen, 1963; Pratt, 1965; Furstenberg,

1976). For many reasons that do not seem easily subject to change, people in this age group are the least frequent users of responsible contraceptive programs.

Dr. Cates said it all when he called our attention to the obvious.

Chastity clearly protects against both STDs (Sexually Transmitted Diseases) and pregnancies. Monogamous heterosexual behavior among couples who use contraceptives will also reduce the risks of STDs and pregnancy to low levels [1984: 318].

Medical science will continue to search for other solutions, but abstinence is the sovereign prophylaxis. Is it appropriate for policy-makers to continue to sneer at it?

Even aside from these weighty public health issues, however, there are significant human costs to our present, permissive policy.

Item: The current social values place enormous pressure on immature young women to submit to sexual suasion without commensurate support for their right to refuse with dignity.

When I studied social development in the more protected era of the late 1950s and early 1960s it was a social advantage for young girls to develop early and enter the world of dating a year or two ahead of their slower developing sisters (Broderick, 1966). But an almost identical study conducted fifteen years later found that early-developing, early-dating girls had lower self-esteem than their late-developing peers and also lower self-esteem than other early-developing girls who did not date and thus postponed the sexual pressures associated with that social practice (Simmons et al., 1979).

Item: Boys are seldom pictured as victims of premature sexualization or of rampant permissiveness because assertive sexuality has typically been viewed as a positive component of the male role prescription. But there is evidence from as far back as the Kinsey studies (Kinsey et al., 1948: 309-310) that boys who become sexually focused early develop a lifetime surplus of untrammeled sex drive, which would appear to serve neither them nor the society well.

Item: Few would contest the observation that the more permissive sexual standards of today have worked against the stability of marriage. One of the most reliable predictors of extramarital sexual adventures is a prolonged period of abasive premarital sexual activity (Athanasiou and Sorkin, 1974; Bukstel et al., 1978; Singh et al., 1976). Leaving aside the negative impacts of permissiveness that are mediated through venereal disease or through coercive premarital pregnancy, there can be little doubt that if the stability of marriage is to be increased it will require a revival of the traditional commitment to an exclusive sexual monogamy as a standard of marital behavior.

CONCLUSIONS

Perhaps societies, like individuals, go through stages in their moral development. In this connection I cannot help thinking of Lawrence Kohlberg's model of moral reasoning (Kohlberg, 1969; Kohlberg and Turiel, 1973). His longitudinal studies found that college-age men and women typically go through a period of rebellion when they discover moral relativism and reject the authoritative doctrines and standards of their youth, returning to a level that he calls post-moral hedonism. Then, after growing up a bit and settling down to adult responsibilities, a new moral posture emerges based not on the moralities of their youth but on their own life experience and emerging priorities. This mature morality is independent of what others think, but it is responsive to the need for social contract and social congress. Is it possible that our whole society has also come through its period of rebellion and hedonism and is beginning to enter into a more adult sense of social responsibility? If so, it may be that it is time to review our own priorities as opinion leaders in that society. Perhaps we are grown up enough to consider whether it would not serve us all better to promote premarital abstinence as a policy that is the most responsive to the needs of our citizens and their right to freedom: freedom from disease, freedom from unwanted pregnancy, freedom to pursue relational skills and human connections with a much muted degree of sexual pressure, freedom to deal with their sexuality and its implications at an age and stage when they have more ego strength and more perspective than they do in their early teens, freedom to pursue and maintain secure lifelong pair bonds reinforced with sexual exclusivity. It seems to me that only those blinded by their own libertarian dogma could fail to see that the time has come for a shift in our public policy. In order to strengthen personal health and well-being, family solidarity, and the general weal it would be prudent and productive to sponsor a return to premarital abstinence as the approved standard of sexual conduct.

REFERENCES

ATHANASIOU, R. and R. SORKIN (1974) "Premarital sexual behavior and post-marital adjustment." Archives of Sexual Behavior 3: 207-225.

BRODERICK, C. B. (1966) "Socio-sexual development in a suburban community." Journal of Sex Research 2: 1-24.

BUKSTEL, L. H., G. D. ROEDER, P. R. KILMANN, J. LAUGHLIN and W. M. SOTILE (1978) "Projected extramarital involvement in community college students." Journal of Marriage and the Family 40: 337-340.

CATES, W., Jr. (1984) "Sexually transmitted diseases and family planning: strange or natural bedfellows." Journal of Reproductive Medicine 29: 5: 317-322.

CHRISTENSEN, H. T. (1963) "Timing of first pregnancy as a factor in divorce: a cross-cultural analysis." Eugenics Quarterly 10: 119-130.

FURSTENBERG, F. F. (1976) Unplanned Parenthood: The Social Consequences of Teenage Childbearing. New York: Macmillan.

KINSEY, A. C., W. B. POMEROY, and C. E. MARTIN (1948) Sexual Behavior in the Human Male. Philadelphia: Saunders.

———and P. H. GEBHARD (1953) Sexual Behavior in the Human Female. Philadelphia: Saunders.

KOHLBERG, L. (1969) "Stage and sequence: the cognitive-developmental approach to socialization," in D. A. Goslin (ed.) Handbook of Socialization Theory. Chicago: Rand McNally.

———and E. TURIEL (1973) "Overview: cultural universals in morality," in L. Kohlberg and E. Turiel (eds.) Recent Research in Moral Development. New York: Holt, Rinehart and Winston.

LANER, M. R. and S. L. HOUSKER (1980) "Sexual permissiveness in younger and older adults." Journal of Family Issues 1: 103-124.

O'CONNELL, M. and M. J. MOORE (1980) "The legitimacy status of first births to U.S. women aged 15-24, 1939-1978." Family Planning Perspectives 12: 16-25.

PRATT, W. F. (1965) "A study of marriages involving pregnancies." Ph.D. dissertation, University of Michigan.

ROBINSON, I. E. and D. JEDLICKA (1982) "Change in sexual attitudes and behavior of college students from 1965-1980: a research note." Journal of Marriage and the Family 44: 237.

SIMMONS, R. G., D. A. BLYTH, E. F. VANCLEAVE, and D. M. BUSH (1979) "Entry into early adolescence: the impact of school structure, puberty and early dating in self-esteem." American Society and Review 44: 948-967.

SINGH, B. K., B. L. WALTON, and J. S. WILLIAMS (1976) "Extramarital sexual permissiveness: conditions and contingencies." Journal of Marriage and the Family 38: 701-712.

WEINSTEIN, A. J. (1984) "Sexually transmittable diseases and other genital infections during adolescence." Journal of Reproductive Medicine 29, 6: 411-415.

WESTOFF, C. F. (1976) "Trends in contraceptive practice 1965, 1973." Family Planning Perspectives 8: 54-57.

It Is Important that Both Men and Women Have Premarital Sex, Especially with the Person They Are Considering for Marriage

ROGER H. RUBIN

I recall one of my professors saying that he would be more concerned if his unmarried, 21-year-old daughter had not had a sexual experience than if she had had one. He considered such an episode a normal developmental occurrence. Adult sexuality is the product of psychological developmental experiences and physiological changes (Kirkendall and Rubin, 1977). It is found in the preadolescent crushes of boys and girls studied by Broderick (1966). Sexual expression flourishes in a society in which half of all Americans between the ages of 18 and 39 are single (Francoeur, 1982). Murdock (1949) found that only about 5 percent of human societies totally ban sexual intercourse for unmarried people. The majority of human societies probably permit it. Therefore, it is an absurdity to claim that under no circumstances should premarital sex be condoned.

DEFINING PREMARITAL SEX

The term "premarital sex" is unclear in its meaning. It "ties sex to a progression toward marriage. It's a concept that doesn't necessarily correspond with what people do, but it may influence how they feel" (Nass et al., 1981: 141).

Premarital implies that marriage is a foregone conclusion. Where does that leave those who will never marry? Do the same rules apply regarding sex between two 14-year-olds and that which occurs between two single 40-year-olds? Why do we not encourage masturbation, petting, and oral sex as socially acceptable alternatives to premarital intercourse? How do we deal with sex after divorce, separation, or death of a partner? How do we categorize coitus with an ex-spouse? Whether or not we call it premarital sex, nonmarital sex, or postmarital sex, it is all condemned in American society.

Although premarital sex is often equated with coitus, it may include kissing, petting, mutual masturbation, homosexual contact, and oral-genital sex, the growing popularity of which is reported by Hunt (1974), Hass (1979) and Bell and Coughey (1980).

Further complicating any meaningful definition of premarital sex is that males may view sexual activities as primarily genital while females may place greater emotional significance on such encounters. Reiss's (1960) classic work on different premarital sexual codes, especially permissiveness with affection, illustrates the length people will go to in order to reconcile values with behavior.

OCCURRENCE OF PREMARITAL SEX

Since the Kinsey reports of 1948 and 1953, premarital sex has become increasingly more socially accepted by males and especially females (DeLamater and MacCorquodale, 1979; Robinson and Jedlicka, 1982). Zelnik and Kantner (1977) found a doubling in premarital intercourse among women under 25 when compared to Kinsey. Zelnik (1979) found two-thirds of American women had intercourse by age 19. Ninety percent of women under age 25 had had premarital intercourse according to the *Redbook* survey of 100,000 women (Levin, 1975). Hunt (1974) found that 50 percent of single women age 18-24 had petted to orgasm. Hendrick and Hendrick

(1983) cite further evidence to these trends in the findings of Bell and Chaskes (1970), Hunt (1974), King et al. (1977), and Clayton and Bokemeier (1980). They also refer to the data of Verner and Stewart (1974), Zelnik and Kantner (1977), and Hobart (1979), indicating increasing rates of premarital intercourse for both sexes when comparing the mid-1960s to the end of the 1970s.

Another trend is toward younger, more casual relationships. Richmond-Abbott (1983) cites studies finding intercourse by age 15 among 38 percent of males and 25 percent of females (Verner and Stewart, 1974), and in the 18-24 year range figures at 95 percent men and 85 percent women having indulged (Hunt, 1974) were reported. Zelnik and Shah (1983) found 50 percent of teenage women and 70 percent of teenage men had premarital intercourse, and 80 percent of these men and women had done so before age 18. Miller (1981) found a mean of 13.3 years for first intercourse among pregnant adolescents.

McCary and McCary (1982) reviewed 21 studies on premarital intercourse among college students reported between 1948 and 1975. They noted a convergence of rates between males and females. Their prediction is that 95 percent of men and women will lose their virginity prior to marriage by the next decade of so. Evidence is increasing that such behavior occurs frequently among people who claim to be emotionally committed to one another (Pauly, 1976). Social commentators like D. S. Smith (1978) conclude that although the behavioral double standard may be disappearing, the attitudinal one is not. Females remain more interested than males in commitment prior to sex.

Among those who are divorced, separated, or widowed, three-fourths have postmarital sex according to Gebhard et al. (1958). McCary and McCary (1982) estimate that this figure exceeds 90 percent today.

THE SOCIAL CONTEXT OF PREMARITAL SEX

Reiss (Reiss and Miller, 1979) developed the theory that an individual's decision to participate or not in premarital sex is societally anchored. The groups one affiliates and identifies with will be instrumental in determining that person's sexual behavior.

There are numerous sociocultural variables to consider if one is to understand the many meanings of premarital sex. For example, 99 percent of Swedish couples live together before marriage (Cherlin, 1981). Cross-culturally, does this mean Swedes are more immoral than Americans? In the United States Blacks are more premaritally sexually active than Whites, and they start younger (Reiss, 1964, 1970; Rainwater, 1966; Shah and Zelnik, 1980; Zelnik and Shah, 1983). Is this because Blacks are less moral than Whites? Perhaps explanations may be found by examining the cultures and socioenvironmental living conditions of these groups.

Social class and premarital sexual intercourse are clearly related. Lower-class males are most likely to be active, while those of the middle class indulge more frequently in noncoital sex. For women of all social classes, intercourse is related to age at marriage, often occurring a year or two before marriage (DeLora and Warren, 1977).

Religion is another major sociocultural variable. The more religious a person is the less sexually permissive that person is (Rice, 1983). However, no one has defined chastity with any precision nor are there consistent sexual laws in the Bible, according to Roy and Roy (1969).

Same-sex peer groups, especially during adolescence, influence sexual decision making (Bell, 1966). The increasing autonomy of groups, such as that of teenagers from their families and other institutions, has promoted sexual permissiveness.

In addition, Strahle (1983) mentions such variables as sexual knowledge, personal sexual history, power in male-female relationships, age, physical attractiveness, educational and occupational aspirations, and sex roles as helpful in understanding premarital sexual activity rates. Add to this list increased longevity and leisure time, sophisticated contraception, legalized abortion, disease control, earlier menarche, privacy, and mobility. Is it any wonder then that we cannot fully understand the significance and meaning of premarital sexual activities without recognizing their social foundations? Many of these serve as valid and justifiable reasons for becoming intimate.

MOTIVES FOR PREMARITAL SEX

Although sex is a biologically based drive, the motives for its expression among humans are myriad. Neubeck (1974) refers to the "psychic ingredients" of the pleasures of sex by listing some of the numerous psychic motives for indulging. These include affection, animosity, anxiety, boredom, duty, adventure, accomplishment, mending wounds, recreation, lust, self-affirmation, and altruism. To confine all these motives to marriage as if that is the only institution confirming one's humanity is ridiculous.

Others have examined additional motives for having sex. Hendrick and Hendrick (1983) mention relief from tension and frustration, dealing with loneliness, controlling and dominating others, getting revenge, escaping oneself, communicating, conveying love and spiritual harmony, and procreating. Kirkendall (1961) sees the use of sex as sometimes a way of trying to salvage a doomed relationship.

Marmor (1969) writes that sex may make a person feel wanted and loved even without a deep commitment. It may serve as an outlet for aggression or an expression of gratitude. Juhasz (1977) views sexual activity as a way to bolster an ego because of an inadequate career or to flee the pressures of a family break-up. In addition, sex may be seen as a source of power, even for those who are often the weakest and most vulnerable.

Finally, for the divorced, widowed, or separated sex can be an escape or a reaffirmation. It may indicate recovery from the lost relationship or discovery of a better sex partner than the past one (Reed, 1976).

POSITIVE ASPECTS OF PREMARITAL SEX

Little has changed in the past few decades since psychologist Albert Ellis (1971) observed in 1953 that when books discuss premarital intercourse they usually end up opposing it. Yet, there is considerable evidence that premarital sex may enhance relationships, including marriage. Athanasiou et al. (1970), polling 20,000 affluent young men and women, found 50 percent believing that premarital sex leads to more successful marriage. Seventy-five percent admitted having had premarital intercourse. Ard (1974) found no marital deterioration related to premarital coitus indulged in by couples married over 20 years. Tavris and Sadd (1977) concluded premarital intercourse had no effect on a woman's marriage. No regrets regarding premarital intercourse were found for the majority of men and women in the Kinsey et al. (1953) study, and Lowry (1969) and Shah and Zelnik (1980) came to the same conclusion. Hass (1979) found the overwhelming majority of teenagers reporting that first intercourse was very enjoyable. Over ninety percent of men and women indicated premarital intercourse improved their relationship, according to Burgess and Wallin (1953). Strong et al. (1983) found that if a couple believes premarital sex prior to a social commitment is desirable then sex may improve the relationship. Finally, Kinsey et al. (1953) alleged from their data that premarital orgasmic experience was valuable in reaching marital orgasm and that early habits and attitudes cannot be dismissed in assessing later capabilities.

DeLora and Warren (1977) conclude that younger people are developing more satisfying sexual relationships today compared to previous generations and cite the work of Hunt (1974) as evidence. He found the vast majority of the young seek sex within a loving and caring relationship. Saxton (1983) writes that trust, affection, and love are associated with sexual intimacy for most American women.

Ellis (1971) is one of the few to state blatantly the benefits of premarital sex. These include release of sexual tension for millions of unmarried American adults and the positive psychological consequences for those who need not be obsessively thinking about sex. Sexual dysfunctioning might be alleviated if people felt more sexually competent and secure via numerous experiences. Ellis advocates the adventure and learning associated with sexual encounters, especially in the realm of marital selection. This may help avoid a hasty rush into marriage due to sexual deprivation. Wilhelm Reich warned in 1945 that it may prove disastrous not to be intimately aware of the sexuality of one's intended life partner. Marriage needs a firm economic, emotional, and sexual foundation today and the older, more experienced one is, the more likely marital success will follow. Ellis (1971) goes on to state that homosexuals may discover their sexual orientation by experimenting premaritally rather than denying reality and tragically disappointing a marriage partner. In heterosexual relationships voluntary premarital sex may help equalize the historical male domination of sexual rules. Even prostitution, pornography, and sex offenses may be reduced in a society more accepting of premarital sex.

Additional benefits of premarital and nonmarital sex may be accrued by society. Brecher and Brecher (1978) praise testosterone as a health hormone. Sexual arousal and activity is the easiest way to increase one's supply. They claim psychosomatic aches and pains may also be relieved by sex. Allen (1983) views sex as exercise and as a stress and tension reliever. In his classic study on premarital intercourse and interpersonal relationships, Kirkendall (1961) found some subjects better able to communicate, be provocative, and be concerned about a partner's feelings once they were sexually involved. The sharing of sexual experiences also had the effect of deemphasizing its importance in the overall relationship.

Through sexual encounters individuals may learn in a special way about their capacity for tenderness, acceptance, understanding, negotiation, and tolerance. It is unreasonable to believe that sexual activity never leads to emotional intimacy. It is perfectly reasonable to believe that some relationships will not be mutually acceptable because of sexual incompatibility. What is considered physically attractive, differences in libidinal drive, and forms of sexual activity deemed appropriate are some of the issues involved.

Finally, sex for fun, pleasure, and recreation is more common than purely procreational sex. As Neubeck (1984: 332) states, "I am in favor of sex even if it is only for 'screwing' as against human violence and hostility. . . . The world is a better place when it is a sexual place."

RESPONSIBILITY AND PREMARITAL SEX

Albert Ellis (1971: 52) asks, "May an informed and intelligent individual in our culture justifiably and guiltlessly have coitus before marriage?" I believe the answer is "Of course, but." Conditions for responsible behavior must precede sexual contact. McCary and McCary (1984) think neither party will be damaged by premarital intercourse if it is rationally discussed beforehand and not in the heat of passion. Decency, fairness, caring, maturity, and a guilt-free attitude toward sex are the basic ingredients.

Minimally, one must have a consenting partner. Responsible consent requires that one can deal with the consequences of one's decision. Contraception and disease control are obvious considerations. But we must also take into account economic resources, child-care ability, emotional stability, maturity and age, communication skills, willingness to marry, and religious, family, and community reactions if coitus results in conception.

How do we increase sexual responsibility in society? Juhasz (1977) suggests teaching decision-making skills, understanding motives, beliefs, self-concept and personal controls on sexual behavior, having a developmental perspective on intimacy needs, and recognizing the familial and social context of sex. This approach conforms with the many thoughts and research data presented thus far.

CONCLUSION

What Burgess and Wallin stated 30 years ago still rings true:

> The relatively small prediction weights warranted by our data on sex experience prior to marriage are in striking contrast with the importance attached by moralists to premarital chastity [1953: 204].

Clearly, the vast majority of people who have had premarital sex have not sustained any injuries. The recognition that such behavior may be beneficial or neutral at best raises the question as to why it is so vehemently opposed. Sociologically, the implication is that premarital sex and intercourse is more an issue related to maintaining control in a society and less one having to do with the actual consequences of premarital sexual activities. Ideally, intimate decisions regarding sex should be determined by the individual's conscience based upon religious, family, social, and personal beliefs. Modern society has no need to dictate an ideology of chastity or sexual permissiveness.

REFERENCES

ALLEN, R. (1983) Human Stress: Its Nature and Control. Minneapolis, MN: Burgess.

ARD, B. N., Jr. (1974) "Premarital sexual experience: a longitudinal study." Journal of Sex Research 10: 32-39.

ATHANASIOU, R., P. SHAVER, and C. TARVIS (1970) "Sex." Psychology Today (July): 39-52.

BELL, R. R. (1966) Premarital Sex in a Changing Society. Englewood Cliffs, NJ: Prentice-Hall.

———and J. B. CHASKES (1970) "Premarital sexual experiences among coeds, 1958 and 1968." Journal of Marriage and the Family 32, 1: 81-84.

BELL, R. R. and K. COUGHEY (1980) "Premarital sexual experience among college females, 1958, 1968, 1978." Family Relations 29, (July) 2: 353-357.

BRECHER, E. M. and J. BRECHER (1978) "Sex is good for your health," pp. 40-42 in Readings in Human Sexuality 78/79: Annual Editions. Sluice Dock, Guilford, CT: Dushkin.

BRODERICK, C. B. (1966) "Sexual behavior among preadolescents." Journal of Social Issues 22: 6-21.

BURGESS, E. W. and P. WALLIN (1953) Engagement and Marriage. Philadelphia: J. B. Lippincott.

CHERLIN, A. J. (1981) Marriage, Divorce, and Remarriage. Cambridge, MA: Harvard University Press.

CLAYTON, R. R. and J. L. BOKEMEIER (1980) "Premarital sex in the seventies." Journal of Marriage and the Family 42: 759-775.

DeLAMATER, J. D. and P. MacCORQUODALE (1979) Premarital Sexuality: Attitudes, Relationships, Behavior. Madison: University of Wisconsin Press.

DeLORA, J. S: and C.A.B. WARREN (1977) Understanding Sexual Interaction. Boston: Houghton Mifflin.

ELLIS, A. (1971) Sex Without Guilt. North Hollywood, CA: Wilshire.

FRANCOEUR, R. T. (1982) Becoming a Sexual Person. New York: Wiley.

GEBHARD, P. H., W. B. POMEROY, C. E. MARTIN, and C. V. CHRISTENSEN (1958) Pregnancy, Birth and Abortion. New York: Harper.

HASS, A. (1979) Teenage Sexuality: A Survey of Teenage Sexual Behavior. New York: Macmillan.

HENDRICK, C. and S. HENDRICK (1983) Liking, Loving, and Relating. Monterey, CA: Brooks/Cole.

HOBART, C. W. (1979) "Changes in courtship and cohabitation in Canada, 1968-1977," in M. Cook and G. Wilson (eds.) Love and Attraction: An International Conference. New York: Pergamon.

HUNT, M. (1974) Sexual Behavior in the 1970's. Chicago: Playboy Press.

JUHASZ, A. M. (1977) "Changing patterns of premarital sexual behavior," pp. 83-86 in Readings in Human Sexuality 77/78: Annual Editions. Sluice Dock, Guilford, CT: Dushkin.

KING, K., J. C. BALSWICK, and I. E. ROBINSON (1977) "The continuing premarital sexual revolution among college females." Journal of Marriage and the Family 39: 455-459.

KINSEY, A. C., W. B. POMEROY, and C. E. MARTIN (1948) Sexual Behavior in the Human Male. Philadelphia: Saunders.

KINSEY, A. C., W. B. POMEROY, C. E. MARTIN, and P. H. GEBHARD (1953) Sexual Behavior in the Human Female. Philadelphia: Saunders.

KIRKENDALL, L. A. (1961) Premarital Intercourse and Interpersonal Relationships. New York: Agora.

———and I. RUBIN (1977) "Sexuality and the lifecycle," pp. 142-148 in Readings in Human Sexuality 77/78: Annual Editions. Sluice Dock, Guilford, CT: Dushkin.

LEVIN, R. J. (1975) "The Redbook report on premarital and extramarital sex." Redbook (October): 38-44, 190.

LOWRY, T. P. (1969) "First coitus." Medical Aspects of Human Sexuality (May): 91-97.

MARMOR, J. (1969) "Sex for nonsexual reasons." Medical Aspects of Human Sexuality (June): 83-87.

McCARY, J. L. and S. P. McCARY (1982) McCary's Human Sexuality. Belmont, CA: Wadsworth.

McCARY, S. P. and J. L. McCARY (1984) Human Sexuality (brief edition). Belmont, CA: Wadsworth.

MILLER, S. H. (1981) Children as Parents: A Progress Report on a Study of Childbearing and Childrearing Among 12-15 Year Olds. New York: Research Center Child Welfare League of America, Inc.

MURDOCK, G. P. (1949) Social Structure. New York: Macmillan.

NASS, G. D., R. W. LIBBY, and M. P. FISHER (1981) Sexual Choices. Monterey, CA: Wadsworth.

NEUBECK, G. (1984) "Perspective: in praise of sex." Family Relations 33, 2: 331-332.

———(1974) "The myriad motives for sex," pp. 89-100 in L. Gross (ed.) Sexual Behavior: Current Issues. Flushing, NY: Spectrum.

PAULY, I. B. (1976) "Premarital and extramarital intercourse," pp. 256-267 in B. J. Sadock et al. (eds.) The Sexual Experience. Baltimore: Williams and Wilkins.

RAINWATER, L. (1966). "Some aspects of lower class sexual behavior." Journal of Social Issues 22, 2: 96-108.

REED, D. M. (1976) "Sexual behavior in the separated, divorced, and widowed," pp. 249-255 in B. J. Sadock et al. (eds.) The Sexual Experience. Baltimore: Williams and Wilkins.

REICH, W. (1945) The Sexual Revolution. New York: Orgone Institute Press.

REISS, I. L. (1970) "The influence of contraceptive knowledge on premarital sexuality." Medical Aspects of Human Sexuality (February): 71-86.

———(1964) "Premarital sexual permissiveness among Negroes and Whites." American Sociological Review (October): 688-698.

———(1960) Premarital Sexual Standards in America. New York: Free Press.

———and B. C. MILLER (1979) "Heterosexual permissiveness: a theoretical analysis," pp. 57-100 in W. R. Burr et al. (eds.) Contemporary Theories About the Family, vol. 1. New York: Free Press.

RICE, F. P. (1983) Contemporary Marriage. Boston: Allyn and Bacon.

RICHMOND-ABBOTT, M. (1983) Masculine and Feminine: Sex Roles Over the Lifecycle. Reading, MA: Addison-Wesley.

ROBINSON, I. E. and D. JEDLICKA (1982) "Change in sexual attitudes and behavior of college students from 1965 to 1980: a research note." Journal of Marriage and the Family 44, 1: 237-240.

ROY, R. and D. ROY (1969) Honest Sex. New York: Signet.

SAXTON, L. (1983) The Individual, Marriage, and the Family. Belmont, CA: Wadsworth.

SHAH, F. K. and M. ZELNIK (1980) "Sexuality in adolescence," in B. B. Wolman and J. Money (eds.) Handbook of Human Sexuality. Englewood Cliffs, NJ: Prentice-Hall.

SMITH, D. S. (1978) "The dating of the American sexual revolution: evidence and interpretation," pp. 426-483 in M. Gordon (ed.) The American Family in Social-Historical Perspective. New York: St. Martin's.

STRAHLE, W. M. (1983) "A model of premarital coitus and contraceptive behavior among female adolescents." Archives of Sexual Behavior 12, 1.

STRONG, G., C. DeVAULT, M. SUID, and R. REYNOLDS (1983) The Marriage and Family Experience. New York: West.

TAVRIS, C. and S. SADD (1977) The Redbook Report on Female Sexuality. New York: Redbook Publishing Co.

VERNER, A. M. and C. S. STEWART (1974) "Adolescent sexual behavior in middle America revisited: 1970-1973." Journal of Marriage and the Family 36: 728-735.

ZELNIK, M. (1979) "Sex education and knowledge of pregnancy risk among United States teenage women." Family Planning Perspectives 11 (November/December): 335.

———and J. F. KANTNER (1977) "Sexual and contraceptive experience of young unmarried women in the United States 1976 and 1971." Family Planning Perspectives 9: 55-71.

ZELNIK, M. and F. K. SHAH (1983) "First intercourse among young Americans." Family Planning Perspectives 15 (March/April) 2: 64-70.

One Should Marry a Person of the Same Religion, Race, Ethnicity, and Social Class

J. ROSS ESHLEMAN

Some of my best friends are ____. Would you want your daughter or son to marry one? These two statements have a ring of familiarity to most of us. Both denote a message of difference: by race, by religion, by ethnicity, by social class, and sometimes even by differences in personality characteristics, ideological preferences, and personal behaviors. The first suggests that we have some friends who are very different from us, and the second questions if that friendship should become intimate enough for marriage. Both statements seem to focus on the central issues of this essay: whether one should marry homogamously and endogamously or whether marrying hetero-gamously and exogamously works equally well. The position taken here is that it is best for you to marry homogamously and endogamously.

Homogamy means, literally, "marrying alike." It stands in contrast to heterogamy, meaning a "union of unlikes." Endogamy means marrying within the group in contrast to exogamy or intermarriage—a marriage between persons of different group affiliations. Within societies, homogamy and endogamy function to maintain the status quo and conserve family and societal values and beliefs. And as long as the family is perceived as an important institution in the United States or in any society, the selection and characteristics of the partners involved in marriage will be an issue of paramount importance.

The research literature on homogamy and endogamy reminds us that partners for marriage are chosen from a pool of eligibles who are much like each other. People marry others of similar race, age, education, socioeconomic background, religious preference, ethnic identity, and so forth in numbers greatly in excess of what could be expected to occur by chance (Eshleman, 1985: chap. 9). The rich seldom marry the poor, blacks seldom marry whites, religiously devout seldom marry nonbelievers, young seldom marry old, and graduate students seldom marry high school dropouts. Why not? Should they do so? Should we not be free to marry anyone we please without regard for race, religion, or class? Do not women's and men's liberation, creative patterns of sexuality, and the range of nontraditional lifestyles demand new freedoms in the choice of a mate?

The answer to questions such as these can be answered from various perspectives. We can respond in idealistic terms and argue for some utopian goal of a marital/societal system that ignores differences of heritage, color, beliefs, wealth, training, or skills. Or we can respond in realistic terms and note social conditions in the United States and around the world that differentiate people by a wide range of criteria. While the former ideal may be a worthy goal, the starting point, it seems to me, is to look at conditions as they exist and approach mate selection from a theoretical perspective of logic, reason, and rational thought and an empirical perspective of observation and evidence. Theoretically we can ask if rational thought and logic support homogamy or heterogamy and if propositions exist to suggest that endogamy leads to better marital outcomes than does exogamy. Empirically, we can ask what exists and what existing research lends support to homogamous/endogamous marriages in contrast to heterogamous/exogamous ones. One way to begin is to examine some of the reasons for the widespread prevalence of marriage between persons of similar characteristics and group identities.

REASONS FOR HOMOGAMY
AND ENDOGAMY

As noted, homogamous and endogamous marriages are the norm. Questions are more likely to be raised about intermarriages, be they racial, religious, class, ethnic, age, or whatever, than about intra-marriages. Societal concerns focus more on the variations from norms and on the different than on the patterns of conformity and on the common. Around the world, mate selection norms tend to grant greater approval to marriage among persons who are similar.

While these norms vary both by culture and by group characteristics within the culture, it is unusual to find norms for exogamy given a higher priority than norms for endogamy. Perhaps the two nearly universal exceptions are to marry someone of the opposite sex (male-female) and to marry outside of the nuclear family (a taboo on incest). Few other exceptions exist to rules favoring the marriage of persons of like characteristics or to rules favoring marriage within one's own social groupings. Why is this so? Why are men and women not created equally and universally available for marriage to anyone else? Why does love not overcome all obstacles and lead most people to ignore social structural differences related to sex, age, religion, race or class?

Many explanations exist to explain the existence of homogamy and endogamy at rates far exceeding those that would be expected simply by chance factors alone. The reasons that follow are not intended to be exhaustive but rather to highlight several leading arguments. Two basic explanations for homogamous-endogamous preferences center on the dual issues of socialization and ethnocentrism.

Socialization is the process of learning how to interact in society, learning what is correct, preferred and desirable, and learning or internalizing the rules of and expectations for behavior in a given society. We learn to interact with others in a given social context, usually in a community of family and friends who are much like us. We learn that eggs are a breakfast food and that dessert comes at the end, not the beginning, of a meal. We learn that to be slim is more attractive than to be fat, to pick one's nose in public is not a highly preferred behavior pattern, and to spit on strangers is not the way to win friends. We learn to believe in one God and be patriotic citizens.

Similarly, we learn to believe that these values and behavior patterns are not merely correct or proper, they are better than the beliefs, actions, and customs of others. In other words, we are socialized to be ethnocentric.

Ethnocentrism is the attitude that one's own culture is superior to others, that one's own beliefs, values, and behavior are more correct than others', and that other people and cultures can be evaluated in terms of one's own culture (Eshleman and Cashion, 1985). Have you any doubts that monogamy is more appropriate than polygamy, that capitalism is superior to communism, or that people who walk around half naked are shameless? Do you not believe that your culture's patterns of marriage and family life, your religious beliefs and practices, and the dress and food preferences of your ethnic group or subculture are superior to those of others? Most of us believe our ways are best. Thus, if my religious beliefs are the "truth," why should I marry someone who is different? If my racial grouping is superior, why should I marry someone inferior? If my ethnic food and dress patterns are most appropriate, why should I marry someone who dresses funny and prefers strange foods? If I am highly educated, wealthy, and attractive, why should I marry someone of little formal training, poor, or unattractive? Believing that our own beliefs, values, and behaviors are more correct than those of others is a key factor in the prevalence of homogamy and endogamy. The preferred mate selection pattern is, therefore, to marry someone highly similar to us, since who we are, what we believe, and what we do is "best."

The propinquity factor is another reason for homogamous/ endogamous marriage. Propinquity, meaning nearness in place or time, suggest that people meet and interact with those near them. And those near are most likely to be highly similar. Parents, often quite consciously, choose to live in neighborhoods and school districts where their children will meet "proper" potential mates. Issues such as interracial busing, school consolidations, and school district boundary changes tend to modify the propinquity composition, thus upsetting many parents by increasing the possibility of their children's marrying persons who are unacceptable.

Pressure from significant others and groups of reference encourage in-group and homogamous marriage as well. Parents, both directly and via more subtle means, encourage their children to interact with persons like them and discourage their children from developing intimate relationships and marital commitments with persons different from them. In extreme cases, pressures to enforce conformity includes the threat of total exclusion from the family. In other cases financial support is withheld, the child is not allowed to bring the potential spouse into the home, criticism is expressed, or parent-child conflict increases. Groups of reference such as religious organizations tend to discourage marriage with outsiders as well. Negative pressures applied may involve exclusion or not being permitted to marry at the altar, and positive pressures may involve special social events, gifts, and public notices of congratulations.

Other social-cultural explanations exist as well to explain the tendency toward and pressures for within-group marriages. Conditions supporting class endogamy, particularly among the middle and higher classes, include the desire to preserve family inheritance, lineage and status. Conditions supporting racial endogamy, at times involving legal restraints against intermarriage, include concerns about offspring and the rearing of children. Conditions supporting religious endogamy, sometimes based on Biblical teachings against being "yoked with unbelievers," includes concerns ranging from a lessening of commitment to the church or religious group to the religious training of children. Social norms exist among all groups in society. Most of these norms tend to provide the greatest positive support and rewards for endogamy. Most of these norms are backed by an assumption that the greatest chances for family cohesion, marital stability, and personal happiness exist among those who marry others similar to themselves.

THE CONCERN OVER HETEROGAMY AND EXOGAMY

Obviously, marriages occur with "opposites" or among those who are outside one's own group. But the conditions under which these marriages occur provide little justification or support for the desirability of these marriages. Spanier and Glick (1980) demonstrate that black females, due to demographic necessity, have a more restricted field of marriage eligibles than while females. They enlarge this field of eligibles by marrying heterogamously: males who tend to be older, who have lower educational attainment, and who have previously been married. None of these conditions argues for marital stability and success; rather, they give support to the idea that higher rates of marital instability among blacks may be associated with their higher incidence of deviation from more homogamous mate selection patterns.

Blau et al. (1982) illustrate how marriage outside one's group is governed by smallness of one's group relative to other groups. They cite studies showing that the proportion of Catholics in a city is a main factor reducing the likelihood that Catholics marry non-Catholics. The same holds true for racial groups and socioeconomic status. The highest socioeconomic strata, which are disproportionately small, are also most likely to marry outside their own class. This research relating exogamous marriage to small group size provides an argument for why people marry outside their group but provides no arguments that suggest it is the most desirable or the best for the persons involved.

In general, factors that foster intermarriage tend to be factors that appear to be related to higher degrees of marital instability. The religiously less devout appear to be both likely to marry outside their group and more likely to exhibit lower patterns of marital stability. Those who marry for what may be termed the romantic love complex are more likely both to marry outside their group and to exhibit lower patterns of marital stability. Those who psychologically rebel against their own group, have feelings of alienation, or are emotionally immature are more likely to marry outside their group and again are more likely to exhibit lower patterns of marital stability. In brief, while a range of explanations exists for intermarriage or exogamy, few of these arguments lend support to the superiority of these marriages over endogamous ones.

THEORETICAL SUPPORTS FOR HOMOGAMY AND ENDOGAMY

What type of theoretical rationale exists to support the idea that likes should marry likes or that it is best to marry one's own social groupings? First, let us approach theory from the general perspective of logic and common sense. Does it not seem logical to assume that if few differences exist in terms of racial, class, ethnic, or religious background, the level of potential conflict will be less? Does it not seem reasonable to assume that two people who share similar interests, goals, and activities have the greatest likelihood of getting along and forming lasting relationships? Perhaps support for this argument comes from one of the most widely used measures of marital or interpersonal adjustment: the Dyadic Adjustment Scale developed by Spanier (1976) and later confirmed by Spanier and Thompson (1982). The scale consists of 32 items centering around four basic components: dyadic consensus, dyadic satisfaction, dyadic cohesion, and affectional expression. Of the 32 items, 28 of them deal with dyadic measures that emphasize agreement, consensus, similarity, and like interests and activities. No items grant a higher adjustment score for differences or for doing things independent of the partner.

Second, is it not logical to assume that parents, friends, and community members will provide greater support to marriages among persons who are similar? Are they likely to raise questions of concern about a relationship between a male and female who are both white, both Catholic, both of Irish descent, and both from similar socioeconomic levels? Of course not. Common sense alone tells us that conflict, social ostracism, and community opposition are least likely to occur among "likes" and are increasingly likely to occur as the degree of difference between the partners increases.

Existing social theory lends support as well for homogamy and endogamy in mate selection. In general, a basic tenet of exchange theory is that in relationships with others, people attempt to maximize their rewards and minimize their costs to obtain the most profitable outcome possible. At first glance, as applied to mate selection, it might appear that the "best deal" is to get something for nothing. If I am poor should I not marry rich? If I am a high school drop-out, should I not marry a Ph.D.? This might appear to be ideal for the person who is poor or who has dropped out of school. But is the marriage likely to be a successful, adjusted one? Are the probabilities of separation and divorce high?

Exchange theory reminds us that in any social exchange, each party needs to receive something perceived as equivalent to that which is given and that the rewards need to be proportional to the cost. This is what Peter Blau (1964) and George Homans (1961) meant when they referred to a "fair exchange" or to "distributive justice." If resources or exchange criteria are unequal or imbalanced, one person is at a distinct disadvantage and the other has power over and is in a position to exploit the other. This is what Willard Waller (1938: 239) was suggesting decades ago in his "principle of least interest." Marriage is a bargaining process, and the one who has the least to offer can be used and exploited. Few people get something for nothing, and those who have nothing or little to exchange are at a distinct disadvantage. The principle of reciprocity is vital to successful relationships of any kind, including marriage. Without reciprocity—having something to give relatively equal to what is received—the marriage will not be successful and its chances for termination are high.

As should be clear, exchange theory has many propositions that suggest homogamy and endogamy. Edwards (1969: 525) quite explicitly stated that

(1) within any collectivity of potential mates, a marriageable person will seek out the individual who is perceived as maximizing his or her rewards;

(2) individuals with equivalent resources are most likely to maximize each other's rewards;

(3) pairs with equivalent resources are most likely to possess homogamous characteristics; and

(4) mate selection, therefore, will be homogamous with respect to a given set of characteristics.

Recent research on friendship choice and marital adjustment tend to present highly similar arguments in favor of equality, equity, and homogeneity. Billy et al. (1984) indicate that research into adult friendship choice indicates a homogeneity bias for demographic characteristics such as age, sex, and marital status; socioeconomic characteristics such as education and occupation; ethnic background; and political and religious preferences. Davidson (1984) investigated the relationship between perceptions of equity in marriage and marital adjustment and found them to be highly related.

Theoretical and empirical arguments both favor homogamy and endogamy in mate selection. The predominant "opposites attracts" theory is that of Winch (1958), who proposed that mate selection tends to be complementary rather than homogamous. The belief that complementary need is typical of most marriages is not consistent with the data, which were extensively reviewed by Murstein (1980) and indicate just the opposite. Minimal research other than that done by Winch himself tends to support his theory. Even that support was meager and derived from an atypical small sample of 25 college couples.

In conclusion, we know that likes tend to marry likes in numbers far exceeding chance. Both empirical and theoretical arguments tend to support homogamous and endogamous marriages. If you uphold the utopian ideal of anyone being a legitimate partner for marriage irrespective of race, class, age, education, religion, and a wide range of other characteristics, do so with a recognition of existing empirical evidence and theoretical perspectives that suggest the potential for negative consequences. If you personally want to violate social norms and marry heterogamously or exogamously because you are "in love," do so with an awareness of the increased probabilities of difficulties less likely to exist in a marriage with someone more similar to you. The suggestion in this article is for you to marry homogamously and endogamously. It is best for you.

REFERENCES

BILLY, J.O.G., J. L. RODGERS, and J. R. UDRY (1984) "Adolescent sexual behavior and friendship choice." Social Forces 62(March): 653-678.

BLAU, P. M. (1964) Exchange and Power in Social Life. New York: Wiley.

———T. C. BLUM, and J. E. SCHWARTZ (1982) "Heterogeneity and intermarriage." American Sociological Review 47 (February): 45-62.

DAVIDSON, B. (1984) "A test of equity theory for marital adjustment." Social Psychology Quarterly 47: 36-42.

EDWARDS, J. N. (1969) "Familial behavior as social exchange." Journal of Marriage and the Family 31(August): 518-526.

ESHLEMAN, J. R. (1985) The Family: An Introduction. Boston: Allyn & Bacon.

———and B. G. CASHION (1985) Sociology: An Introduction. Boston: Little, Brown.

HOMANS, G. C. (1961) Social Behavior: Its Elementary Forms. New York: Harcourt, Brace and World.

MURSTEIN, B. I. (1980) "Mate selection in the 1970s." Journal of Marriage and the Family 42(November): 777-792.

SPANIER, G. B. (1976) "Measuring dyadic adjustment: new scales for assessing the quality of marriage and similar dyads." Journal of Marriage and the Family 38(February): 15-28.

———and P. C. GLICK (1980) "Mate selection differentials between whites and blacks in the United States." Social Forces 58(March): 707-725.

SPANIER, G. B. and L. THOMPSON. "A confirmatory analysis of the dyadic adjustment scale." Journal of Marriage and the Family 44(August): 731-738.

WALLER, W. (1938) The Family: A Dynamic Interpretation. New York: Cordon.

WINCH, R. F. (1958) Mate-Selection: A Study of Complementary Needs. New York: Harper & Row.

One Should Marry on the Basis of Love and Compatibility of Intellect and Personality, Regardless of Background

RICHARD MARSHALL DUNHAM
JEANNIE S. KIDWELL

In this chapter we will argue that qualities of the mind and the personality of the one we love are more important for a successful marriage than the circumstance of background similarities. It is true that there is a great deal of evidence that marriage between demographically similar individuals has a better survival rate. Perhaps this is because we know more about these unions; most marriages take place between people who share cultural, racial, religious, and social class backgrounds and who are similar in age. However, similarity of background does not cause success in marriage, it merely correlates. Perhaps it only brings people together and provides them with the common tasks and goals around which the threads of love may be woven. Perhaps people who share common origins also share common traits such as attitudes, interests, and intellectual styles, which grow out of similar childhood experiences. These compatibilities, it seems to us, are more crucial to the success of a relationship than the mere presence of matched demographic conditions.

There are two kinds of reasoning that support the idea that those who are similar in personality and intellect, and who love each other, are more likely to be successful in marriage. The first of these are the correlational studies that suggest that people who are matched on some personal characteristics are more likely to succeed in marriage. Such studies do not exist for love because there are no objective measures. The second line of reasoning is based on studies of psychological and social processes. These processes reflect the deeper causal flow within the individual's personality and relationships. They define not only the conditions for the onset of a loving relationship but also for its successful continuation.

Our focus will be on processes. We believe that love is a complex and continuing process, not merely a fleeting encounter with excitement and bliss. Anyone who has experienced the blessing of new love knows also the joy of seeing or experiencing life in similar ways. But the mere existence of love and compatible attitudes and interests is only enough for a start. It is what one does about them that assures the long-term success of the relationship. If nurtured, romantic love can be a sound basis for marriage. The reader may have already noted that our view applies more clearly to deeper, more intrinsic relationships, and less to relationships that are more utilitarian in nature (Cuber and Harrof, 1968).

Tennov (1980) has provided a valuable recent discussion of love. She concluded that there is a difference between being in love (romantic love) and loving someone (defined as concern). One is an involuntary personal or psychological state, the other an act or intent that is chosen. Loving may occur with or without being in love. She coined the term "limerance" to refer to the romantic component of love that may be absent in the act of loving.

Limerance implies intensity, passion, longingness, poignancy, exclusivity, and a sense of acute aliveness, all of which are usually present between people who are in love. The limerant experience is often said to be fragile. In fact, many writers have denied that it relates to the success of a relationship, and some have even referred to it as irrational, narcissistic, impractical, or ephemeral—in short, a poor basis for marriage. Although Tennov found that it may last a lifetime, the average duration is only two years. We believe that it is possible for couples to cultivate and sustain the enlivening and compelling qualities of limerance. We also believe that limerance is the energy that drives the personal growth and the development of family and community that typically follow from an enduring, intrinsic relationship. We will discuss the conditions that favor its occurrence and continuation.

THE FOUNDATIONS OF LOVE

In part, the ability to experience and sustain love emerges from the personal and intellectual qualities of the people who come together in love. These qualities emerge in the developmental history of each individual, as described in the works of Erik Erikson (1959), Carl Rogers (1972), and other developmental theorists. For our brief writing, suffice it to say that the qualities are attained in successful completion of developmental stages up to and including the early adolescent emergence of personal identity. It is particularly important that one have shared comfortable intimacy in the family and/or with special other people in childhood. Paradoxically, the ability to love implies not only that one has learned to sustain intimacy within the family of origin, but that one has learned to recognize and accept one's self as unique and able to be separate from those with whom one has had intimacy in childhood. This separateness does not require the failure of these early important relationships, only the recognition of one's own essential and inevitable individuality. Self-reliance and self-trust may be products of this recognition and, with it, some sense of being effective and responsible as an individual in all relationships (Branden, 1980; Rogers, 1972).

The qualities attained up to and including the completion of a sense of personal identity constitute basic personality characteristics. When they are shared, they provide common building blocks for a couple who are striving to be successful in love. The maturity of the individuals allows them to maintain personal growth and separateness in the presence of mutuality.

ON BEING COMPATIBLE

We have discussed the importance of a sufficient developmental attainment in each partner as a foundation for a successful marriage. This is an important similarity. When both partners discover their similarities, their attraction to each other and their tolerance of each other are increased. In support of this contention are studies showing that the matching of some personal qualities is correlated with success in a relationship. Still, the level of prediction and understanding achieved in this research is not impressive. We find that the value of matched personal qualities cannot be taken alone as a basis for understanding the strengths or limitations of a relationship. Similarities alone are not enough. We may pass up lots of similar people for the "right one."

This brings us to one of the great mysteries of love—how it can be so selective. The selectivity of romantic love impresses us when we wonder what makes the one with whom we are falling in love so special. It may also rise when we find love occurring suddenly and unexpectedly. There is a rightness about it, it is compelling, it feels intuitively correct. Part of the answer may lie in the existence of simultaneous, though paradoxical, requirements for both similarities and differences. We will use Neal Miller's approach/avoidance conflict resolution model to help clear up the mystery.

Miller's model suggests that we learned our basic tendency to approach (be with, be intimate with, be open to, trust) in previous important relationships, such as those with our parents, grandparents, or in other special relationships. The approach tendency grew in response to the many rewards and comforts that occurred as we experienced affection, acceptance, approval, and our own growing competence in the contexts of those vital earlier relationships. It is active within us, a legacy of our past, shaping our future.

The approach tendencies we learned in early, important relationships generalize readily to all other human contacts, but the more strongly to people who are more like those who originally shaped the approach tendency within us by their care for us. Thus a woman may find herself drawn to men with curly hair and beards because of a strong similarity to a favorite, caring grandfather. According to Carl

Jung, these choices are often guided by archetypes set deep in our preconscious thoughts.

As the approach tendency grows within us in response to love, an avoidance tendency also grows, but in response to punishment, criticism, domination, and rejection. The avoidance tendency is stronger as the amount of these negative exchanges increases. When it becomes stronger than the approach tendency, we seek to escape the relationship. The avoidance tendency also generalizes, but less so than the approach tendency. The avoidance tendency has it strongest effect on relationships with people most like those who were important in our childhood.

The Miller model predicts that we will experience the greatest fascination with or attraction to someone who is of optimal dissimilarity, neither so similar as to elicit our home-learned aversions, nor so different as to fall beyond the range of those who call out our home-learned attraction. The optimal dissimilarity must be greater where greater aversions were learned, as with punitive, nonaccepting parents. It may be minimal when parents were very loving, democratic, and open.

The Miller model helps us understand how an initial fascination can occur in romantic love. It describes the conditions for the successful start of a meaningful love. It even tells us what leads up to the suddenness, the power, the exquisiteness, and the mystical quality of infatuation. Even more important, it tells us something about helping love to thrive. The newly formed relationships will survive for only a while on the home-learned attractions and aversions. It must build its own history of exchanges if it is to survive as more than a fantasy. It is in the building of a romantic love—what we do about it—that greatness in it is achieved or lost.

There is another way to understand the importance of similarities and differences. This part of our analysis relates more clearly to the question of compatibility. It is a scientific fact that we become more relaxed in the presence of the expected, the familiar, the comfortable. This relaxation is a basic appetite that shows up from infancy onward. We need enough relaxed, confirming occasions to feel safe, secure, and self-confident.

It is equally true that we become more activated, interested, or even anxious, when things occur that are beyond our understanding or expectation. The activation mobilizes our mental and physical energies to cope with and understand the unexpected. In our efforts to cope we bring the new within the expected, and within us. We become more competent by virtue of our encounters with the unexpected.

Sufficient activation keeps us emotionally alive, mentally alert, and growing. We may experience the activation as fascination, infatuation, zest, and as a keen aliveness. It may also take stressful forms. It may come as jealousy, poignancy, anxiety, guilt, or anger. It is impossible to say that some of each of these are not part of our human lot. We may even need them all within our experience in order to become all that we might wish. We need both relaxation and activation, in balance, in our lives. Relaxation follows a matching of our circumstances with our expectations, and activation occurs when our expectations and circumstances are not matched. The matched condition occurs more readily in homogamy, or at any time we are with those most like us. It is all just "old shoe"—comfortable, if a bit boring. The unmatched condition follows from differences and brings the adventure to romance.

And so we find that romantic love, with its critical balance of similarities and differences, provides the conditions for the experience of emotional security and comfort, on the one hand, and excitement and growth, on the other. Less than a critical balance would be either pallid or excessively stressful, and would leave us either bored or personally insecure. In our interpretation, the intuitively appreciated value of differences is that each is bringing to the other gifts that may guide them in rounding out their individual qualities.

BUILDING ON OUR STRENGTHS

We have shown how success in a love relationship requires more than a simple matching of personalities. Compatibilities consist of a critical mix of similarities and differences. These are the basic building blocks upon which a couple can construct a life with mutually satisfying goals and common tasks, and in which each can grow as an individual.

We illustrate this growth process using elements of learning theory. In learning theory, we find that any response is more likely to recur in a situation in which it is effective. We are more likely to do the things we have found ourselves to be competent in doing. It is less often recognized but equally true that we form attachments to the things that are present during our competent behavior. We love books if we have learned to read well; we love the equipment of our best sport. Each effective response in a situation involving the one we love ties us more closely together.

If we have learned a response from someone we love by imitation, the effect is enhanced. This happens when we pick up some of their usages, knowledge, skills, or better qualities. It happens, also, when both partners respond the same way in the same kind of situation.

When a couple shares intellectual and personality compatibilities, they will often respond in surprisingly similar ways to a given stimulus. This can be observed at parties or other social gatherings as well as in one-on-one intellectual exchanges. Knowing what elates, excites, or even offends each other can be shared by a simple glance or facial expression. When the matching of behaviors and attitudinal responses occurs, mutual approach and acceptance is strengthened. We feel alike and confirmed in our competence, and we are compelled to be together.

It is also important to note that in learning theory the ignoring of an inappropriate response contributes to its cessation. This process, called the extinction of the behavior, is an active one in a loving exchange. Thus, love, as interpreted in learning theory, provides for both accentuating the positive and ignoring or downplaying the negative. A loving partner may openly admire a skillful, well-coordinated dance step but overlook the inability to hit a tennis ball over the net.

This pattern of reinforcing the adaptive and extinguishing the minor unadaptive behaviors is sometimes called "catching them being good," and is part of the fabric of love. Habitual punishment for behaviors that are not wholly adequate or appropriate is an opposite and destructive interpersonal state, which has sometimes been called the "criticism trap." It tends to aggressively replace the more constructive and caring pattern and tends to evaluate a given behavior in terms of its inadequacy rather than its partial adequacy or its value in approximating some ultimate, beneficial response. Shared ineffective behavior, or mutual domination, criticism, and punishment gradually have damaging effects. We tend to avoid relationships that make us more incompetent, and we wish to feel different from the person who is dominating or critical toward us.

In reality, all relationships provide some mix of positive and negative. Love and growth thrive when the more caring, approving, competent exchanges predominate. Stendahl (1822) referred to this condition more poetically in his term—crystallization—whereby one's best qualities grow under the influence of love like a growing population of crystals.

These effects are subtle and limited in magnitude for any one shared occasion. However, if the shared occasions are numerous, the total effect can be great. For this reason, the investment of one's time and care in a loving relationship pays off. Having enough high-quality time together is vital, and the neglect of a relationship will gradually stifle it. People who remain in love are people who protect their time together and assign a high priority to the relationship.

THE SEASONS OF LOVE

Being aware of the effects of maintaining the predominantly positive spirit of the relationship may be a crucial factor as it proceeds from one natural phase to another. A characteristic of the development of a relationship is that it may proceed from *forming* the relationship through initial attraction and sharing, to *storming* through the differences that may have been ignored or suppressed in the beginning, to *norming* as the differences are resolved and we become more deeply matched, to *performing* as the more fully developed strength of our relationship is used in moving toward common goals and interests.

The forming phase tends to be thought of as the most romantic phase. It is the phase celebrated in poetry and song. It has the excitement of discovery and the special enhancing of similarities, as dealing with differences is diplomatically deferred. Poignancy or desperation are often experienced at this phase when one is not able to "get enough" of the lover because arrangements for being together have not yet been worked out. These obstacles enhance the urgent need to be together and to share everything. This is sometimes called the honeymoon phase.

The storming stage destroys many relationships. It is most severe when the predominance of positive events is permitted to erode. It is also destructive when the skills in communication, negotiation, and decision making are insufficient to move along the resolution of differences or when the emotional maturity levels of the partners are very different. It is more extensive when there are many differences to be resolved and more vulnerable when the differences are serious, such as when one partner is oriented to power or material well-being and the other toward humanitarian or altruistic considerations.

The norming period of a relationship begins when the first differences have been successfully resolved, and continues along with the storming process for as long as there are differences thereafter. In the storm-norm phase the challenge is to resolve differences in values, to continue to build upon compatibilities, and to grow personally in the process.

When we are successful in the storming stage the benefits are enormous. We know each other more deeply. Our self-disclosure is fuller and freer. Where differences exist, one partner may hold a more realistic or effective attitude. The better attitude is more likely to survive the storm, especially if the other partner can "take on" the better attitude. Thus, storming leads to growth in each. We are personally better for having gained the better behaviors from our pool of two repertoires, or having invented new ones more effective than those of either. Progress in this phase may be retarded if one partner is overly deferential or not sufficiently open.

The performing phase occurs any time we do things together with mutual understanding. This is where common interests and intellectual sharing can be of lasting benefit. Couples who have many interests in common are fortunate, and more so if they understand the importance of building upon these together.

In this writing we have attempted to show how love—growing out of compatible traits such as intellect, maturity, interests, and values— provides a sound basis for a fulfilling and enduring marriage. The value of these compatibilities is that couples can build upon them in a dynamic growth-oriented way. This is less true of the more static background factors such as age, socioeconomic status, and race. Using some developmental and learning theory principles, we have discussed the importance of early developmental history; emphasized the value of both similarities and differences; illustrated the importance of working at building a relationship through deliberate behaviors, such as emphasizing positive traits and ignoring negative ones; and shown how couples can use their compatibilities in strengthening their relationship through its various phases. It is not any particular similarity of personality or intellect that is crucial, but the optimizing of the matching of qualities. Love, like an enduring architectural wonder, can survive and can fulfill its promise when it is actively cultivated.

REFERENCES

BRANDEN, N. (1980) The Psychology of Romantic Love. Los Angeles: J. P. Tarcher.

CUBER, J. F. and P. B. HARROF (1968) Sex and the Significant Americans. Baltimore: Penguin.

ERIKSON, E. H. (1959) "Identity and the life cycle." Psychological Issues 1: 18-164.

KINGET, G. M. (1979) "The 'many splendored thing' in transition or 'the agony and the ecstasy' revisited," in M. Cook and G. Wilson (eds.) Love and Attraction. New York: Pergamon.

MELVILLE, K. (1983) Marriage and Family Today. New York: Random House.

MURSTEIN, B. I. [ed.] (1971) Theories of Attraction and Love. New York: Springer.

ORLINSKY, D. E. (1979) "Structural features of the romantic love relationship," in M. Cook and G. Wilson (eds.) Love and Attraction. New York: Pergamon.

ROGERS, C. R. (1972) Becoming Partners: Marriage and Its Alternatives. New York: Dell.

SAXON, L. (1983) The Individual, Marriage and the Family. Belmont, CA: Wadsworth.

STENDAHL, (1822) De l'amour. Paris: Librairie Armand Colin.

TENNOV, D. (1980) Love and Limerance. New York: Stein & Day.

II. Marriage and Divorce

This section of the book has three parts: the importance of the family in a person's life, marriage with traditional marital sex roles versus nontraditional sex roles, and the effect of divorce on children.

The first topic raises the question about whether the satisfactions of marriage outweigh the benefits of the single life. The next topic looks to the nature of the marital state by discussing the traditional family where the male functions as head of household and breadwinner while the woman is the homemaker, wife, and mother. This traditional orientation is contrasted with three alternatives—the out-of-home achieving woman, the notion of equality in the marital relationship, and the somewhat unusual notion that marital success is primarily up to the husband. The last topic brings up the question of whether couples' rights to happiness in case of marital breakdown outweigh the rights of the children to an unbroken family.

DISCUSSION QUESTIONS

(1) Considering all the advantages that Dr. Stein mentions for the single life, why does anyone get married?

(2) What function does marriage serve so well that most divorced people remarry? Would all divorced persons remarry if they could? What does this say about some functions that marriage does not serve?

(3) To what extent is getting married or staying single a rational choice?

(4) What are some advantages and problems of having a traditional-sex-role marriage?

(5) How does the achievement of women outside of the home threaten traditional marriage? How would a traditional marriage person answer the author?

(6) Equality sounds good. What are some problems with an equality-based marriage?

(7) Dr. Newman suggests that males should be primarily responsible for the success of the marriage. How would our society be different if most males agreed with him?

(8) Consider some social engineering ways to help people make more rational decisions about how to allocate sex roles, since it is likely that roles may be allocated differently during their marital career.

(9) Is "honor thy children" a good adage for parents, and should they implement it by remaining married for the sake of the children? Develop the argument favoring this adage.

(10) Discuss how children might be better off if their parents were happy even though divorced.

(11) Under what conditions would you suggest to parents that they stay together or get divorced for their children's sake?

(12) Relate the mode of selecting marital partners, marital sex roles, and divorce. Form some general statement of your own or from family theory.

CLASS ACTIVITIES

(1) Play out a skit with several young single people who are achieving in their work. Have them discuss how much better off they are than their married friends. When they are finished, have the class ask them questions.

(2) Have two class members take the roles of two older people who are celebrating their fiftieth wedding anniversary. Have the class interview them about the sources of satisfaction and problems. Invite a real couple to come to class.

(3) It is the year 2085, and you are the person in charge of who should get married and who should remain single. What criteria would you use for deciding?

(4) Invite a traditional married couple to come to class and discuss their family life together including whatever problems they have had or may be facing as well as their satisfactions.

(5) Select one student to represent the employer of a number of women. Have this employer discuss with a group of students representing husbands how the home and work settings could be made more positive for their wives.

(6) Have students draw pictures depicting family scenes indicating different ways in which equality of marriage may be worked out.

(7) Have each student write a poem or short story illustrating a way a husband can help create a positive marriage. Have the class discuss and analyze them in terms of the readings.

(8) Have a debate among the advocates of each position about marital sex roles. The debaters are to take a position with which they do not agree.

(9) Work out the plot for a film focusing on the postdivorce life of the parents.

(10) Have a panel discussion involving real children of divorced couples, class members from divorced families, or those taking the role of children from a divorced family. Note their ambivalences.

(11) Have the class be members of a convention of children whose parents were divorced. Ask them first to develop a children's and parents' rights plank. Then have the convention try to resolve differences in small committees.

(12) Have students draw family scenes, paint a picture, or write a poem illustrating their viewpoint about any two of the three topics of this section.

The Single Life Has More Potential for Happiness than Marriage and Parenthood for Both Men and Women

PETER J. STEIN
MERYL FINGRUTD

Joan is a 31-year-old professor of psychology at a well-known urban college. Aside from preparing for her classes, doing research, and writing, she belongs to a professional organization, body-builds at a nearby health club, works against apartheid in South Africa, and has a small but active friendship network. She dates three different men: one who is ready to settle down, one who cannot deal with commitments, and one who is married.

Robert is a 36-year-old urban planner. He prides himself on having made a stable professional career after many years of confusion and struggle. His main problem at the moment is whether or not he is capable of loving one woman for the rest of his life. He dates a lot, but has few relationships that last longer than six or eight months. He would like to get married, not only to get overbearing friends and relatives off his back or to prove to some of his colleagues that he is not a latent homosexual, but because he is at heart a romantic and would like to believe that one can still find love and happiness in modern society.

Joan and Robert are typical of the men and women who make up the growing population of singles. This widening network of unaffiliated young people has been the subject of hundreds of magazine and journal articles that ask questions such as, Who are they, Why don't they marry, What sort of lifestyle do they construct, Are they lonely and unhappy, and Do they have it better than married people? The September 1984 issue of *Ms.* offered an analysis of the ten most attractive cities for single women, with information on job possibilities, civil rights, safety, and convenience of transportation. *New York* (September 22, 1984) recently presented some data on the severe discontent among single New Yorkers. A new book by Douglas Austrom (1984), who conducted a study of Canadian singles, reports that, contrary to earlier data, singles were every bit as healthy as married people but that married people were happier with the quality of their lives. Robert Staples (1981), writing on black singles, comments that a basic reason for the increase in singleness among blacks is the degree of conflict prevalent in male-female relationships. The conflict reflects perceived differences in values, interests and goals; differing definitions of needs, and the shortage of eligible men for middle-class women.

Peter Stein, in his book *Single Life* (1981), writes that singles and marrieds both face key issues of adulthood—friendships, intimacy, sexuality, work, careers, living arrangements, emotional and physical health, whether or not to become a parent, and aging—but the social contexts within which those issues are addressed are dramatically different. Stein emphasizes that singles typically have no significant other with whom to make such decisions. Singles tend to make such decisions alone, though with the help of family members, friends, or therapists, but they themselves must bear the consequences of the decisions.

The latest census data indicate the increasing tendency for young adults to delay marriage. In 1984 the median age at first marriage for men was 25.4; for women it was 23.0. The proportion never married has increased for each group in the age range 20 to 44, as indicated in Table II-A.1.1.

TABLE II-A.1.1   Percentage Single (Never-Married), 1984 and 1970

Age Groups	Women	Percentage Change 1970-1984	Men	Percentage Change 1970-1984
20-24	56.9	+21.1	73.2	+20.1
25-29	25.9	+15.4	37.8	+18.7
30-34	13.3	+ 7.1	20.9	+11.4
35-39	7.5	+ 5.7	11.6	+ 4.4
40-44	5.6	+ 5.3	6.9	+ 0.6

SOURCE: Saluter (forthcoming).

An increasing proportion of single adults live alone, and the rate of increase is largest among younger men and women. For ages between 25 and 34 the percentage living alone or with nonrelatives quadrupled between 1970 and 1984. The rate of increase among lone householders was five times as rapid for people under 45 (217 percent) as compared to those 45 and over (43 percent).

In this article we want to examine some aspects of single life in order to appraise the quality and texture of this social status. Single life opens up many opportunities and closes others. We want to note some of these opportunities, even if single people have not yet exploited these possibilities for constructing a satisfying life. We are concerned in the pages that follow primarily with singles who are middle-class men and women between the ages of 20 and 44 who, unlike most of their counterparts, remain unmarried. We are going to assume that these singles have some measure of economic self-sufficiency and social psychological autonomy and are located in or near a supportive network of friends and/or family (Adams, 1976; Peterson, 1982; Barkas, 1980). We do not assume that single life is a sociosexual utopia, but that it is a way of life that offers enormous possibilities for happiness, productivity, and self-actualization.

One of the most basic, positive features of single life is that it does not restrict opportunities for development and change. The years after high school and college are typically a time for people to clarify careers, lifestyle choices, and political and sexual identities. By staying single, an individual has more freedom to experiment, reflect, and make substantial changes in beliefs and values.

In sociological terms we would say that the single has a greater opportunity to construct new identities. Each new encounter (and we are thinking especially of dating situations) provides the possibility for the single to stress different parts of his/her biography, to present other sides of the self, to engage different interests, values, emotions. This greater control over the process of identity construction is a luxury that marriage, with its ideology of stability, continuity, and responsibility to others, does not often provide. However, this freedom may come with its own constraints: The single may find that it is difficult to be so many selves, may long for a more integrated, stable definition of self. Using a national sample of never-married adults, Arthur Shostak (forthcoming) found that singles develop a variety of coping mechanisms to relieve problems of identity loss and confusion. Friends and other support networks provide an ongoing community of significant others.

Singles often cite freedom as the greatest benefit and pleasure of single status. Singles are not only able to alter their identity, but without the obligations of spouse and family they can move more freely in the society. Married people are more involved in the web of social life, more embedded in a complex system of statuses, roles, obligations, and expectations with family, relatives, and friends. One man comments:

> As a single man I could hop on a plane to Florida at Thanksgiving for a couple of hundred dollars. Now it would cost me $720 to get the whole family there. And the kids would want to go to Disneyworld. So we're staying at home—I'm staying at home.

Singles need to be embedded in some kind of network or group in order to feel attached to and involved in social life, but their embeddedness occurs largely through their own choice and design.

Singles are often accused of having no sense of responsibility except to themselves and, as such, live a rather selfish existence. We do not agree with this characterization. Single life can be "self-ish": oriented toward serious thinking about how to tap all of the resources and possibilities housed within the person. Indeed, the single could learn little about his/her part in society other than the fact that there are infinite possibilities to experience. But this is not generally the case.

First, families and friends often put greater demands on singles precisely because they are so "free." The expectation is that a single person is more readily available and can drop everything to come to the aid of friends in crisis or families in need. That a single person might have a life for which he or she is responsible is frequently negated, as though only married couples with families have "real" lives.

Second, we believe that the single learns how to rely on his/her self, to become his/her own best friend, to gain an intimate knowledge of what makes life meaningful. The single is closer to the decision-making process because there are fewer institutionalized constraints, obligations, and patterned responses that the single can use as a guide. The single is more often alone with his/her decision. As such, single life allows for the development of creativity and maturity. The single, like the artist, is encouraged to design from scratch, work slowly and thoughtfully on the creation of the object, view the results and then, if necessary, start again, having learned the consequences of relying upon a particular medium of expression. Just as the artist matures through experimentation, taking risks, stretching the imagination, so the single learns to accept responsibility for having made certain decisions and develops the courage to change when the results are disappointing.

Single life offers the individual more leisure time. Studies of consumption patterns show that singles are a large portion of the market for travel and vacation offers. They are also apt to take courses at universities and neighborhood centers and to engage in political activity. There are two positive side effects here. First, single life can encourage the growth of a cosmopolitan personality. Singles are not people who work all day, come home to have dinner with the family, and remain at home to pay bills. Singles can be the explorers and archaeologists of cultural and community life. Second, singles are more available for community. They have the time to join in "extracurricular" activities, and because single life can be lonely, they often are highly motivated committed members of groups that provide social contact.

Single life is, at first glance, incompatible with the sociologist's notion that human beings are social animals. We subscribe to the idea that human beings are compelled toward social contact and indeed need others to help with the exigencies of everyday life. It is paradoxical, then, that single, not married life allows the time and motivation for participating in communities. Married life has a tendency to become more focused on one's family, particularly with the arrival of children. This narrowing need not be part of married life; certainly, families could become tied to one another in important ways, and strong neighborhood groups could arise. But in modern society with its increasing suburban sprawl, there is less of a chance for a strong neighborhood sense to develop. Adults are, rather, torn between the time they spend at work and the time they can devote to family life. The ecology of home and workplace does not allow families easy, consistent access to others, and the work day is both mentally and spatially separated from home, family, neighborhood.

The single, though on the surface a solitary figure, has more chance to form community links because he or she does not have to devote after-work energies to maintaining a family. Singles form alternative families or subcommunities by linking up with others who have time and energy for something beyond workplace obligations. But single life can be isolating and anonymous. Cargan and Melko (1982) in a study of 400 households in Dayton, Ohio, that included 114 never-married men and women found that, while singles had more fun, they were also more lonely. Because single life does not come with a built-in network of significant others, single people can deeply feel and know the value of community and will attempt to seek it out when they can.

Taken together, available time, freedom to move in and out of lifestyle choices, and participation in community point toward another interesting possibility provided by single life. Daniel Berrigan once said that single people more easily become revolutionaries. While we do not think singles are necessarily the revolutionary vanguard, we do see single life as having the potential for the development of critical consciousness. Because there is a less clear picture of single life and fewer institutionalized norms and expectations, singles do more ad-libbing. Marriage is still a highly valued lifestyle that most people expect to join at some point in their lives. A study by Thornton and Freedman (1983) found that marriage continues to be valued by the majority of Americans and that 90 percent still expect to marry and have lasting marriages.[1] Gallup (1982) reported that the most important social value for Americans is "having a good family life" (82 percent). This means that single life is less normative or less mainstream. Marginality usually makes individuals more critical and questioning of the taken-for-granted realities of everyday life.

Hence, single life can encourage people to think carefully and deeply about their society and develop new ways of being. For example, the single is confronted daily with America's emphasis on "coupling": Restaurants, especially expensive ones, are not set up for and may not be as welcoming to a single person. Singles are often relegated to the bar, the counter, or a dark table in the corner. Going out alone at night is sometimes depressing and even frightening. Single women, especially, are prey to harassment by men when they are not accompanied (protected) by a man. Therefore, everyday life becomes a territory for critical reflection and reevaluation through the eyes of the single. Singles in some sense trouble the smooth flow of social life, given that so much of it is organized around couples. Confronted with this prevailing definition of reality, singles are forced to construct alternative meanings on a temporary or long-term basis.

Finally, we cannot leave this discussion of single life without mentioning the issue of sexual freedom. Singles frequently cite this feature as a benefit as well as a difficulty in their lives. Sexuality and sexual mores are especially troubling in modern society, and theory and practice are likely to be out of sync. For example, Jacqueline Simenauer and David Carroll (1982), who studied 3000 single men and women, found that about 75 percent of the men said they are indifferent or actively opposed to having sex on the first date, yet about 66 percent sleep with a woman on the first to third date and 80 percent have sex by the fifth date.

Freedom to have variety in sexual partners is exciting and life enhancing. If they are not desperate and there are opportunities to find sexual partners, the ability to choose to have sex makes one feel in control of one's life. Singles do not have to have "affairs"; they do not have to hide the fact that they want to make love with someone. But sexual freedom is only as pleasurable as the social setting allows. Singles may find that while they are available for sex, others are not. Singles may be insecure about their attractiveness, sexual skills, sexual desirability, given that there is no steady partner to validate one's attractiveness, sexuality, and desirability. The social construction of one's sexuality requires validating others'. Sex can be unsatisfying, even alienating, when there are many and changing partners. Singles are frequently reminded of the possibilities of venereal disease, AIDS, and infections connected to sex, especially when they do not know enough about their partners. Finally (and this is not unrelated to the sex/disease connection), singles must be ready to face the fact that many adults came from backgrounds in which sexuality was viewed as dirty, sinful, or unspoken. They must be prepared to confront their backgrounds and the residue of religious and parental invocations. To choose sexual freedom means that singles must reeducate themselves and their partners about the location and meaning of sex and sexuality in everyday life. There is even now no clear, wise social discourse on sexuality. Singles can be important contributors to the discourse on these issues, especially if they are already doing some serious evaluations of themselves and their lives.

Much more can be said about the complexity of single life, and we have merely touched on some of the issues involved. Singleness does present possibilities for better knowing oneself, for clarifying values and life choices, and for participating in social life. Though far from a tension-free existence, we believe that the benefits of single life are real and profound.

NOTE

1. A majority of mothers and their 18-year-old daughters "considered the decision to marry or to remain single as a real and legitimate choice between acceptable alternatives"; this perception of the relative merits of marriage and single life is quite different from that held by Americans in the past.

REFERENCES

ADAMS, M. (1976) Single Blessedness. New York: Basic.
AUSTROM, D. (1984) The Consequences of Being Single. New York: Long.
BARKAS, J. L. (1980) Single in America. New York: Atheneum.
CARGAN, L. and M. MELKO (1982) Singles: Myths and Realities. Beverly Hills, CA: Sage.
Gallup Report. (1982) What's Important to Americans. Report 1982, March.
HASS, A. (1983) Love, Sex and the Single Man. New York: Franklin Watts.
PETERSON, N. L. (1982) The Ever Single Woman: Life Without Marriage. New York: Quill.

SALUTER, A. F. (forthcoming) Preliminary data for report on "Marital status and living arrangements: March 1984," U.S. Bureau of the Census. Washington, DC: Government Printing Office.

SHOSTAK, A. (forthcoming) "Singlehood: the lives of never-married employed Americans," in S. Steinmetz and M. Sussman (eds.) Handbook of Marriage and the Family.

SIMENAUER, J. and D. CARROLL (1982) Singles: The New Americans. New York: Simon & Schuster.

STAPLES, R. (1981) The World of Black Singles: Changing Patterns of Male/Female Relations. Westport, CT: Greenwood.

STEIN, P. [ed.] (1981) Single Life: Unmarried Adults in Social Context. New York: St. Martin's.

THORNTON, A. and D. FREEDMAN (1983) The Changing American Family. Population Reference Bureau, Vol. 38, No. 4, October.

U.S. Bureau of the Census (1984) "Marital status and living arrangements: March 1983," in Current Population Reports, P-20, no. 389. Washington, DC: Government Printing Office.

Marriage and Parenthood Are Necessary for a Happy Life for Both Men and Women

WALTER R. SCHUMM

There are many good reasons for staying single in spite of our culture's bias against singleness and single persons. Because of many subtle and not-so-subtle pressures on individuals to get married and to have children, well over 90 percent of us will marry at some point and usually have children, a percentage that is probably much higher than it should really be. Single persons retain a certain degree of flexibility that can enable them to serve others in special ways and to enjoy a lifestyle out of reach of the typical married person. In some situations singleness may be preferable to marriage and family life for most individuals (I Corinthians 7). However, in the present circumstances in the United States, I believe that marriage and family life are preferable for the average person.

Now there are, of course, good and poor reasons to marry and to have children. While St. Paul highlighted his concern for the risks of premarital sexual relations in I Corinthians 7—risks that I think are quite valid (Schumm and Rekers, 1984)—I think that sexual drive is a poor primary reason for marrying. I think that the best frame of mind for making a mature choice of a partner would occur once one had decided that one could live happily as single or married, not when one felt he or she was so sexually frustrated that marriage to anyone would be an improvement over the current frustration. I also think that marrying for reasons of social pressure is unwise. I remember how at William and Mary during my senior year I heard stories of how left out some of the unengaged senior women began to feel as more and more of their peers were announcing their pinnings or engagements. It was alleged by some to get to a point where the two groups were no longer on friendly speaking terms with each other.

We can turn to research for some general pointers on the issue. One will generally find that the overall life satisfaction of married couples is higher than that of singles (Campbell et al., 1976: 398; Andrews and Withey, 1976: 286), although the extent of the differences can be debated. However, on measures other than self-reported satisfaction, it appears that single males are particularly distressed on the average, while single women are better off than married women, on the average (Bernard, 1972). Many of the men I have talked to have indicated that marriage increased their productivity at work by freeing them from the anxiety and time demands associated with an active dating life. One would suspect that the opposite may be true for women, particularly after having had children, since most of the child care and household chores still remain the wife's responsibility even when she is employed full-time. It is also obvious to me that children are necessary for societal growth (where else are all the future teachers, doctors, farmers, soldiers, and factory workers going to come from?); therefore the state has a legitimate interest in general regarding population control.[1]

However, most of us do not get married or have children because we want the state to have more future workers or because some research study predicted that we will be happier if we marry. We usually respond—or at least would like to think we do—to more personal concerns.[2] Even the concept of having children in order to have someone to take care of oneself when one is older may have less validity than we often assume; certainly, one may be very disappointed if one assumes that one's children will automatically provide the desired level of assistance (Quinn, 1983). At the present time I think there are four benefits of marriage and family life for the average person that make that state more desirable than singleness. While it is possible to obtain similar benefits while single, I think for the average person the circumstances of marriage and family life are more conducive to obtaining the benefits than are the typical circumstances of singleness. Thus, I am not trying to argue *against* singleness as much as *for* marriage and family life.

The first reason is that I believe we were made to be social beings with a need for varying levels of interpersonal interaction with others. While we all need friendly interaction with a wide variety of people, I believe that we also need very close interaction with a smaller number of persons who are quite different from ourselves. Family life in the traditional sense guarantees an opportunity for very close involvement with people quite different in sex and age. It would be much easier to live with persons of the same sex and age, I suppose, but having to live with persons with basic—even biological—differences requires us to step out of our own narrow perspectives and evaluate our lives from a wider perspective.[3] Without such opportunities, I think we are going to feel a sense of incompleteness, of not having used all of our interpersonal facilities. Perhaps this is one reason that the biblical creation story describes Adam as created with a need for Eve, a need only partly related to sexual fulfillment (Genesis 2:20-25). We need the support that can come only from a person who has known us for a long time in a variety of close encounters, a person who is quite different from us but equal.

Related to the first idea is a second benefit. While many people are turning to various encounter groups for interpersonal growth, I think that the best laboratory for continued interpersonal growth can be found in the marital relationship. Growth is often painful, though, so this is not a popular reason to marry. However, as (if I recall correctly) Samuel Johnson once said "Marriage has many pains, but celibacy has few pleasures." Some will avoid marriage to spare themselves these hassles and do so correctly (I Corinthians 7:28). But for most, these hassles can be a source of increasing maturity and personal development. Unfortunately, we tend to think such hassles are the product of our own particular marriage and not shared by others in their marriages.[4] Thus, we often see couples bailing out of a relationship within weeks of marriage, simply because things did not seem to work themselves out automatically. Sadly, such couples are thereby forfeiting the growth they could have gained if they had decided to work together cooperatively to support each other in that growth.

As part of a premarital counseling course that I have been teaching at Kansas State, my students and I enjoy adding to a list of things that have to be decided in marriage. The list began with about fifty things when I took a similar course at Purdue and has now expanded to over 400 items. For each item, one can decide who is going to do it, when it is to be done, how often it is to be done, how well it should be done, and who decides if it has been done satisfactorily. Things can be done together, by each other taking turns at it, or by just one person. Items include such chores as taking out the garbage or doing laundry and more abstract things, such as establishing a balance between intimacy and individuality. Taking the 400 items with at least five types of questions for each item, one obtains at least 2000 decisions that must be made at some time in marriage. The single person can do whatever he or she pleases in most of the areas, but the married person must give and take with his or her partner in these areas.[5] With a roommate one has many of the same decisions, but the decisions can be postponed if necessary until one gets a new roommate, so that the situation is not quite the same. One is forced to weigh alternatives and ask tough questions about what is really important to oneself, what one's priorities really are or are going to be. Decisions often have to be made under less than ideal circumstances, when one is exhausted, frustrated, and confronted by a similarly situated partner whose tact may have run out. Learning how to respond with loving, sensitive, thoughtful, unselfish words and actions under such circumstances draws upon the deepest reserves of one's character.

I used to think that I was almost intrinsically unflappable and very mild tempered—until I got married! I was mild tempered and did not show much anger very often because I had never been in circumstances that really tested my patience and selflessness as marriage can. Having been married a few months I came to realize that I was not nearly as good as I had thought beforehand. I also realized that it is much more difficult to produce the considered, tactful responses one is supposed to (according to modern communication principles as in the Minnesota Couples Communication Program by Miller et al. [1975] or according to scripture) respond with in marriage than it is in the artificial setting of the classroom or in more superficial relationships. Since learning such principles is so much easier than putting them into practice, I fear that many

relationships have foundered once one partner learned such principles and blamed the marriage or the spouse for the unexpected
difficulty encountered in trying to apply the principles on a daily
basis. I am inclined to think that character is not forged on the
playing fields of Eton as much as it is forged in the heat of the kitchen
and the bedroom. While I think such things should be welcomed as
opportunities for personal growth (James 1:2-5), I think many of us
avoid them and the associated emotional pain by leaving the
marriage, downgrading our marital interaction to a more superficial
distance, or forcing our marriage into very conventionalized patterns
that maintain the appearance of smug satisfaction but serve to hide
the fact that the marriage is devoid of vitality beneath the surface
(Matthew 23:27).[6]

I think that the marriage relationship should be considered
primary, even though some think it exists primarily for the procreation of children. Here, I would note that God created marriage
before family (if one accepts the truth of the Genesis account) and
that, while not having children might be very disappointing, it
should not be taken as severely as Hannah did (I Samuel 1:8). Of
course, some will choose to marry and remain childless or child-free,
depending on one's terminology—certainly a viable option. Why
then do I prefer marriage *and* family life?

First, I think that children teach us a great deal about ourselves as
adults. They can be our best, though most painful, critics and our best
supporters, even should our spouse die or the marriage end in divorce.
Their success or failure in life will affect our sense of lifetime
accomplishment (Proverbs 23:24). But more interesting, they remind
us of many of our adult behaviors that are products of our harried
world and reflect back to us patterns of behavior into which we have
slipped. They dare to ask "Why?" about almost everything, forcing us
to consider if the reasons we once did something are still relevant
today. They will accept our guidance without reservation (at least
occasionally!) because they are willing to trust us totally, whereas
adults would have to check things out pretty carefully before
committing themselves. In some things their responses to us are
closer to the way ours should be to God than ours often are, as
accustomed as we are to being skeptical and cautious about things
that cannot be tangibly investigated (Matthew 18:3), even though not
all such responses are desirable (I Corinthians 13:11). They can enjoy
simple things over and over, while we hurry along, forgetting to stop

and smell the flowers along the way. They also remind us of how much we have had to learn from scratch in order to become fully functioning adult persons, but the zeal with which they strive to take their first step and other steps of growth often puts our motivation to shame. They can also stretch our patience even further than our spouses can. (Try to calm a baby sometime when you cannot figure out why the baby is distressed and upset.) How you react in the midst of the very irritating crying noise and your sense of helplessness and felt incompetence will show you a great deal about your reservoirs of patience and love.

Children also force us to evaluate our priorities and goals. Although we all may like to think that our occupations are terribly important—and they may be—in their consequences, the fact remains that most of us can easily be replaced with few really noticing much difference in results. I am quite sure that if I left Kansas State, for example, my department would have no trouble filling the vacant position with someone else of equal or better competence, given the large number of unemployed Ph.D.s and the small number of vacant professorships. However, the same cannot be said for our situation as spouses or parents, especially the latter. We can be replaced as a spouse (I Corinthians 7:39) perhaps but never as a parent. The effect of parenting can extend to several generations (Deuteronomy 5:8). One way that I illustrate the relative effect of choices and their consequences is what I (tongue-in-cheek) call my mathematical model of morality (Figure II-A.2.1). The consequences of one's actions can have impact over varying periods of time and over a wide array of persons and groups of people. Some jobs amass a lot of prestige and income if they draw upon the resources of a large audience (professional athletics, popular novelists, automobile manufacturers, and so on), but for them the question is the extent to which audience members are really affected over time. Other people influence a smaller number of persons but have a deeper influence that may last longer (for example, physicians and teachers). Marriage and family life involve perhaps the smallest number of persons but have the longest effect over time and, therefore, may be considered relative to most jobs to have the largest effect altogether.

The world needs parents who will train wanted, loved children, who according to virtually all research (Rollins and Thomas, 1979) end up as the most responsible, caring adults. The importance of

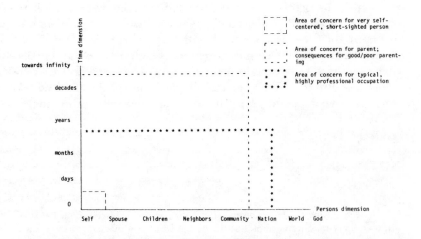

Figure II-A.2.1 Mathematical Approach to Morality Model

raising children well is highlighted in Malachi 2:15 ("seeking godly offspring").

Some of my comments may seem to some to be rather unusual reasons for marriage and family life. Indeed, they are meant to be, since many of the popular reasons (sex, love, happiness) are less valid and certain than they might seem at first glance. Having a marriage and family life means learning how to love unselfishly in creative ways under difficult circumstances in ways that help others grow personally (as opposed to "guilting" them or stifling them). Singles can do similar things, but marriage and family life place you in circumstances where you can hardly avoid learning such things. General MacArthur is alleged to have said that he was more proud of being a father than of being a great general in world history. When your 3-year-old child runs out of your home with great excitement, exclaiming "Daddy, Daddy! Daddy's home!" or "Mommy, Mommy! Mommy's home!" you can begin to understand how that is much more important and precious than all the notoriety and money that you might gain by staying single and focusing your extra energy and time resources on your occupation.

On the other hand, marriage and family life should not be entered by those who do not care much for loving and personal growth, because the consequences of careless parenting can be very unpleasant for oneself as well as for one's children. I have seen children disown their parents and even change their last names to avoid the dishonor they feel is associated with a parent who raised them abusively. I have also seen such parents die very lonely, solitary deaths that were essentially unmourned except for the wasted potential of their lives. But for those who are willing to accept the challenge, I think that marriage and family life are preferable to remaining single.

NOTES

1. Given the interest of the state in maintaining population levels sufficient to staff future military-industrial complex activities, it is surprising that so little direct state involvement (at least in the United States) has occurred in the area of abortion, aside from any moral considerations.

2. Many couples do space their children's births to fit deadlines for tax breaks—one example of a direct pressure to rearrange our lives to fit federal regulations, even though we may convince ourselves that we are thereby beating the system.

3. I think that marriage between male and female sets up a creative tension between the sexes that lends itself to the creation of a balanced approach to solving problems. On the other hand, male-male or female-female marriages are alleged by many homosexuals to lead to a predominance of same-sex traits for solving problems that may make understanding each other easier but may not lead to such well-balanced approaches to resolving difficulties (on the average).

4. In a recent unpublished study conducted at Emporia State University, I served as program evaluation consultant to a marriage enrichment program for newlywed couples. Though the program seemed to fail in terms of most of the numerous outcome variables we tested, most couples felt they gained greatly from learning for the first time in a concrete sense that other newlywed couples were going through the same hassles they were, which helped them realize that their marriages were not as unusually difficult as they had previously perceived them to be.

5. Years ago, when who did what chore was determined by gender and cultural norms, marriage may have involved fewer decisions than it does currently, with everything up for grabs, so to speak. The list of 400+ decisions may be obtained from the author by sending a written request, your address, and $2.00 to cover handling and postage to Premarital List, c/o Dr. Walter R. Schumm, Department of Family and Child Development, Kansas State University, Manhattan, Kansas 66506.

6. I occasionally hear of "perfect" marriages among Christians, especially staff members of religious organizations. Frankly, I question the reality orientation of anyone who claims to be the perfect spouse or to have the perfect marriage in any absolute sense. I have known of marriages in which one person, usually the husband, thought so and was rudely awakened one day to find his spouse leaving him, having endured enough of his perfection. As persons and as couples, there is always room for two things: disagreement and improvement.

7. The idea of mathematics comes from the concept of calculus, in which integration serves to determine how much area (of consequences in the model) falls under a curve over various ranges (dimensions in the model). More sophisticated, less narrow moral codes will take larger areas of potential consequences into account when moral decisions are being considered; that is, they integrate by their own decision rules over a wider set of ranges.

REFERENCES

ANDREWS, F. M. and S. B. WITHEY (1976) Social Indicators of Well-Being. New York: Plenum.

BERNARD, J. (1972) The Future of Marriage. New York: World.

CAMPBELL, A., P. E. CONVERSE, and W. L. ROGERS (1976) The Quality of American Life. New York: Russell Sage.

MILLER, S., E. W. NUNNALLY, and D. B. WACKMAN (1975). Alive and Aware. Minneapolis, MN: Interpersonal Communications Programs, Inc.

QUINN, W. H. (1983) "Personal and family adjustment in later life." Journal of Marriage and the Family 45: 57-73.

ROLLINS, B. C., and D. L. THOMAS (1979) "Parental support, power, and control techniques in the socialization of children," in W. R. Burr et al. (eds.) Contemporary Theories About the Family, vol. 1. New York: Free Press.

SCHUMM, W. R. and G. A. REKERS (1984) "Sex should occur only within marriage," in H. Feldman and A. Parrot (eds.) Human Sexuality: Contemporary Controversies. Beverly Hills, CA: Sage.

The Traditional Family with the Woman as Homemaker and the Man as Breadwinner Is Best for Most Families and for Society

JAYNANN M. PAYNE

> To insist that marriage and family still express our highest moral ideals is to awaken hostility and opposition [Michael Novak, 1976: 39].

Polarization has taken place in our society over sex roles, family values, and lifestyles. One group, the traditionalists, claim there are time-tested moral imperatives that have their validity rooted in natural and divine laws. The other group, the moral neutralists, hold that life and laws should be subject to the interpretation of an evolving social context or personal freedom and expediency. This ethical earthquake has created much upheaval in the family sector. When people disagree over what is right and wrong and why it is right and wrong, confusion and anxiety are common (Flinders, 1979: 1-3).

In spite of the trendy social experimentation going on as a result of women's liberation and other egalitarian movements, there are significant examples of the "staying power" of the traditional family roles and values. Medford Spiro's 25-year study of the Israeli kibbutz attests to the powerful attraction of traditional gender-based family values.

> The original kibbutz settlers were avowedly committed to eliminating every traditional role, gender distinction, and element of traditional family living. Based on a strong feeling that traditional roles stifled identity and discriminated against women, most pioneer doctrines were designed to radically revolutionize the female role. Dresses and cosmetics were replaced by shorts and shirts; children played, ate, and slept in age-graded houses; infants were nursed by whichever women had sufficient milk; married women retained their maiden names and kibbutz memberships independently of their husbands. Marriage was minimized by eliminating the traditional marriage ceremony and such terms as *husband* or *wife*. Public displays of affection were avoided.
>
> Over half a century later, in this particular kibbutz the second- and third-generation sabras have almost totally reversed these doctrines and practices. Among the implications for intimacy and role behavior are:
>
> A 50 percent decline in divorce, and a public climate "actively opposed to divorce."
>
> Care and concern for the couple's own children, seeing them as important to personal fulfillment rather than as obstacles to emancipation.
>
> Increased birthrate to a typical three or four children, with five or six not unusual.
>
> Family sleeping within the same house.
>
> Adoption of women of "feminine" clothing and grooming.
>
> Domestication of apartments, with emphasis on baking, cooking and gracious hosting.
>
> The return of "my husband" and "my wife," traditional wedding celebrations, public display of affection, preference for marital housing and privacy.

As if to confirm the desirability of this virtual revolution, the pioneer generation seems to rather enjoy the changes made by their "apostate" children and grandchildren [Brown, 1981: xii, 51-53, 96, 109].

This study is an excellent illustration of the difference between practice and principle. Is the traditional role wrong in principle? The answer is no. Has the practice of the principle always been positive? No. I am not going to defend malpractice of a correct principle, but just because people do not live the principle is no reason to throw out the principle.

There are at least seven valid reasons that traditional roles promote greater stability and happiness in family relationships. The following paragraph sums up the definition of traditional roles that I will use in this chapter.

Traditional marriage in Western culture means loyal monogamy. The role of wife and mother is one of commitment to the husband and children as a full-time homemaker, at least until the children are raised. She is a nurturer, teacher, homebuilder, and a role model of a fully feminine woman. Tradition and natural authority define the father's role as the head or leader of the home; a masculine role model, a protector, provider, and one who sets parameters and standards of discipline, although this does not preclude fathers' nurturing and mothers' disciplining their children. Traditional values affirm the sanctity of life; hence children are the cherished product of the conjugal union and are to be nurtured, protected, and trained to responsible adulthood and productive citizenship—to become of maximum value to themselves and their society.

A significant study completed in 1975 by Harold and Margaret Feldman of Cornell University tested the effect of absent and present fathers on their children. The Feldmans found that those fathers who were at home but did not interact with their children had the same effect on their offspring as those fathers who were absent (e.g., through death or divorce). Fathers who interacted extensively with their children made a positive difference in how their children felt about school, their brothers and sisters, their peers, and their parents.

The Feldmans suggest that "the increasing movement of women into the occupational system may provide an impetus for men to take a more active part in the family, thus contributing to the fuller functioning of both sexes" (Feldman and Feldman, 1975: 17).

BACKGROUND

Today nearly 53 percent of U.S. mothers work outside the home, and 43 percent with children under six years of age are now employed, according to a national pool commissioned by General Mills (1981: 9-12). A significant finding was that the majority of women want to and will continue work outside the home, not only for economic reasons but for personal satisfaction, marriage and childrearing responsibilities notwithstanding. Dr. Brent Barlow, a panelist at the TV news conference for this poll, commented, "Women finding more fulfillment in the workplace than in the home is quite an indictment of the husband, for he has failed to value the role of homemaker and mother." Women, like men, value those places where they feel valued.

A majority of respondents felt that both parents working outside the home has had negative effects on families. Feminists disagree. Their reasons were tied up in self-identity and the children's greater independence (General Mills, 1981).

The fundamental questions are, What has been the effect on marriage and family relationships of women leaving the homemaker's role and achieving in the workplace of men? And why are marriage and family best when the husband and wife play traditional roles?

- *Proposition 1*: Positive feminine identity does not require leaving the home or the traditional female role.

Dr. Urie Bronfenbrenner (1976: 47) commented,

> In encouraging self-fulfillment and self-gratification, women have been encouraged to move away from the home and family into the workplace, having been told by the feminists that this is liberation from "drudgery, and second class citizenship." Women will not achieve liberation if what they aspire for are the values and the behaviors of the men who have been locking them out of the man's world.

Betty Friedan, the leading spokeswoman of the feminist movement, has reevaluated the illusions of the *Feminine Mystique* and arrived at the realities of *The Second Stage*. In *Women's Day*, October 13, 1981, she gives some insights into "what went wrong with the women's movement." In reality it has failed to claim the hearts and minds of millions of women. Women are no longer trapped at home, but they have new problems that were neither anticipated nor addressed by the women's movement. She states,

> Even among those who have broken through to the executive suite, I sense the exhilaration of superwomen giving way to a tiredness, a certain brittle disappointment, a disillusionment with dressing for success, assertiveness training, and the rewards of power.
>
> An older woman in Ohio said: "I was the first woman in management here. I gave everything to the job. It was exciting at first, breaking in where women never were before. Now, it's just a job. But it's the devastating loneliness that's the worst. I can't stand coming back to this apartment alone every night. I'd like a house, a garden. Maybe I should have a kid, even without a father. At least then I'd have a family. There has to be some better way to live" [Friedan, 1981: 56].

Two significant books, *Sexual Suicide* (Gilder, 1973) and *The Castrated Family* (Voth, 1977), deplore the unisex trend for its psychological and societal damage. Dr. Voth decries the "castration" of both men and women from their primary biologic roles by women's demands for liberation from homemaking and becoming more masculine and aggressive, and due to men and women competing with each other in the marketplace. The social effects of this gender-blurring are reflected in the high divorce rate and the increase in homosexuality. George Gilder (1973: 43) states,

> The women's movement, pornographers, sexologists, and the gay liberationists, promote the male abdication from the family and monogamy. The androgynous ideal of women's liberation—with its polymorphously copulating "human beings"—is a destructive fantasy. There are no human beings, there are just men and women, and when they deny their divergent sexuality, they reject the deepest sources of identity and love. They commit sexual suicide.

One of the significant findings of the General Mills (1981) poll was that the workplace definitely influenced when and whether a woman had a child or not.

Betty Friedan (1981: 58) said,

Many women "choose" not to have children because they simply can't afford to stop working or because they can't count on adequate child-care facilities. But can women find their total fulfillment, identity and security in jobs and careers as they have been constituted by and for men?

It would appear then that traditional roles affirm a more healthy gender identity by encouraging fully developed masculinity or femininity, including the capacity to mate and live in a complementary relationship rather than a competitive one. This creates emotional space for love and human intimacy. It also develops a more accurate self-identity and capacity for forming lasting relationships. Voth (1977: 18) concluded, "The fate of mankind depends upon the durability of the heterosexual relationship."

- *Proposition 2*: Traditional roles encourage a stronger commitment to the marriage relationship.

Traditional couples also experience greater long-term satisfaction and fulfillment. Linda Wolfe, writing on love and work in *New York* magazine (February 16, 1981) says that the dual-career couple is severely stressed: "Instead of co-existing blissfully, many working couples are wrestling continuously with professional rivalry; guilt about neglecting each other or their children, friends and relatives; and performance anxiety both on the job and in the home." Many women report marital problems as a consequence of leaving home to "go out into the world of men." Others engage in affairs to affirm their sexual liberation as well. The divorce rate would seem to indicate a definite erosion of the marital commitment among working couples.

What our society today is reaching out for is the reality of human intimacy. Sexual activity without commitment and without communication is illusion, says Victor L. Brown, Jr. (1981). He describes reality as the process of identifying consequences and illusion as the process of ignoring, denying, or misinterpreting consequences.

Realities of human intimacy are love, trust, service, sacrifice, and discipline. Opposed to these realities are the glamorous illusions marketed by our society that equate intimacy with an obsession with self, an insistence that every appetite is legitimate and must be gratified, and, most tragic of all, the belief that the laws of human relations can be violated without damaging consequences [Brown, 1981: xii].

The Judeo-Christian ethics of chastity and fidelity, which are the foundation of the traditional roles in marriage, encourage commitment. Sexual integrity, because it is exclusive, places greater value upon the marriage partner and therefore increases the capacity to form lasting and caring relationships.

- *Proposition 3*: The traditional role of husband and father offers greater personal fulfillment and stronger commitment to the family unit.

To the extent that the women's movement has removed the man as the head of the home, it has devalued both roles. Gilder (1973: 204) said, "The great irony of the women's movement is that it may effect a relative increase in the power of men and an absolute decrease in the freedom and happiness of both sexes."

It is crucial to understand the sexual role of money, according to Gilder: "A man who does not make as much money as the relevant women in his life or class, or his place of work, will often abandon his job and will pursue his women chiefly in the predatory masculine spirit that the feminists so understandably deplore" (p. 97).

It is chiefly in the nuclear household, where a father desires to claim his children, where he is the *key provider*, that his fatherhood is direct and unimpeachable. He identifies, loves and provides for his offspring. His role as provider then becomes almost as crucial for the maintenance of the family as the mother's role. He thus can feel equal to the mother within the family and he can join it without damage to his sense of himself as a man [p. 88].

Gilder also shows that when a man has a family to provide for he is apt to work more consistently and productively than "a man oriented toward his next fix, lay, day at the races, or drinking session with the boys." Gilder also comments that the severing of sex from the very idea of parenthood fragments it and restores the primitive pattern where "men roam in gangs or hunting parties."

Marriage attaches males to families, the source of community, individuality, and order in a free society. As we are increasingly discovering in our schools, prisons, mental hospitals and psychiatric offices, the family is the only agency that can be depended upon to induce truly profound and enduring changes in its members. The family is the only institution that works on the deeper interior formations of human character and commitment. Thus it is the only uncoercive way to transform the individuals, loose in social time and space . . . into voluntary participants in the nurture of society [p. 73].

As was suggested by the Feldmans, the movement of women into the workplace may have impelled some fathers to accept a more interactive role with their offspring. The paradigm of Rapoport et al. (1980), which outlines the father's role as primarily protector and provider, has undergone some shift. With the popularity of Spock's child-care books new emphasis has been given to the father's nurturing role. It has been noted that parenting literature in the United States underwent a change. A new orientation is emerging based on the assumption that "children are not a mother's responsibility, nor a father's. They are parents' responsibility." This healthy shift still requires the long-term commitment of the father (Beail and McGuire, 1982).

- *Proposition 4*: The full-time mother finds greater fulfillment and growth in her biological role.

A full-time mother has more time and inclination to establish the bonding that is so important to both mother and child. A homemaker will generally want to nurse her infant and will have the time to develop this close relationship, which is so essential. "The holding, rocking, washing, bathing, loving, cuddling association reassure the child that he is important, he is loved and he can trust. He will then build a close relationship with others" (Voth, 1977). The elements of what social scientists call optimum mothering are these six characteristics: "A *loving relationship* which leads to *attachment*, which is *unbroken*, which provides *adequate stimulation*, in which *the mothering is provided by one person* and which *occurs in the child's own family*" (Rutter, 1981: 18). This object constancy and close physical contact is also the theme of Jean Liedloff's *The Continuum*

Concept. She shows the optimum growth of babies of "primitive" mothers who are born and reared in the "continuum" of the human biological experience (i.e., with constant physical contact for the first year). Bronfenbrenner (1977: 43) emphasizes that

> every child should spend a substantial amount of time with somebody who's crazy about him. . . . there has to be at least one person who has an irrational involvement with that child, someone who's in love with him and whom he loves in return. . . . You can't pay a woman to do what a mother will do for free.

Nothing is closer to the heart than the hearth. Once a mother leaves the home she can no longer deal on the heart level. Society encroaches on our freedom to deal on the heart level, and the home is the greatest environment for the family to develop sensitive and caring feelings for others. Victor L. Brown, Jr. (1981: 109) commented,

> *It is arrogant nonsense to imply that this woman who has voluntarily chosen her home and family as her highest priorities is inadequate or narrow or lacks the courage to engage life.* It is offensive when writers, whose worlds are voluntarily circumscribed by the workplace, challenge the meaning of *a homebuilder's soul-stretching, spirit-deepening life. The intelligently committed wife and mother—homebuilder—knows a world unknown to those who would call her a less distinctive individual.*

- *Proposition 5*: A traditional, full-time homemaker can create a very cost-effective family environment.

Sydney Reynolds (1979), mother of eight children and wife of a professor, outlines well why she chose the career of wife and mother:

> I asked some of my college-educated women friends why they chose to be full-time wives and mothers. Here are some advantages they see in this special career.
>
> 1. You have the opportunity to create the physical environment in which you live and work and in which your family spends much of their time. . . . The homemaker also has the opportunity to influence

greatly the spiritual and emotional environment of her family. Creating a haven from the pressures of this world is a real service that takes time and energy as well as a primary commitment to the home.

2. A homemaker can make a *valid economic contribution* to her family which may *exceed that of a second salary*, with its attendant problems of increased tax bite, transportation, payment for sitters, enlarged wardrobe and convenience foods. She elene Hall Bartholomew of White Plains, N.Y. writes: "I sometimes like to remind myself that a penny saved is no longer a penny earned—it's two pennies! For every dollar I save by gardening, sewing, home decorating and maintaining, comparison shopping, bread baking, child counseling, tutoring, and self-educating, I save double the amount, as savings are not taxable income. In addition, a capable, full-time homemaker can save thousands in terms of cost-prevention. By meeting the physical, mental, emotional and spiritual needs of her family now, she can do much to avoid medical, psychiatric, legal and rehabilitative expense later. . . . The government is never as efficient or effective as the individual, but too often people forget that when voting for new programs."

3. A woman at home—not in the work force—can have a great impact on society. Why not work with my children now, as their mother, instead of later as their social worker? Why not keep them out of jail with some good solid training now rather than learn how to "spring them" later as their lawyer? I am, of course, overstating my case to make the point that an ounce of prevention is worth a pound of rehabilitation.

It is cost-effective families that build a cost-effective community, state, and nation. We can solve problems of national economy only by solving them in the home. It is in the family that we develop the capability to be productive and useful citizens. Michael Novak (1979: 14) has stated, "The family is the only Department of Health, Education and Welfare that really works!"

- *Proposition 6:* Traditional roles create more opportunity for optimum nurturing of children.

What are the effects on children who are being raised by "surrogate mothers"? Childhood authorities Bowlby (1973), Berger (1980), and Fraiberg (1977) substantiate the damaging consequences of maternal deprivation and prolonged separations. Fraiberg points to the poor performance of child-care programs with these comments (in Berger, 1980: 154-155):

> I have to say it: many of these centers, even the ones licensed, are not providing for the real emotional needs of infants . . . for a sustained, close involvement with a caring person. Young children who get to know such a person then lose that person, show anxiety, agitation, tearfulness. When those children keep meeting someone, then losing someone . . . there are going to be emotional consequences; lack of confidence in the future: a degree of withdrawal from the future, a degree of withdrawal from the world.

The mothering for the younger child must be a continuous, stable, daily giving of love and interest to the child; it is not the kind of mothering you can concentrate into a tired hour of "quality time" following a long work day outside the home. The myth of "quality time" is frequently presented in women's magazines as part of the message to women that they can have it all (McGraw, 1980).

Brenda Hunter, author of *Where Have All the Mothers Gone?*, discusses the working mother's problem of disengagement from her child:

> If a woman is going to leave her child for 8 to 10 hours a day, she is going to be in anguish if she doesn't disengage from her child in order to have anything left for the office. Doing this day after day creates an emotional distance between the mother and child. The mother in effect is saying to the child: "My work is more important to me than you are." If you are going to devalue mothering you have to devalue the object of all that love and care, and that is just what has happened [McKay, 1964: 445].

Children quite often blame themselves for the disengagement as they do in the case of divorce. Betty Friedan (1981) relates the struggle of women who try to juggle dual careers:

> One young mother, whose children are three and six, rebelled against her lack of "power" and "value" as a housewife by becoming an accountant. Now she is caught in the superwoman bind. "I keep

complaining that my husband is not doing enough in the house," she said. "Why do I always have to be the one to scrub the bathroom or take the kids to the doctor? I drew up contracts, dividing all the chores in half. But when he was the one who bought the kids new socks and took them for their shots, I fell apart. It's hard to give up being the real parent, the one responsible for the children, the important one."

Bronfenbrenner's study showed that children who spend more of their elective time with their peers than with their parents developed negative attitudes and were more likely to get into trouble. When youngsters are left to find their habits, values, and lifestyles from the "social contagion" of their peers, there are very negative consequences because children are immature and impressionable and are not carriers of sound moral judgments (Moore and Moore, 1981: 35).

The burgeoning home-school movement attests to the concern parents have for their children's education. Raymond and Dorothy Moore, authors of *Schools Can Wait* and *Home Grown Kids* state that for the first eight to ten years of life—at least until their children's values are formed—most parents, even average ones, are by far the best teachers for their children (Moore and Moore, 1981). The Jencks (1972) study on inequality states, "The most important determinant of educational attainment is family background."

Victor L. Brown, Jr. (1981: 96) asks us to consider society's disparagement of nurturant roles in the light of the deep human need for intimacy:

What contributes to healthy, happy individuals and family? And what fosters the development of human intimacy? . . . It would be black humor, if it were not painful, that our day may see men, weary of the lonely workplace, groping toward the intimacy of family, while women, harrassed by economic or emotional disparagement of their nurturant role, grope toward the very illusions which men are abandoning. If this is so, where will the rising generation experience intimacy? Educators already report the struggles they have with alienated, rootless "latchkey children" who go home each day to an empty house. What price is being paid?

If we do not provide traditional roles, children will have a difficult if not impossible task of developing a positive healthy self-identity. The Hebrew law "Honor thy father and mother" intuitively sensed the validity of this notion. Where is self-identity if children do not or cannot honor their parents?

- *Proposition* 7: Traditional parents make a significant long-term contribution to society when they create a stable, productive, and happy family.

Perhaps we can enlarge our vision of the long-term effects of devoted mothering by looking back in time to our colonial history.

One of the most remarkable examples of the sphere and influence a mother has is in the life of Sarah Edwards, the wife of Jonathan Edwards, a minister and early colonist. Sarah raised 11 children while her husband busied himself with writing and ecclesiastical duties, becoming the *famous one* of the family. She stayed in the background as a homemaker—valuing each child's individuality and intelligence, educating both sons and daughters, but also teaching them to work responsibly. A genealogical study later tracked down 1,400 descendants and compared them to another family who were notorious for criminality and welfare dependency. The Jukes family *cost* the state of New York a total of $1,250,000.00 in *welfare* and *custodial charges*, while the Edwards descendants boasted the following:

  13 college presidents
  65 professors
 100 lawyers and a dean of a law school
  30 judges
  66 physicians and a dean of a medical school
  80 holders of public office
   3 United States senators
     mayors of three large cities
     governors of 3 large cities
     a vice-president of the United States
     a controller of the United States Treasury, not to mention
     the countless numbers who were successful in business and
     the arts.

Only 2 of these 1,400 were "black sheep," which eloquently testifies to the power of one woman who wasn't afraid of a few diapers [Eyre, 1983: 10-11].

A noted religious authority states, "The most humble home where a loving father and mother preside over a united family, has far greater value to mankind than any other institution. No other success can compensate for failure in the home" (McKay, 1964). As the above example indicates, there is a direct correlation between success in the family and achievement in society. It follows then, as Harold B. Lee said, "The most important work we will ever do will be within the walls of our own homes" (Lee, 1973: 91).

CONCLUSION

To the extent that a woman's achievement outside the home undermines gender identity; breeds unhealthy competition between the sexes; encourages infidelity to the marriage commitment; eliminates the male role as provider, protector, and head of the family; denigrates or devalues the nurturant and homebuilding role of the mother; or neglects the children's needs for a loving, continuous, and caring relationship, then her achievement will not be a correct choice. Each person must answer for himself or herself this question: Can the laws of human relations be violated without damaging consequences?

Quoted authorities and empirical evidence serve only to stimulate our thinking. The answer lies within the heart. And by what criteria do we judge? Pragmatism is a good copilot but an unsafe and dangerous pilot. Secure movement toward a better future resides in correctness and not expediency. The theme, Does it work? should always be subservient to the theme, Is it right? Each of us must make a choice. Whatever our answer is, time and experience will reveal the correctness or incorrectness of our choice.

REFERENCES

BEAIL, N. and J. McGUIRE (1982) Fathers—Psychological Perspectives. London: Junction.
BERGER, B. (1980) "The family as a mediating structure," in Democracy and Mediating Structures. Washington, DC: American Enterprise Institute for Public Policy Research.

BOWLBY, J. (1973) Attachment and Loss, vol. 2. New York: Basic Books.
BRONFENBRENNER, U. (1977) "Nobody home," Psychology Today (May): 43.
———(1976) "Liberated women—how they're changing American life," U.S. News and World Report (June 7): 47.
BROWN, V. L., Jr. (1981) Human Intimacy—Illusion and Reality. Salt Lake City, UT: Parliament.
EYRE, L. (1983) A Joyful Mother of Children. Salt Lake City, UT: Bookcraft.
FELDMAN, H. and M. FELDMAN (1975) "The effect of father absence on adolescents." Cornell University.
FLINDERS, N. J. "Moral perspectives and educational practice." Pleasant Grove, UT.
FRAIBERG, S. (1977) Every Child's Birthright: In Defense of Mothering. New York: Basic Books.
FRIEDAN, B. (1981) "Being superwoman is *not* the way to go," Woman's Day (October 13).
General Mills (1981) Families at Work, The American Family Report. Minneapolis, MN: Author.
GILDER, G. (1973) Sexual Suicide. New York: Quadrangle.
HUNTER, B. (1982) Where Have All the Mothers Gone? Grand Rapids, MI: Zondervan.
JENCKS, C. S. "The Coleman Report and the conventional wisdom," in M. Mosteller and D. P. Moynihan (eds.) On Equality of Educational Opportunity. New York: Random House.
LEE, H. B. (1973) "Be loyal to the royal within you," in Talks of the Year. Provo, UT: Brigham Young University Press.
McGRAW, O. (1980) The Family, Feminism and the Therapeutic State. Washington, DC: Heritage Foundation.
McKAY, D. O. (1964) "Blessed are they who do His commandments." Presented at the Improvement Era Conference Talks, June.
MOORE, R. and D. MOORE (1981) Home Grown Kids. Waco, TX: Word Books.
NOVAK, M. "The American family, an embattled institution," in M. Novak, The Family, America's Hope. Rockford, IL: Rockford College Institute.
———(1976) "The family out of favor." Harper's (April): 39.
RAPOPORT, R. et al. (1980) Fathers, Mothers and Society: Perspectives on Parenting. New York: Random House.
REYNOLDS, S. S. (1979) "Wife and mother: a valid career option for the college-educated woman." Presented at the Brigham Young University Forum, Provo, UT, April 3.
RUTTER, M. (1981) Maternal Deprivation Reassessed. New York: Penguin.
VOTH, H. M. (1977) The Castrated Family. Kansas City, KS: Sheed Andrews & McMeel, Inc.

Achievement of Women Outside the Home Is the Phantom Factor in Marital Breakdown

SHARON K. HOUSEKNECHT

Women have always been motivated to achieve. However, they have not traditionally devoted their energies to academic and employment pursuits but rather to the perfection of social skills—for example, being a charming hostess (Stein and Bailey, 1975). As long as achievement strivings were limited to activities that are culturally defined as feminine (i.e., social skills), achievement behavior for women was consistent with the feminine role. Women's efforts to achieve did not elicit a strong negative reaction because they did not conflict with the traditional norms prescribing proper behavior for males and females.

Over the past few decades, however, women's achievement strivings in the United States have expanded to include what has heretofore been considered masculine areas of achievement. More and more women have been obtaining higher levels of education, and the proportion of women in the labor force, particularly wives and mothers, has been increasing at a phenomenal rate. Accompanying these surges in female education and employment has been a dramatic rise in the divorce rate. Perhaps not surprising is the widespread conclusion that the increase in marital breakdown is due to the greater involvement of women in the educational and labor-market spheres.

An interpretation such as this might be expected given that achievement of women outside the home violates the traditional division of labor between the sexes. The primary role of males in this society has been the breadwinner role, while for females it has been the wife-mother role. Furthermore, it is easy for people to believe that something undesirable/deviant (education and employment of women) causes something else undesirable/deviant (marital break-down), especially when the factors vary together. What is sometimes forgotten is that correlation is not causation. The fact that increased levels of female education and employment have occurred at the same time that the divorce rate has risen does not mean necessarily that the former is the cause of the latter. Before determining that one variable causes another, other possible causes must first be taken into account and ruled out. The belief that achievement of women outside the home causes marital breakdown serves certain social functions, however, and recognizing this fact helps us to understand the reluctance of some to reconsider other possible causes.

The purpose of this chapter is to present a theory of marital breakdown that emphasizes the importance of marital roles rather than women's roles outside the home. Evidence will be compiled to support the notion that female achievement in education and employment is only a phantom factor in marital breakdown. It will be argued that roles inside the home, not roles outside the home, are the real cause.

HISTORICAL ORIGINS OF THE MYTH

Before discrediting the idea that female career achievements lead to marital breakdown, it is important to explore its historical origins. Certainly, there is no doubt but that sweeping changes in women's educational and employment opportunities have occurred over the past thirty years. The timing and extent of these shifts, as well as the parallel increase in the divorce rate, will be reviewed here.

EDUCATION

For several decades now, the high school completion rate for women has risen steadily. In 1981, 85 percent of the women 25-34 years old had completed high school (U.S. Bureau of the Census, 1982). The most dramatic increases in women's educational achievement, however, have occurred at the college level. The proportion of women aged 25 to 34 who completed college more than tripled between 1950 (6 percent) and 1980 (20 percent). Within the college category, the greatest change has been in graduate training. For example, between 1970 and 1980 women's enrollment in graduate programs more than doubled up (112 percent); the increase at the undergraduate level was 52 percent (U.S. Bureau of the Census, 1981).

As enrollment of women in college has increased, so has the number of degrees earned by women (National Center for Education Statistics, 1981a, 1981b). Almost half of the baccalaureate and master's degrees awarded in 1979-1980 went to women. Although only 30 percent of the doctoral degrees were earned by women, even this level represented a considerable increase for them, an increase that was especially pronounced in the 1970s.

EMPLOYMENT

American women have made significant gains in school enrollment and educational attainment, but an even more dramatic indicator of their changing social and economic status is the extraordinary increase in their labor force participation rates. Between 1950 and 1980 the number of women in the labor force increased by 144 percent (U.S. Department of Labor, 1980; U.S. Bureau of the Census, 1982).

In addition to the rise in rates, there also has been a change in the pattern of women's participation. Oppenheimer (1970), for example, points out that prior to 1950, if a woman worked at all, it was, with few exceptions, before marriage and children. Beginning in 1950, however, her statistics indicate that marriage and childbearing were decreasingly likely to lead to a permanent withdrawal from work outside the home. The traditional pattern was even less pronounced in 1960 and has continued to decline to the present. In 1950 less than one-fourth (22 percent) of married women were employed; in 1980 the proportion had risen to one-half. The general category "married women," of course, includes many women who are in the retirement stage of life. If only married couples with at least one spouse employed are considered, the proportion of wives working outside the home in 1981 was 67 percent. Fully two-thirds of these employed wives were full-time workers (U.S. Bureau of the Census, 1984).

The parental status of employed women has changed, too, over the past thirty years. There have been substantial increases in the labor-force participation rates for women with children, even preschool children. While only 12 percent of the married women with children under six were in the labor force in 1950, the proportion had expanded to almost half by 1980 (45 percent). Considering mothers of school-age children, 62 percent were in the labor force by 1980.

DIVORCE

The evidence presented here clearly demonstrates that women's achievements outside the home have increased dramatically over the past three decades. Paralleling the upward trends in female education and employment has been a rapid rise in the American divorce rate. The divorce rate in 1962, the year before the long-term increase began, was 9.4 per 1000 married women aged 15 and over. By 1974 it had more than doubled (22.6) and then continued to increase at a slower rate during the middle to late 1970s, peaking in 1981. Interestingly, the 1970s marked the first time in American history that more marriages ended every year in divorce than in death (Cherlin, 1981).

Most of the recent increase in divorce has been among younger women; for example, proportions divorced are highest for women in their thirties and early forties (U.S. Bureau of the Census, 1983). It is important to note that the age category that has accounted for the major increase in divorce closely corresponds to the age category that has accounted for the major increases in female achievements outside the home. The greatest surges in educational attainment and labor-force participation rates in the 1960s and 1970s were among women aged 20 to 44 (U.S. Bureau of the Census, 1980, 1983).

SOCIAL FUNCTION OF THE MYTH

The major thesis of this chapter is that women's participation in the education and economic institutions does not have a detrimental effect in and of itself on the marital relationship. Although increases in female education and employment have accompanied the rise in the divorce rate, it is incorrect to conclude that the former causes the latter. Why, then, is this notion so commonplace? The widespread popularity and staying power of this myth can be explained by the fact that it fulfills an important social function—keeping women in their place.

Women's roles have traditionally been defined in terms of support, nurturance, and caregiving. In contrast to males, whose activities were carried out mainly in the public sphere, women were expected to concentrate their time and energy fulfilling the needs of their spouses and children within the family context. This particular family role structure is clearly depicted by Parsons and Bales (1955: 151):

> Considered as a social system, the marriage relationship is clearly a differentiated system. . . . [the] *more* instrumental role in the subsystem is taken by the husband, the *more* expressive one by the wife. . . . [the] husband has the primary adaptive responsibilities, relative to the outside situation . . . whereas the wife is primarily the giver of love.

In fact, Parsons (1949) argued that sex-role segregation such as this is a functional necessity for marital stability in our society. For this reason, he held that most women must be relatively excluded from the occupational system, "at least in a status-determinant sense." The major mechanism preventing disruptive competition between husband and wife, according to Parsons, is sex-role segregation, where the dominant male role is the occupational role and the dominant female role is that of housewife and mother. He concludes that if marital stability is to be maintained, married women must either avoid work or work at an occupation that is not status competitive. Clearly, Parsons articulates a point of view that is held by many people.

Given the pervasiveness of this orientation, it is not surprising that there has been a strong reaction to the enormous increase in women's roles outside the home. One way of conceptualizing this reaction is to see it as the old versus the new individualism (Pankhurst and Houseknecht, 1983). The old individualism is based upon the individual rights and prerogatives of the adult male. In contrast, the new individualism also respects the individual rights and prerogatives of adult females and, increasingly, of children and the elderly. Pankhurst and Houseknecht (1983) point out that the new individualism is more egalitarian than the old, for it allows variations in lifestyle patterns that the traditional patriarchal forms oppose. In fact, they believe that the current clash between the old and new individualisms is essentially a struggle between patriarchy and egalitarianism. Promoting the notion that women's achievements outside the home lead to marital breakdown, therefore, is functional in the sense that it helps to sustain the traditional patriarchal family ideology.

WOMEN'S ACHIEVEMENT AND
MARITAL SUCCESS: A REASSESSMENT

This essay has set forth two reasons women's achievement activities outside the home are equated with marital breakdown. First, upward trends in female education and employment have been accompanied by a rapid rise in the divorce rate. Second, the myth performs a key social function; consistent with patriarchalism, it helps to keep women in a secondary role. It is important to note at this point that the existence and accuracy of an idea are two different issues. Exploring its historical origins and social functions, as we have here, helps us to understand its existence but does not verify its correctness. In fact, evidence is accumulating that women's achievement in the educational and employment spheres is only a phantom factor in marital breakdown. This section will review this evidence but first will propose an alternative explanation for marital breakdown.

A THEORY OF MARITAL ROLES
AND MARITAL BREAKDOWN

The position of this essay is that it is roles inside the home, not roles outside the home, that are the real cause of marital breakdown. The argument that blames women's educational and employment opportunities misses the mark. It is not women's roles outside the home but their own and their families' reactions to such roles that are crucial. This reaction, of course, depends upon what is considered to be proper wife behavior. If expectations are traditional, there is not likely to be much tolerance for role interchangeability. The primary role for women under these circumstances would be caring for spouses and children within the family context; the primary role for men would be that of breadwinner. Most women who go to school or participate in the labor force would have difficulty fulfilling all of the obligations that are associated with the traditional wife/mother role.

Many husbands are strongly opposed to having their wives vary from the conventional pattern. When husbands' expectations for suitable role performance on the part of their wives lack flexibility, there is little chance that women can smoothly integrate their achievement activities outside the home with their wife role. Marital conflict is likely to result. Traditional marital role requirements, then, are the decisive factor in marital breakdown, not employment and education of women per se. This is an important distinction because it means that women who are not held to the traditional wife role requirements can go to school and be employed without experiencing a detrimental effect on their marriages. In other words, female achievement activities outside the home in and of themselves do not cause marital breakdown.

The Traditional Wife Role

Effects on marital quality. Traditional marital role requirements for the wife are enforced through socialization and social control. In other words, many women have internalized or come to believe that fulfillment of traditional role expectations is necesssary. Those who deviate from expectations are penalized in an effort to get them to conform. When women are involved in career-related activities more than they want to be or more than their families think they should be, there exists the potential for reduced marital quality.

There is an abundance of evidence showing that the demands of the traditional wife role do not allow for female employment other than as a secondary commitment. For example, women perceive greater conflict between work and home maintenance roles than males perceive (Herman and Gyllstrom, 1977). Part-time employment is one way that women try to handle this conflict; in fact, Orden and Bradburn (1976) note that this may be the way for women to achieve optimum adjustment in marriage. Nye (1963), too, found that part-time employed mothers were higher on happiness than either mothers who were employed full-time or mothers who were not employed. Part-time employment, then, is a way for women to minimize competition between their employment-related activities and their traditional wife/mother role.

Underemployment is another tactic that women use to reduce conflict between traditional marital role requirements and achievement activities outside the home. A recent study that distinguished between traditional and nontraditional jobs (Philliber and Hiller, 1983) found that women in nontraditional jobs were more likely to move to a lower status position, to leave the labor force, or to become divorced than were women in traditional positions. In addition, many women in nontraditional jobs shifted to traditional jobs. Nontraditional jobs, of course, are less likely to allow easy exit and easy reentry at the time of child rearing, and this means that it is more difficult for women to integrate them with their traditional marital role requirements. That conflict of this type exists for women at the highest levels is indicated by Statham et al. (1984). Their sample of highly educated women revealed that 41 percent of the ever-married women with children underutilized their training in some way—part-time employment, working in jobs that did not use their training, having unsatisfying jobs, and withdrawing from the labor force. These kinds of solutions would almost certainly have a negative impact on marital quality in the long run if the wife is attitudinally committed to achievement activities outside the home. On the other hand, if she did not organize her activities so as to allow her to fulfill the traditional wife role expectations held by her husband, conflict would ensue. Whichever of these adaptations is adopted, the reduction in marital quality can be attributed to traditional wife role requirements.

In sum, women's commitment to achievement activities outside the home frequently is incompatible with expectations for the traditional wife role. In fact, high career aspirations have been found to be positively related to role conflict for women but negatively related for men (Holahan and Gilbert, 1979). Quite likely it is for this reason that an unusually high proportion of highly educated women remain single (U.S. Bureau of the Census, 1980; Houseknecht and Vaughan, 1984). However, Houseknecht and Macke (1981) stress that it is not employment status per se that is important in determining the marital adjustment of professional women, but rather the extent to which family experiences accommodate the wife's employment. Having a supportive husband was found to be a major factor; a tolerant husband, of course, means that role expectations for the wife would tend to be more flexible. The impact of wives' achievement behavior on marital quality, then, is dependent on the extent to which their achievement behavior violates traditional wife role expectations—either their own (as in the case of women who are working only out of financial necessity) or those of their husbands.

Effects on marital stability. In their literature review, Moore and Hofferth (1979) concluded that there is no clear-cut body of evidence indicating that female employment leads to marital instability (i.e., divorce/separation). They do note, however, that couples in which the wife earns high wages or works a long week and couples in which the husband has a relatively low income or a history of unemployment run an increased risk of divorce. (In the latter case, among one-earner couples it would be expected that the wife and not the husband would be unemployed.) As with marital quality, these findings suggest that the effect is dependent on the extent to which the wife's achievement behavior violates traditional role expectations.

The more education that women have, the more likely it is that they will be in the labor force (U.S. Bureau of the Census, 1983). Furthermore, it has been established that a higher level of education among women leads to a higher level of commitment to work (Hubback, 1957; Myrdal and Klein, 1968). Relatively high levels of work commitment, in turn, probably mean less inclination and time to fulfill traditional wife role expectations. For these reasons, focusing on women with higher levels of education can be very informative in understanding how traditional role requirements lead to marital breakdown.

Interestingly, women with five or more years of college have the second-highest rate of separation and divorce among all women in the United States. Their rate of marital disruption is surpassed only by women who have not graduated from high school (Houseknecht and Spanier, 1980). A recent study (Houseknecht et al., 1984) asked 663 women graduates about the timing of their career and family events. It was found that marriages usually break up after, not before, women begin graduate school. In addition, once- and still-married women were consistently more likely to complete each career step (school enrollment, graduation, and first job) before they married than were women who had experienced marital disruption. The authors interpret these findings as indicating that disruption is more likely to occur if a marital pattern is established before the woman starts graduate school, perhaps because there is an abrupt change in the established interaction pattern, which probably was defined in terms of traditional roles.

This same study revealed that a husband's willingness to be supportive of his wife's career significantly reduces the probability of marital instability. In fact, a husband's cooperation is so crucial that, when it is taken into account, the timing of marriage in relation to school is no longer important. Husbands who are willing to change their traditional role expectations when their wives take on a new role reduce the likelihood of marital instability. This research lends further credence to that the contention that it is not women's achievement activities outside the home but, rather, the flexibility of traditional role requirements that is the determining factor in marital instability.

The Traditional Husband Role

Failure to fulfill traditional wife role obligations has implications for the husband role as well as the wife role. According to Orden and Bradburn (1969), the freedom to choose to work is important in understanding the relationship between female employment and marital adjustment. "Choice" here can be understood to mean not only that women are happier when they are doing what they want to do but also that husbands are less likely to experience threats to their traditional husband role. When the wife's employment is due not to choice but rather to financial necessity, the husband may view himself as a less-than-adequate provider. The wife may or may not view him the same way but, in any case, this sort of tension is not conducive to marital quality (Nye, 1963; Orden and Bradburn, 1969; Scanzoni, 1970; Burke and Weir, 1976; Hauenstein, 1976; Safilios-Rothschild and Dijkers, 1978; Staines et al., 1978; Rallings and Nye, 1979).

The fact that the wife is working out of choice does not necessarily mean, however, that her spouse will not be apprehensive about his primary role of provider. Recent findings indicate that wives' employment contributions to family status can restrict the chances of husbands' occupational mobility (Sharda and Nangle, 1981). The traditional wife role involves various types of support for the husband's career. When women are pursuing achievement activities outside the home, they are less able to participate in what Papanek

(1973) has referred to as the two-person career. The requirements of the traditional husband role limit the sharing of family work and also exert pressure on wives to perform in ways that will increase their husbands' competitive advantage in the occupational sphere (Mortimer et al., 1978). The absence of the supportive role of traditional wives is viewed as an obstacle to husbands' career success (Hunt and Hunt, 1977; Scanzoni, 1978).

Traditional marital roles emphasize provider activities for males and wife/mother activities for women. The point of this section is that, when women pursue achievement activities outside the home, both marital roles are affected. Since marital quality seems to be most related to congruence between the role expectations of one spouse and the role performances of the other spouse (Lewis and Spanier, 1979), inflexible role expectations for one's partner (and for oneself) can lead to dissension. In other words, expectations for the traditional wife role can negatively affect marital quality/stability when they are not met. Related research has shown, in fact, that the impact of wives' employment on their own and their husbands' depression depends on whether or not it is consistent with their preferences (Ross et al., 1983).

CONCLUSIONS

Sociologists have long recognized the age-old tension between the individual and the group. Those who argue that education and employment opportunities for women must be limited lest the family suffer, of course, are emphasizing the importance of family considerations over individual well-being. The thesis of this chapter has been that it is not women's achievements outside the home that are disruptive but, rather, inflexible expectations for the traditional wife role inside the home.

It cannot be denied that, in asserting their rights, women are providing the impetus for the transition from one family pattern to another. Too, since we are currently in a period of transition with regard to marital roles, resistance to the changes is not surprising. However, there is no reason to expect that there will not be reorganization or that the reorganization phase will be characterized by conflict. Reorganization that takes individual needs into account would reduce the seeming antagonism between individual rights for women and family well-being. Just as the traditional family role structure addresses similar rights for males, a reorganization could eventually incorporate such rights for women, too.

Merton's (1968) "postulate of indispensability" is that it is a mistake to assume that any particular social structure is necessary or indispensable for the fulfillment of any given functions. In other words, to alter the traditional family role structure is not to destroy the family. There is more than one arrangement that can carry out familial functions. Although the institution of marriage is currently in a period of transition as far as traditional marital roles are concerned, we need to keep our eye on the ultimate goal of reorganization—a reorganization that gives both women and men greater role flexibility and freedom.

REFERENCES

BURKE, R. J. and T. WEIR (1976) "Relationship of wives' employment status to husband, wife and pair satisfaction and performance." Journal of Marriage and the Family 38: 279-287.

CHERLIN, A. (1981) Marriage, Divorce, Remarriage. Cambridge, MA: Harvard University Press.

HAUENSTEIN, L. S. (1976) Attitudes of Married Women Toward Work and Family. Reports 1 and 2. Ann Arbor: University of Michigan, Department of Psychology.

HERMAN, J. B. and K. K. GYLLSTROM (1977) "Working men and women: inter- and intra-role conflict." Psychology of Women Quarterly 1: 319-333.

HOLAHAN, C. K. and L. A. GILBERT (1979) "Conflict between major life roles: women and men in dual career couples." Human Relations 6: 451-467.

HOUSEKNECHT, S. K. and A. S. MACKE (1981) "Combining marriage and career: the marital adjustment of professional women." Journal of Marriage and the Family 43: 651-661.

HOUSEKNECHT, S. K. and G. B. SPANIER (1980) "Marital disruption and higher education among women in the United States. Sociological Quarterly 21: 375-389.

HOUSEKNECHT, S. K. and S. VAUGHAN (1984) "The impact of singlehood on the career patterns of professional women." Presented at the Annual Meeting of the American Sociological Association, San Antonio, TX.

———and A. S. MACKE (1984) "Marital disruption among professional women: the timing of career and family events." Social Problems 31: 273-284.

HUBBACK, J. (1957) Wives Who Went to College. London: Heinemann.

HUNT, J. G. and L. L. HUNT (1977) "Dilemmas and contradictions of status: the case of the dual-career family." Social Problems 24: 407-416.

JOHNSON, B. and E. WALDMAN (1981) "Marital and family patterns of the labor force." Monthly Labor Review 104: 36-38.

LEWIS, R. A. and G. B. SPANIER (1979) "Theorizing about the quality and stability of marriage," in W. R. Burr et al. (eds.) Contemporary Theories about the Family, vol. 1. New York: Free Press.

MERTON, R. K. (1968) Social Theory and Social Structure. New York: Free Press.

MOORE, K. A. and S. L. HOFFERTH (1979) "Effects of women's employment on marriage: formation, stability and roles." Marriage and Family Review 2: 1, 27-36.

MORTIMER, J., R. HALL, and R. HILL (1978) "Husbands' occupational attributes as constraints on wives' employment." Sociology of Work and Occupations 5: 285-313.

MYRDAL, A. and V. KLEIN (1968) Women's Two Roles. London: Routledge and Kegan Paul.

National Center for Health Statistics (1984) Monthly Vital Statistics Report, vol. 32, no. 9. Advance report of final divorce statistics, 1981. Washington, DC: Government Printing Office.

———(1981a) Digest of Education Statistics. Washington, DC: Government Printing Office.

———(1981b) Earned Degrees Conferred 1979-80. Washington, DC: Government Printing Office.

NYE, F. I. (1963) "Personal satisfactions," in F. I. Nye and L. W. Hoffman (eds.) The Employed Mother in America. Chicago: Rand McNally.

———and L. W. HOFFMAN (1963) "Adjustment of the mother," in F. I. Nye and L. W. Hoffman (eds.) The Employed Mother in America. Chicago: Rand McNally.

OPPENHEIMER, V. K. (1970) The Female Labor Force in the United States. Population monograph series, no. 5. Berkeley: University of California.

ORDEN, S. R. and N. M. BRADBURN (1969) "Working wives and marriage happiness." American Journal of Sociology 74: 392-407.

PANKHURST, J. G. and S. K. HOUSEKNECHT (1983) "The family, politics, and religion in the 1980s: in fear of the new individualism." Journal of Family Issues 4: 5-34.

PAPANEK, H. (1973) "Men, women, and work: reflections on the two-person career," in J. Huber (ed.) Changing Women in a Changing Society. Chicago: University of Chicago Press.

PARSONS, T. (1949) "The social structure of the family," in R. Anshen (ed.) The Family: Its Function and Destiny. New York: Harper & Row.

———and R. F. BALES [eds.] (1955) Family, Socialization and Interaction Process. New York: Free Press.

PHILLIBER, W. W. and D. V. HILLER (1983) "Relative occupational attainments of spouses and later changes in marriage and wife's work experience." Journal of Marriage and the Family 45: 161-170.

RALLINGS, E. M. and F. I. NYE (1979) "Wife-mother employment, family and society," in W. R. Burr et al. (eds.) Contemporary Theories about the Family, vol. 1. New York: Free Press.

ROSS, C. E., J. MIROWSKY, and J. HUBER (1983) "Marriage patterns and depression." American Sociological Review 48: 809-823.

SAFILIOS-ROTHSCHILD, C. and M. DIJKERS (1978) "Handling unconventional asymmetries," in R. Rapoport and R. Rapoport (eds.) Working Couples. New York: Harper & Row.

SCANZONI, J. (1978) Sex Roles, Women's Work, and Marital Conflict. Lexington, MA: D. C. Heath.
———(1970) Opportunity and Family. New York: Free Press.
SHARDA, B. D. and NAGLE, B. E. (1981) "Marital effects on occupational attainment." Journal of Family Issues 2: 148-163.
STAINES, G. L., PLECK, J. H., SPEPARD, L. J. and O'CONNOR, P. (1978) "Wives' employment status and marital adjustment: Yet another look." In J. B. Bryson and R. Bryson (eds.) Dual-Career couples. New York: Human Sciences Press.
STATHAM, A., S. VAUGHAN, and S. K. HOUSEKNECHT (1984) "The ordering of significant life events among professional women as a determinant of involvement in career." Presented at the Women Work Symposium, University of Texas, Arlington.
STEIN, A. H. and M. H. BAILEY (1975) "The socialization of achievement motivation in females," in M.T.S. Mednick et al. (eds.) Women and Achievemetn. New York: Halsted.
U.S. Bureau of the Census (1984) Current Population Reports, Series P-23, No. 133. Washington, DC: Government Printing Office.
———(1983) Special Demographic Analysis, CDS-80-8. Washington, DC: Government Printing Office.
———(1982) Current Population Reports, Series P-20, No. 374. Washington, DC: Government Printing Office.
———(1981) Current Population Reports, Series P-20, No. 362. Washington, DC: Government Printing Office.
———(1980) Current Population Reports, Series P-20, No. 356. Washington, DC: Government Printing Office.
U.S. Department of Labor (1980) Perspectives on Working Women: A Databook. Bulletin 2080. Washington, DC: Government Printing Office.

II-B.2b

Husbands and Wives Should Have an Equal Share in Making the Marriage Work

CHARLES LEE COLE
ANNA L. COLE

We view marriage as an intimate partnership of two persons who are mutually committed to growth as individuals and as a relationship. Both partners work on building and sustaining the marriage. If only one partner were committed to making the marriage work, the relationship would fail to achieve its full potential for meeting the needs of both partners. Thus, each partner has an equal (but not necessarily identical) share in making the marriage work.

In this chapter we will address the issue of how marriage has changed from an institution governed by external role constraints and obligations to an internally motivated relationship held together by the internal dynamics of the couple's interaction patterns of striving to meet each other's emotional needs. We will begin our discussion by defining what we mean by successful marriage, and then will discuss the importance of equality in marriage. Our next section will briefly focus on some major social forces that have shaped our current expectations of marriage. We then will discuss some of the basic dynamics required for successful marriage as we have defined it.

DEFINING SUCCESSFUL MARRIAGE

Many components make up what we mean by successful marriage. Because we see marriage as a dynamic process rather than a static entity, we prefer not to define marriage in one way, but to use four different conceptualizations of "good," "healthy," or "successful" marriages.

Lederer (1981: 46) describes a good marriage as possessing six characteristics that he sees healthy marriages as having in common:

> 1) both partners feel that they are getting most of what they want from the relationship, 2) both partners are productive in ways which are important to them as individuals (some experience individual produc- tiveness through professional career or hobbies, while others experi- ence it by being in charge of home and family), 3) both partners are comfortable about sharing their satisfactions with one another, now as well as in times to come, 4) both partners are comfortable about sharing the tasks and trials which are unpleasant to the other, 5) both spouses get satisfaction from being supportive to each other, and 6) both spouses have the ability and willingness to adapt to the never-ending changes and circumstances which affect their relationship.

He also notes that there is an "endless variety" of ways couples achieve these characteristics and that what one couple perceives as meeting their mutual and individual needs may not make much sense to anyone else and does not need to.

Lewis (1979: 28) lists three factors necessary for a healthy marriage. The findings of his research on healthy families suggest that "shared power and intimacy are cornerstones and for many couples, sexuality is a third important dimension." These dimensions were found in marriages he studied that seemed to "work best." He notes that these marriages had been "constructed" by the partners and provided for continued growth throughout life as well as strength in coping with life's stresses.

Mace (1982a) delineates three core ingredients necessary for achieving a successful companionship marriage: (1) a commitment to individual and couple growth, (2) an effectively functioning communication system, and (3) the ability to make creative use of conflict. Mace calls these a "primary coping system," and we will be mentioning them again in a later section on the dynamics of contemporary marriage.

Hof and Miller (1981: 9-10) discuss what they call an intentional companionship marriage, which they define as

> a relationship in which there is a strong commitment to an enduring marital dyad in which each person experiences increased fulfillment and satisfaction. There is a strong emphasis on developing effective interpersonal relationships and on establishing and maintaining an open communication system. The ability to give and receive affection in an unconditional way, to accept the full range of feelings toward each other, to appreciate common interests and differences and accept and affirm each other's uniqueness, and to see the other as having equal status in the relationship.

They go on to point out,

> There is a commitment to expanding and deepening the emotional aspects of the relationship, including the sexual dimension, and to developing and reinforcing marital strengths. The relationship is characterized by mutual affection, honesty, true intimacy, love, empathy, and understanding. There is an awareness of changing needs, desires, and aspirations, and appropriate responses to them. There is also a sense of self-worth in each partner and a balance of autonomy and interdependence, with each partner accepting equal responsibility for the success of the relationship.

> The intentional companionship marriage is imbued with a conscious realization that marriage is not a static system with inflexible roles, but rather is a dynamic, changing relationship, calling for continued commitment to openness, creative use of differences and conflict, negotiation of roles and norms, and continued individual and couple awareness and growth. . . . there is an intentional commitment by both

partners to work on the process of the relationship, and to develop the skills needed to insure the continued growth and vitality of the relationship [Hof and Miller, 1981: 9-10].

THE IMPORTANCE OF EQUALITY
IN CONTEMPORARY MARRIAGE

Mace (1982a) points out that our expectations for marriage are high. He lists three interrelated qualities commonly sought when people marry. At the top of his list is equality, since he contends that love and intimacy, the other two qualities, are impossible as he defines them in a hierarchical relationship. Love, of course, can be present in an unequal relationship, but is very different from love without domination or submission, with respect for one another as equals. Intimacy or "shared privacy" is impossible to achieve without the strong trust developed between equals.

Relationships in which the partners are not perceived as equals are not growing relationships. Instead, they stagnate into dullness and boredom by maintaining the status quo and, consequently, fail to meet the emotional needs of either partner. If the spouses perceive that they are not equal partners and that one is more capable than the other, they then interact in ways that perpetuate this assumption. The overresponsible one quickly takes charge of all situations, not allowing the one assumed incapable to learn how to take responsibility. The underresponsible one assumes that the other spouse is so capable that there is no need for him or her to learn responsible behavior. Since the relationship is based on assumptions, neither partner has the opportunity to grow and change either as an individual in the relationship or as a partner. In such a marriage, partners either find satisfaction and growth outside of the relationship, minimizing the importance of the marriage in their overall lives, or through finding satisfaction and growth opportunities outside the marriage decide to divorce.

We do not consider equal to mean that spouses must be identical and split all responsibilities down the middle. Instead, we mean that both partners are valued for the special qualities they bring to the marriage and are given the fullest range possible of opportunities to continue to grow as individuals. In addition, each couple has the opportunities to build a marriage based upon shared values. For example, some couples may choose to have husband and wife have equal responsibility in parenting and provider roles. Some couples may choose to have either the husband or wife as primary parent and lifestyle maintainer while the other serves as the primary provider for the family. Some couples may choose to be child-free so that both may devote a major portion of time to their careers. The possibilities for the division of responsibility are infinite.

MAJOR SOCIAL FORCES SHAPING EXPECTATIONS OF MARRIAGE

In the eighties there has been increased emphasis on companionship as the central focus of marriage. Family sociologist Ernest Burgess (Burgess and Locke, 1945) coined the term "companionship marriage" forty years ago, predicting an ideological shift from a view of marriage being valued because of its instrumental qualities (i.e., successful if the instrumental roles of provider, homemaker, mother, father, and so on were well executed) to the view of marriage being valued because of its expressive qualities (i.e., successful if the expressive needs of each spouse, such as love, emotional support, companionship, and intimacy, are met within the relationship). A great deal has happened in those forty years to confirm Burgess's prediction and to shape our expectations of what a successful marriage is.

We will not describe in detail the many social forces that have impacted marriage, but instead will selectively cite a few of them that we see as having a major influence in changing the nature of the marital partnership from instrumental to expressive.

Economic constraints have eroded the buying power of the consumer, and the rising expectations for higher standards of living have forced more and more couples to rely upon the incomes of both husband and wife. Technological innovations—such as TV, home computers, microwave ovens, prepackaged meals, and the increasing array of household appliances aimed at reducing the amount of time required for cooking, cleaning, and maintenance of the household—have had enormous effects upon the time required to do the household tasks.

The development of reliable contraceptives, beginning with the birth control pill in 1957, have given couples more choice in controlling their reproductive and parenting decisions and have made it possible for women to plan careers in addition to home-making and parenting. Having reproductive freedom has allowed couples to plan whether to parent and to plan the spacing of children. These changes have had enormous impact upon the expectations couples have about the instrumental functioning of the family unit.

The changes in the expressive domains of marriage, however, are of the most concern to us in this chapter and seem to be more related to the human liberation movements (both the women's liberation movement that emerged in the sixties and the men's liberation movement that emerged in the seventies), the human potential movement that emerged in the sixties, and the marriage enrichment movement that began to take shape in the seventies.

The women's liberation movement opened up new frontiers for women that moved beyond roles as mother, wife, and homemaker to sharing work roles in wider opportunities previously open only to men. The men's liberation movement provided men with the opportunity to become more expressive and opened up new frontiers for sharing work roles in the maintenance of home and family. Both of these movements liberated men and women so that they could become more complete persons rather than being locked in stereo-typed male and female roles.

The human potential movement emphasized individual growth as opposed to needing to fulfill roles imposed by family or society. As the "me generation" developed, commitment to marriage based on fear of disapproval from family and society lessened, and many feared that the ideal of family would disintegrate and that marriage would become obsolete. Instead, an awareness began to develop that both individuality and the companionship afforded by marriage could be realized in a companionship marriage in which the commitment comes from the two partners and the focus is on meeting emotional needs as well as on sharing instrumental tasks.

The marriage enrichment movement gained momentum as it became obvious that new insights and skills were necessary to build a companionship marriage. The marriage enrichment movement also provided couples with the much-needed basis for couples to support other couples by working together to nurture and support each other's marital growth. This gave couples a wider range of role models for developing a companionship marriage and the awareness that marriage is dynamic rather than static. Through marriage enrichment events—such as weekend retreats, growth groups, and support groups—couples acquire training in interpersonal skills such as communication, conflict management, and problem solving.

DYNAMICS REQUIRED FOR A SUCCESSFUL COMPANIONSHIP MARRIAGE

As stated previously in the section defining successful marriage, Mace (1982a) suggests that a primary coping system is prerequisite to the development of a successful companionship marriage. He delineates a primary coping system as (1) a commitment to growth, (2) an effectively functioning communication system, and (3) the ability to make creative use of conflict. In this section we will briefly discuss these three elements as well as other dynamics we believe are important components of a companionship marriage.

COMMITMENT TO GROWTH

The purpose of traditional marriage was primarily to maintain social order, and its stability was of prime importance (Mace, 1982a). Couples were encouraged to "settle down" after marriage. A companionship marriage, however, cannot succeed without continual growth, since it is based upon the development of all the potential of both individuals and of the relationship. Such growth takes sustained effort, and both partners must be committed to the hard work and challenges involved.

AN EFFECTIVELY FUNCTIONING COMMUNICATION SYSTEM

Foote and Cottrell (1955) coined the term "interpersonal competence" to describe the required skills for developing and maintaining a successful companionship marriage. Interpersonal competence means skill in relating to others. Interpersonal competence implies that the skills used in developing a meaningful relationship serve as a foundation upon which the marriage is shaped by patterns that a couple develop.

As indicated by our earlier definitions of successful marriage, it is clear that a companionship marriage of equals requires more interpersonal competence than does a marriage of partners who are not perceived as equal. In a marriage of unequal partners most, if not all, decisions are made by only one partner with little or no input sought or valued from the other partner. In a companionship marriage of equals both partners make input into most, if not all, decisions affecting the relationship, requiring more communication skills.

In joint decision making, both partners share the responsibility for solving problems, including the development of strategies to approach the problem and the actual implementation and carrying out of decisions. To do this, both spouses must be able to communicate effectively. Some of the interpersonal skills needed include the ability to state a point of view congruently, being able to suspend judgment until all the information is in, giving full attention to the partner when he or she is talking and giving full consideration to the partner's input, and conveying a sense of understanding and appreciation. Such skills are essential in building trust, developing true intimacy, and building self-other esteem (Guerney, 1977).

CREATIVE USE OF CONFLICT

Since differences are viewed as healthy and essential ingredients for building relationship vitality, it is crucial that a couple know how to use their differences as a source of marital strength rather than letting their differences drive a wedge between them. This means that the couple must be able to understand the dynamics of conflict and conflict resolution. Mace (1982b) points out that anger is a useful tool, much like a smoke alarm that can sound a warning that something is wrong and needs to be investigated before serious damage is done to either the individual or the relationship. Without skills, however, a couple will not be able to move past the angry feelings to investigate and find solutions.

Mace (1982b) notes that most conflicts are resolvable if the partners have the necessary skills to listen to each other's point of view and work for a solution that both can agree on. He also points out when a solution is not easily found a couple has the option of agreeing to disagree. He suggests that in a companionship marriage, in which both partners are respected and accepted, it is not acceptable for either partner to use force, power, or manipulation to coerce the other into submitting to the partner's will. As a couple learns to respect individuality, agreeing to disagree becomes easier to accept since partners do not believe that they always have to agree. In many instances, issues that once seemed insurmountable later seem insignificant; thus, the conflict dissipates with the passage of time.

DIFFERENCES IN TEMPORAL AND SPATIAL PATTERNING

Marriage is a dynamic relationship that must be responsive to the changing needs and rhythmic patterns of daily interaction of the couple. Differences in temporal and spatial patterning (Constantine, 1983) of the two spouses must be negotiated by the couple so that they establish a time and a place in which things are done. For example, if one spouse prefers to go to bed earlier and arise earlier than the other, the couple may be out of sync in their natural temporal cycles. This can create tensions when coordinating schedules for participating in joint activities.

A couple with different spatial orientations may disagree about what each part of the house is to be used for, how important it is for the house to be tidy and orderly, who owns what and how it should be used, areas considered private for each person, and areas considered to be jointly shared.

DIFFERENCES IN ENERGY LEVELS

Both the temporal and spatial patterns established will need to take into account individual energy levels and how each spouse prefers to expend, recharge, and monitor his or her own energy reserves. If the couple have differences in how they like to unwind and relax or in doing physically and mentally taxing tasks, they likely will experience an imbalance in their energy levels. This has implications for the couple's choice of lifestyle, and respect for energy differences will need to be learned.

DIFFERENCES IN LEARNING STYLES

Reiss (1981) and Duhl and Duhl (1979) point out the importance of couples' understanding their differences in learning styles. Learning styles reflect how an individual seeks, takes in, and processes new information. In some marriages both spouses learn the same way. In other marriages the spouses have very different learning styles. For example, one partner may prefer to examine issues slowly and in depth, while the other partner's natural style is to examine issues quickly and trust intuition. It is crucial for both spouses to respect and gain an appreciation of the other's styles. Differences enhance the learning potential of each partner.

BALANCING SEPARATENESS-TOGETHERNESS NEEDS

Each marriage needs to establish patterns for separateness (doing things apart as individuals pursue their own unique interests) and togetherness (doing things as a couple where the companionship is valued and desired by both spouses) that take into account their own temporal, spatial, and energy patterning as individuals and as a couple. It is important for a couple to achieve a balance in separateness and togetherness. This time alone is vital for developing individual interests and becomes an important input for enriching time together.

CONCLUSIONS

Marriage takes hard work, and it is impossible to achieve a mutually satisfying relationship without commitment by both spouses to continued growth. The norms of marriage have changed, so now each couple must develop their own norms and patterns that best meet their own individual and relationship needs.

REFERENCES

BURGESS, E. W. and H. J. LOCKE (1945) The Family: From Institution to Companionship. New York: American Book.

CONSTANTINE, L. L. (1983) "Dysfunction and failure in open family systems, I: application of a unified theory." Journal of Marriage and the Family 45: 725-738.

DUHL, B. S. and F. J. DUHL (1979) "Integrative family therapy," in A. Gurman and D. Kniskern (eds.) Handbook of Family Therapy. New York: Brunner/Mazel.

FISHMAN, B. and R. FISHMAN (1983) "Enriching marriage as a reciprocally resonant relationship," in D. Mace (ed.) Prevention in Family Services: Approaches to Family Wellness. Beverly Hills, CA: Sage.

FOOTE, N. and L. S. COTTRELL (1955) Identity and Interpersonal Competence. Chicago: University of Chicago Press.

GUERNEY, B. G., Jr. (1977) Relationship Enhancement. San Francisco: Jossey-Bass.

HOF, L. and W. R. MILLER (1981) Marriage Enrichment: Philosophy, Process, and Program. Bowie, MD: R. J. Brady.

LEDERER, W. J. (1981) Marital Choices: Forecasting, Assessing, and Improving a Relationship. New York: W. W. Norton.

LEWIS, J. M. (1979) How's Your Family? New York: Brunner/Mazel.

MACE, D. R. (1982a) Close Companions. New York: Continuum.

———(1982b) Love and Anger in Marriage. Grand Rapids, MI: Zondervan.

REISS, D. (1981) The Family's Construction of Reality. Cambridge, MA: Harvard University Press.

MARITAL SEX ROLES

II-B.2c

Successful Marriages Are
Primarily the Job of the Man

PHILIP R. NEWMAN

Premise 1: Isn't a successful marriage the product of the woman's hard
work? Doesn't the woman spend her time maintaining the marriage
relationship, taking care of the children, and creating the home
environment? The woman must be the one who makes a marriage
successful.

Premise 2: Doesn't it seem logical that the responsibility for the success of a
marriage rests with both partners? A successful marriage must rely on
active efforts by both partners to work together and to resolve conflicts
through negotiation and compromise. The two partners have to get
along with each other, resolve their differences, and plan their lives in
mutually acceptable ways to make a marriage successful.

The first premise is an example of stereotypic thinking. The
second premise is an example of logical speculation. Both are
common ways of conceptualizing who is responsible for the success of
a marriage. As often happens when we examine the research evidence,

however, we find a surprising and unexpected dynamic. The husband is the pivotal person in determining whether or not a marriage will be successful. A successful marriage is, then, the responsiblity of the husband.

Men often seem to have more power in the early phases of a marriage. This may be due to cultural expectations, age, training, and occupational status. The happiest marriages are characterized by equalitarian decision-making patterns or husband-dominant decision-making patterns. The least happy marriages are characterized by wife-dominant decision-making patterns (Gray-Little and Burks, 1983). Hyman Rodman (1972) pointed out that much of the woman's experience in a marriage will depend on how the husband shares his power in the relationship. If the husband fails to become involved in his marriage relationship, or if he fails to behave in accordance with role expectations by assuming decision-making responsibility, he increases the likelihood that his marriage will be unsuccessful. If the husband shares decision-making power with his wife, or if he retains decision-making power for himself, he is likely to create a marriage that is satisfying to both partners.

William Barry (1970) in his review of the marriage literature concludes that the success of a marriage relationship as defined by mutual satisfaction seems to depend primarily on four key characteristics of the husband. These include the happiness of his own parents' marriage, his educational level, his socioeconomic status, and the stability of his personal identity. Barry (1970) and Bell (1983) find that the problems of adjusting to the stresses of marriage are greatest for women. However, whether the wife is able to adjust successfully to marriage depends upon the support and understanding her husband provides.

In this chapter each of the key characteristics will be examined in order to see how they enable husbands to create successful marriage relationships.

HAVING A GOOD MODEL

The success of the husband's parents' relationship is an important correlate of his own marital success. A good model for marital success in his family of origin will be helpful in guiding a husband's efforts toward making his marriage a success. This makes sense. The expectation that marriage can succeed is cultivated through the years. In a successful marriage there is a wealth of opportunity for the children to observe the philosophy, skills, and techniques that help make the relationship work well. Successful spouses must be able to supply emotional support, resolve conflict in mutually satisfying ways, and understand the conditions that promote personal development for all family members.

These tasks and many others that make up the process necessary for a successful marriage require commitment and skills. If the husband has had opportunities to observe and participate in a successful family process in his childhood home, he will be able to use his knowledge and skills in his own marriage rather than be required to learn them from the beginning when he enters marriage. He is likely to have a general expectation that says a marriage can be successful. Husbands who have grown up in families with unsuccessful marriage relationships may have to do remedial work when they marry in order to correct inappropriate expectations and conceptualizations about how the marriage process works.

EDUCATIONAL ATTAINMENT AND SOCIOECONOMIC STATUS

Two other characteristics of the husband that are important correlates of successful marriages are educational attainment and socioeconomic status. The more educated the husband is and the wealthier he is, the greater is the likelihood that he will be able to make the marriage relationship succeed.

Education and socioeconomic status are positively related to each other. The greater the husband's educational attainment, the greater is his access to the opportunity structure of the society. The more opportunity the husband has, the greater is the likelihood that he will achieve a job that pays well and provides a sense of security about the future. This will help the family attain the resources its members need. If family members are able to accomplish their goals and develop a lifestyle that meets their needs, they will tend to be happy and satisfied. Reiss (1980) and Scanzoni and Scanzoni (1981) review numerous studies that show a positive relationship between socioeconomic status and both length of marriage and marital satisfaction.

Men learn more in school than how to be effective in the world of work. Many skills and ideas a man learns in school are likely to help him to be a successful marriage partner. As part of his college curriculum a man is likely to learn about love, sex, understanding another person's point of view, empathy, child rearing, negotiation, communication, and a wide variety of other processes that are important to the success of a marriage relationship. Courses in psychology, sociology, economics, political science, and family relations often help a man develop a knowledge base that will help him become a successful person as well as a successful worker. Courses in literature and philosophy stimulate a man's thinking about abstract issues concerning the quality of being. Men gain intellectual insight and skills in formal educational settings that help them meet the challenges of married life as well as work life. Abstract learning is often effective in generating a multifaceted understanding of these processes.

Reviewing the last two sections, we find that there appear to be two factors that have been identified thus far that help a husband make a marriage successful. The first factor is the amount of prior learning that he brings to his marriage. The second factor is the resource base he can provide to meet the needs of his wife and his children.

A STABLE PERSONAL IDENTITY

The final factor that is related to the success of a marriage is the stability of the husband's personal identity. Later adolescence is the life stage during which the formation of a personal identity is most preoccupying for individuals. It is important to recognize, however, that the process of self-definition begins in infancy and continues into later adulthood.

Personal identity is an abstract concept that is sometimes difficult to grasp. Two brief statements by Erikson give us a sense of what he means by the concept.

> The final identity of the individual is not the sum of his previous identifications but is a more highly differentiated complex in which earlier identifications become part of a more unified whole [Erikson, 1971: 166].

> The young individual must learn to be most sure of himself where he means the most to others—those others, to be sure, who have come to mean most to him. The term identity expresses such a mutual relation in that it connotes both a persistent sameness with oneself (self-sameness) and a persistent sharing of some kind of essential character with others [Erikson, 1959: 102].

The formation of a personal identity, then, involves a process of integration that leads to a new component of the personality. In addition, one's identity serves as an anchor that allows one to experience a sense of continuity in social relationships. There is also a cultural component of personal identity. One's personal definition includes the roles and accompanying expectations in which individuals are involved, as well as the roles and expectations in which they anticipate involvement.

Identity commitments are established in the areas of work, ideology, sex-role, marriage, child rearing, friendship, social network and education (Newman and Newman, 1984). It is important to note that, according to this definition, identity is not simply a process of occupational choice. Personal identity includes an orientation toward interpersonal relations as well as life tasks. In fact, one's personal identity is crucial in setting personal goals and guidelines for selecting a marriage partner, deciding about having and raising children, and establishing friendships. A good deal of adult social life is determined by how one defines oneself in relations with others. One's personal identity provides an internal continuity to one's adult behavior as a spouse, parent, friend, church member, neighbor, business associate, ethnic group member, and citizen.

Identity achievement occurs after a period of self-questioning and decision making that leads to personal commitments. This is called the psychosocial moratorium. The individual does not necesssarily decide who he or she will marry or what kind of work he or she will do by the time identity achievement occurs. In a sense, this process establishes a structure of personal identity. However, the actual content of one's personal identity may not be filled in until specific choices are made during the adult years. The structure of one's personal identity guides the specific choices.

People who prematurely make structural commitments in the aforementioned areas, usually by accepting parental choices, develop a foreclosed identity. These people experience commitment but not the process of personal decision making. People who fail to make commitments, who are unable to identify their strengths and weaknesses, and who do not achieve a structure for their identity experience role diffusion. These people may or may not experience a decision-making struggle, but they definitely do not make commitments.

Research in the area of identity development suggests that there may be some interesting differences between men and women. Douvan and Adelson (1966) conclude that women tend to develop a sense of intimacy before a sense of identity, while men tend to develop a sense of identity before a sense of intimacy. Rossi (1968) and Raush et al. (1975) found that women tend to enter marriage having completed less work on occupational identity than men. Marcia (1980) argues that the predominant concerns of most adolescent girls involve the establishment and maintenance of interpersonal relationships. He also hypothesizes that the process of achieving personal identity takes longer for females than males. Matteson (1982) and Rogow et al. (1983) found support for the position that interpersonal concerns are important for men's identity as well as for women's. In fact, interpersonal concerns seem to be as important for men's identity as occupational issues.

There is one finding that has been observed time and time again by a number of researchers using Marcia's method for assessing ego-identity status. Men who are described by identity achievement or psychosocial moratorium score highest on self-esteem and lowest on anxiety. Women who are high on self-esteem and low on anxiety are described by identity achievement and identity foreclosure. The psychosocial moratorium or identity crisis seems to be more personally threatening and more worrisome for women than it is for men.

These few paragraphs provide a brief description of the major landmarks in identity research. I believe these findings can be synthesized in a way that will help us gain an understanding of why the responsibility for the success of a marriage lies with the husband. I do not think women develop a sense of intimacy before they develop a sense of identity. I argue that men and women have tended to deal with identity issues in a different order and, perhaps, with differing emphases. During the initial phases of identity formation, women tend to focus more on interpersonal issues, while men tend to focus more on occupational issues.

If women are more skillful than men in interpersonal relations, and/or if society expects women to deal more effectively with interpersonal relations, we might expect to find women dealing with interpersonal issues first as they develop the structure of personal identity. We would also expect that women would be more preoccupied than men with interpersonal issues related to identity. If men are more skillful than women in instrumental activity, and/or if society expects men to deal more effectively with task-related issues, we might expect to find men dealing with task-related issues first as they begin the preoccupation with self-definition. We might also expect that men would be more preoccupied than women with issues related to their own instrumentality during the period of identity formation.

In the past few years, times have changed to the point where a majority of American women work outside of their homes in their own occupations. Does this mean that cultural expectations for the behavior of women have changed? To some extent the answer is "yes," but to some extent it is "not yet." Cultural expectations exist in people's minds, and it will come as no surprise that many Americans still hold the same kind of sex-role expectations they did fifteen years ago regardless of whether or not women's activity has changed. It will take time for these expectations to change. As this happens, we may find that the preoccupations involved in identity formation become more similar for men and women. However, if the temporal course of identity development is different for men and women, as Marcia hypothesizes, we may continue to observe the same differences that are currently noted.

The process of self-definition seems to be more difficult for women than for men. The self-questioning and role experimentation that is essential for identity formation produces a confrontation between a woman's own internal expectations for feminine behavior and the new alternatives she may consider particularly in the area of occupational choice. This confrontation produces periods of uncertainty, self-doubt, and self-criticism that are reflected in anxiety and low self-esteem. Men do not face this same confrontation. They are expected to select an occupation and can do so without internal conflict that results from working on the task itself.

Men are vulnerable to problems if they do not develop an identity structure that includes an orientation toward interpersonal issues. There are some traditionally male professional groups, for example, whose members become so preoccupied with occupational goals that they fail to adequately consider interpersonal commitments. Many physicians demonstrate extreme occupational commitment. There is a body of literature developing within the American Medical Association that documents the psychological problems of the spouses and children of physicians. This an example of an occupational commitment that is extreme. Such a preoccupation seems to preclude adequate work on the interpersonal aspects of identity. This is then reflected in failing marriages and in the development of psychopathology within families.

Here lies the key to understanding why a stable self-identity is important in helping the husband create a successful marriage relationship. Men are likely to have established stable self-identities as they enter marriage. Women are more likely to be working on identity issues as they enter marriage. This occurs partially because women tend to marry men who are older than they are. Another reason is that the identity problem is somewhat more difficult for women at this time in history. Finally, it may be related to a natural difference between the sexes in the time it takes to resolve identity issues.

Having experienced the process of developing a sense of personal identity, the husband is able to help his wife during her struggle. He is able to provide security, reassurance, emotional support, and ideas. He may help her by sharing some skills he has learned about cognitive role experimentation or he may encourage her efforts to explore career options. He may provide information about how to pursue a career. A male with a stable self-identity is able to provide the security he needs to support himself emotionally in the difficult times of the years ahead.

People who have achieved a sense of personal identity tend to be competent and independent. They tend to feel good about themselves and demonstrate the highest levels of ego functioning. By helping his wife achieve a sense of personal identity, a husband is planting the seeds of long-term health in his marriage relationship.

CONCLUSION

I have presented an argument for the position that a successful marriage is the responsibility of the husband. This position, although not commonly held, is supported by the research literature. The husband appears to be the person whose behavior is most responsible for the success of his marriage. One area of importance involves the husband's role in the decision-making structure of the relationship. He must be able to accept responsibility for making the decisions or he must share this responsibility with his wife. Either condition leads to marital satisfaction. The husband must also be able to provide support and encouragement to his wife while she accomplishes the more difficult adjustment process. Finally, the husband must be able to match his wife's skills for engaging in intimate interpersonal relations. If the husband has these skills, chances are good that his marriage will work; if he does not, chances are good that the marriage will fail.

Three things affect the husband's ability to be successful in his marital responsibility. First, the husband's prior learning experiences affect his performance as he tries to create a successful marriage. The primary settings for these learning experiences include the family in which he grows up and the schools that he attends. The husband is more likely to be involved in a successful marriage if his parents' marriage was successful. The more educated the husband is, the greater is the likelihood that his marriage will be successful. Second, the husband is able to ensure a sense of security and need fulfillment for family members by being able to provide a workable resource base. A sense of security and need fulfillment are necessary for the attainment of a sense of satisfaction. Third, the husband is able to help his wife successfully achieve her own sense of identity by providing the support and understanding she needs during the identity struggle. The formation of a sense of personal identity seems to be more difficult for women than for men, and it appears to take a longer time. Consequently, many women are likely to marry before they have completely established their personal identities. The husband must provide support, encouragement, and security for his wife's efforts. The husband's orientation can help his wife meet the challenges she must face. The outcomes of attaining a sense of personal identity include a sense of independence and competence. These qualities help the wife experience positive feelings about herself and allow her to function in the best possible way.

The husband maximizes the probability of success of his marriage by helping his wife function at her best, by having access to necessary resources for group satisfaction, and by knowing how to behave in an intense interpersonal environment.

REFERENCES

BARRY, W. A. (1970) "Marriage research and conflict: an integrative review." Psychological Bulletin 73: 41-54.

BELL, R. R. (1983) Marriage and Family Interaction. Homewood, IL: Dorsey Press.

DOUVAN, E. and J. ADELSON (1966) The Adolescent Experience. New York: Wiley.

ERIKSON, E. H. (1971) "The syndrome of identity diffusion in adolescents and young adults" and "The psychosocial development of children," pp. 133-215 in J. M. Tanner and B. Inhelder (eds.) Discussions about Child Development, vol. 3. New York: International Universities Press.

——(1959) "The problem of ego identity," pp. 101-164 in Psychological Issues Monograph Series, vol. 1, no. 1. New York: International Universities Press.

GRAY-LITTLE, B. and N. BURKS (1983) "Power and satisfaction in marriage: a review and critique." Psychological Bulletin 93: 513-538.

MARCIA, J. E. (1980) "Identity in adolescence," pp. 159-187 in J. Adelson (ed.) Handbook of Adolescent Psychology. New York: Wiley.

MATTESON, D. R. (1982) "From identity to intimacy: it's not a one-way street," in H. A. Bosma and T.L.C. Graafsma (eds.) De ontwikkeling van identiteit in de adolescentie (The Development of Identity in Adolescence). Nijmegen, Netherlands: Dekker and van de Vegt.

NEWMAN, B. M. and P. R. NEWMAN (1984) Development through Life: A Psychosocial Approach. Homewood, IL: Dorsey Press.

RAUSH, H. L., W. A. BARRY, R. K. HERTEL, and M. A. SWAIN (1975) Communication, Conflict, and Marriage. San Francisco: Jossey-Bass.

REISS, I. L. (1980) Family Systems in America. New York: Holt, Rinehart & Winston.

RODMAN, H. (1972) "Marital power and the theory of resources in cultural context." Journal of Comparative Family Studies 3: 51-69.

ROGOW, A. M., J. E. MARCIA, and B. R. SLUGOSKI (1983) "The relative importance of identity status interview components." Journal of Youth and Adolescence 12: 387-400.

ROSSI, A. S. (1968) "Transition to parenthood." Journal of Marriage and the Family 30: 26-39.

SCANZONI, L. D. and J. SCANZONI (1981) Men, Women, and Change: A Sociology of Marriage and Family. New York: McGraw-Hill.

DIVORCE

Couples Who Have Children Should Stay Together Even If They Are Unhappy with Each Other

MARY JANE S. VAN METER

Whether or not couples should stay together for the sake of the children is a question rarely heard debated in contemporary society. Parents are less child-oriented and more self-oriented today, as compared with previous generations (General Mills, 1977). As evidence of this trend, Glick (1984) predicts 59 percent of all children born in the early 1980s may expect to live with only one parent for at least a year before reaching age 18. More than a million new children experience family dissolution firsthand each year (Bureau of the Census, 1980). The voluntary dissolution of marriages is something parents can control, and possibly might if the consequences to their children were better understood.

The high visibility of divorced persons and the availability of legal divorce in contemporary American society may have facilitated the "myth of the romance of divorce" (Hetherington et al., 1978: 174).

Current literature, films, and emphasis on doing your own thing generate expectations that presume one will find personal freedom, self-realization, and perfect harmony outside of the present relationship.

Although most studies mention the distinct painfulness of the process of breaking an attachment between husband and wife, regardless of the length of the marriage, major victims may be the children. Any effort to compile the evidence of the adverse effects of divorce on children forces an awareness of the great gaps in knowledge and the real deficits in divorce data.

Only by focusing attention on the nature of the effects of divorce on children can a case be made that parents should stay together for the sake of the children. In this chapter I will discuss a number of variables that may influence the outcome for children.

CONCERNS TO CONSIDER

Time of separation, developmental issues, sex differences, biological or adopted status, the predivorce family environment, the divorce process itself, and the new environment all seem to affect children.

TIME OF SEPARATION

Parents may divorce one another and become ex-spouses, but once an individual becomes a parent that person is always a parent, never an ex-parent, regardless of how old the child becomes. Some indication is available to suggest that the *separation*—that is, the visible departure of one parent—may be the time of greatest stress for children (Kelly and Wallerstein, 1976), and the amount of stress may depend on the age of the child.

DEVELOPMENTAL ISSUES

The Wallerstein and Kelly (1980) study is the only longitudinal study that includes an initial interview with children and with parents at the time of separation of the parents, a second interview a year and a half after the separation, a five-year follow-up study, and most recently, a ten-year interview (Wallerstein, 1984). These data points have clearly indicated that divorce must be seen not as a single event, but as a sequence of experiences involving a transition in the lives of both children and adults. Their study paid particular attention to the different reactions of children at various developmental levels, despite a possibly biased subject sample from Marin County, California, and the lack of a comparison or control group (see Levitan, 1979).

Preschool children are typically frightened and bewildered by the separation and sometimes blame themselves for what had occurred (Wallerstein and Kelly, 1980). The young child is less likely to consider the motives and feelings of parents, therefore, is likely to self-blame. Their egocentric perceptions at this stage are apt to enhance their feelings of responsibility for the divorce (Longfellow, 1979). Clinical evidence (Kalter, 1983) suggests this feeling of personal culpability may even persist into other stages of development as the child grows older. Guilt and responsibility, however, are not a universal finding, but a clinical finding (Wallerstein, 1984). Rather, children universally are scared. As 75 percent of preschool children in one study had not been told about the impending divorce and awoke one morning to find one parent had left, it was not surprising to find many had fears of abandonment and were afraid to go to bed at night (Wallerstein and Kelly, 1980).

Slightly older children, six to eight years of age, experienced profound sadness and longing for the absent father; they felt abandoned and rejected (Kelly and Wallerstein, 1976). Some of these children, unable to express anger at the father for being left, held considerable anger toward the mother. More common were fears of antagonizing or challenging the custodial mother.

The older latency children in this study displayed worry about their unstable family condition and about their own futures, along with genuine sympathy and compassion for a troubled parent. In the overall seven- to ten-year-old group, Wallerstein and Kelly (1976) report that none of the children was relieved by the divorce despite a situation of severe marital conflict in many of the families. In fact, only 34 percent of school-age children were happy and thriving five years after the divorce, while 37 percent were depressed (Wallerstein and Kelly, 1980).

The findings of Kalter (1983) corroborate that nearly all school-age children involved in divorcing families indicate, to varying degrees, sadness, anger, feelings of rejection by the noncustodial parent, insecurity about whom they could count on for care, and the pain of conflicted loyalty toward each parent. In Kalter's interview-based studies, 200 children of divorce were asked in a 25-item questionnaire how two imaginary children would feel about the experience of parental divorce. The same negative feelings of shock, pain, sadness, and anger, and wishes for their parents to get back together were revealed.

The period of adolescence is normally characterized by a gradual process of withdrawal from dependence on parents, of defining and establishing one's own identity, and a need for external stability during the time of physiological and psychological changes. These are the main features of normal adolescence that are seriously impaired by parental divorce. The time to grow up is shortened by the marital disruption, the loss of one parent, usually the father, and the lessened availability of discipline and controls make it an especially difficult period.

To each person among the 22 adolescents in the Wallerstein and Kelly (1974) study, divorce was experienced as an extraordinarily painful event. The main affects involved great anger at the parents for breaking up the family at a point critical to the adolescent, considerable sadness and sense of loss, and a sense of betrayal by one or both parents. These researchers indicated their initial surprise at finding the extent of unhappiness among adolescents, given the widespread expectation that preschool and school-age children would experience more distress. Though it was anticipated that the process of increasing independence and withdrawal by adolescents from their parents would lessen the pain, it became clear that the very acute distress was indeed very real.

Adolescents, at a more advanced psychological, sexual, and social stage than younger children, became swept up in the parents' own concerns. Observation of a mother and father changing established patterns, forced to take on new roles, and creating new sexual alliances causes problems with the teen's own identity formation. Anxiety about their own future marriage, worry about money, and loyalty conflicts are further issues with which the adolescent must contend.

No data are currently available on the feelings of adult children when their middle-aged or aging parents divorce, perhaps those parents who stayed together for the sake of the children until the children were emancipated. Based on findings to date, the expectation that the adult child would also have feelings of anger, sadness, and loss would be reasonable.

SEX DIFFERENCES

How boys and girls may be affected differentially by the divorce is a concern of interest to many researchers. Though they noticed few differences, at the time of separation Wallerstein and Kelly (1980) found very clear follow-up differences between boys and girls.

Boys were significantly more opposed to the divorce than their sisters; they felt significantly more stressed within the post-divorce family and more of them remained intensely preoccupied with the divorce. More boys longed intensely for their father, more boys felt rejected by their father. More boys were preoccupied with fantasies of reconciling the broken marriage. More boys were depressed [Wallerstein and Kelly, 1980: 165].

These findings concur with others (e.g., Hetherington, 1979), which indicate that the impact of divorce is more pervasive and enduring for boys than for girls. Boys of divorced parents show a higher rate of behavioral disorders and problems with interpersonal relations, both at home and at school with teachers and peers, than do girls from divorced families. Among the reasons girls are able to function better may be that (1) little girls, unlike boys, are able to cope with the loss of the father through the mechanism of denial through fantasy in which they dream of his return one day; and (2) the character of the relationships of girls with one or both parents is such they are less the object of a mother's wrath than are boys. Girls who had good relationships with their father prior to divorce were more likely to experience continuity afterward. Boys, on the other hand, had to abruptly face a changed response by the father (Wallerstein and Kelly, 1980).

Sex differences disappear after five years. Other issues then converge to create a complex constellation of factors that determine either a good or poor outcome for children.

BIOLOGICAL OR ADOPTED STATUS

Dreams of reunion and fantasies of the lost biological parents may be a part of the life experience of any adopted child who seeks the missing link in ego continuity and identity (Tessman, 1978). Add to the adoption experience the divorce of the adoptive parents, and an even greater burden of abandonment, sadness, and loss is likely to occur. No empirical data exist to indicate whether or not adopted children are more stressed than the biological children of divorcing parents. One possible prediction is that adopted children would feel greater anger over the divorce as they endure the disruption and/or loss of yet another parental set.

PREDIVORCE FAMILY ENVIRONMENT

Few studies have attempted to consider the impact of the predivorce family environment as an important variable in measuring the impact of divorce on children. Homes that are rife with marital conflict may embroil the child in the ongoing parental struggle. Children who are exposed to frequent marital quarreling may be placed in a position of conflicting loyalties, with one parent attempting to persuade the child to form an alliance against the other parent. Additionally, children with perceptions of greater conflict in their families, regardless of the family structure, have significantly lower self-esteem (Raschke and Raschke, 1979; Berg and Kelly, 1979).

Nye, in his 1957 study of adolescents' adjustment in broken and happy or unhappy, unbroken homes, found adolescents in single-parent or reconstituted families significantly better adjusted in areas of psychosomatic illness, delinquent behavior, and parent-child adjustment. More recently, a review of literature suggests that family discord may be a more important determinant of the effects on children than marital structure (Goetting, 1981).

Much of the literature regarding the effects of divorce on children has assumed, since the Nye study, that divorce was preferable to a conflicted family environment. The impact on children of the loss of the "happy" family may be more devastating than the disruption of the conflict-ridden family. Landis (1960) found that the degree of divorce-related trauma experienced by adolescents was greater among those who regarded their families as being happy prior to the divorce than for those who saw their homes as having open conflict between the parents. A divorce in a family perceived to be happy is most likely to be a catastrophic divorce, which Sprenkle and Cyrus (1983) found resulted in more severe trauma, anger, and pain. The divorce with no prelude may be seen as senseless and especially devastating to the self-esteem and readjustment capacity of those family members affected (Sprenkle and Cyrus, 1983).

CHANGED FAMILY ENVIRONMENT

Parental divorce is not just one painful stressor on its own, but leads to other stress-provoking events to which each child must adjust. The most obvious and most devastating change that occurs to children of divorce is the separation, and too frequently, the loss of one parent. With children remaining with the custodial mother in over 90 percent of cases, the loss of the father from the home sets in motion a series of other changes associated with the divorce.

The downward economic mobility of divorced mothers and children lies at the heart of the remaining life changes. Her decreased income may reflect inability to seek employment due to caring for young children, her entry into a competitive labor market with outdated or inadequate skills, or the lowered earnings of employed women as compared to men, coupled with either the father's failure to pay, or the inadequacy of, child support. Research has documented that the poverty of the female-headed family may result from divorce (Brandwein et al., 1974).

A residential move to more affordable living space is often required for the single-parent family. This may entail a change of schools and the loss of friends who might otherwise have been able to act as a support system for the children experiencing divorce.

For the children, loss of the mother to the work force may mean the loss of her attention, in addition to that of the father. The lack of companionship in shared family activity contributes to the feeling of loneliness the child experiences. The loss of parental attention may contribute not only to the child's lower self-esteem, but indicates as well the diminished supervision with the absence of the custodial parent.

After divorce, a redefinition of family is required for all of the participants. How this is accomplished depends on the relationship between the parents (Ahrons, 1983). A cooperative and mutually supportive relationship between divorced parents reduces the crisis potential, whereas ongoing conflict as a major part of the child's life does not bode well for that child's adjustment.

A major component of the redefinitional process appears to be the parents' ability to maintain a child-centered relationship. For most, the continuing parent-child relationship is less intimate and more task-oriented (Ahrons, 1980). This may, of course, happen in the relationship with both the custodial and noncustodial parent.

The family redefinition process frequently includes remarriage and the introduction of stepparents, and often stepsiblings, into the postdivorce family. Loyalty conflicts for the child may get in the way of establishing good relationships with stepkin unless the parents are able to maintain a good relationship.

Another part of the redefinition process may include relationships with the child's extended family. The female custodial parent is most likely to continue, and possibly increase, her interaction with her own kin and maintain contact with her former in-laws at a lower level of interaction (Spicer and Hampe, 1975). For the child, lack of contact with the absent father results in the loss of contact with his kindred and an imbalance in that child's kin network (Anspach, 1976).

Thus, as the vast majority of noncustodial fathers move away, physically and emotionally, from everyday involvement in the child's life, so also may the parental grandparents be separated from the degree of interaction with their grandchildren that they had formerly experienced. The continuing active role of the father appears crucial to the maintenance of ties between his parents and his children. As the kin-keeping function is usually ascribed to women in the family, this unfamiliar task may remain unattended when it falls to the male.

Divorce in the lives of children usually means a substantial redefinition of the family to include some or all of these family forms: single-parent family, binuclear family, and stepfamily. At the same time, divorce typically brings a redefinition of extended family that means diminished contact with paternal grandparents.

LONG-TERM CONSEQUENCES

The latent consequences of childhood family disruption by divorce only recently are becoming known. Any divorcing parent who believes the children will get over it is taking a very cavalier, indeed, wishful stance.

Ten years later, children who were 9 to 18 years old at the time of the divorce have persistent and strong feelings of sadness and vivid memories of the divorce and the pain with a predominant mood of regret, sadness, and loneliness (Wallerstein, 1984). Having witnessed a disrupted marriage in their own homes as children, they are concerned with how to select a marital partner more carefully and most admitted to spending many hours thinking about it. They plan living with a lover, late marriages, and a long delay afterward before having children to ensure certainty about the relationship (Detroit Free Press, 1984). Parental divorce appears as a stressful event that endures throughout one's lifetime (Kulka and Weingarten, 1979), and there is a consistent finding of intergenerational transmission of marital instability. Children from divorced homes are more apt to experience divorce in their own marriages (Kulka and Weingarten, 1979; Mott and Moore, 1979; Mueller and Pope, 1977). Children of divorce do not learn the interpersonal skills of bargaining and negotiation, problem solving and conflict resolution.

CONCLUSION

Evidence is abundant that divorce has a profound, lifelong effect on children. Though it is tempting to insist parents stay together—particularly in the face of evidence of the deep longing for intact family, the pain, and the sadness children of divorce express—the conclusion must be that not all parents should do so. Family violence and sexual abuse, in which the abuser is unwilling to seek or is unresponsive to therapeutic treatment, are certainly examples where it is unhealthy for families to remain together.

The reality of contemporary life suggests that divorces will continue to occur in families with children. The issue then becomes finding the most humane way of disengaging from the family and altering attachments in such a way as to inflict the least amount of pain.

A complex configuration of factors, rather than one single thread, appears to determine good outcomes for children (Wallerstein and Kelly, 1980). In general, the factors influencing positive consequences are subsumed in the overall quality of life in the postdivorce family. Among the many components presaging good outcomes are

(1) that the divorce ends the conflict between the parents;
(2) that there remains continuity with both parents;
(3) that there is not a drastic reduction in the standard of living; and
(4) that the children have a restoration of parenting.

Perhaps those children of divorced families seen ten years later were grasping an important idea for this age: One should select a marital partner very carefully and then wait a period of time before having children. Their view suggests that prior to the decision to have children a deeper level of marital commitment needs to be achieved— for the sake of the children.

REFERENCES

AHRONS, C. R. (1983) "Divorce: before, during, and after," in H. I. McCubbin and C. R. Figley (eds.) Stress and the Family, vol. 1. New York: Brunner/Mazel.
———(1980) "Divorce: a crisis of family transition and change." Family Relations 29, 4: 533-540.
ANSPACH, D. F. (1976) "Kinship and divorce." Journal of Marriage and the Family 38, 2: 323-330.
BERG, B. and R. KELLY (1979) "The measured self-esteem of children from broken, rejected, and accepted families." Journal of Divorce 2, 4: 363-369.
BRANDWEIN, R. A., C. A. BROWN, and E. M. FOX (1974) "Women and children last: the social situation of divorced mothers and their families." Journal of Marriage and the Family 36, 3: 498-514.
Bureau of the Census (1980) Social Indicators II. Washington, DC: Government Printing Office.
Detroit Free Press (1984) "Children of divorce are cautious to marry." April 29: 8E.
General Mills (1977) The General Mills American Family Report 1976-1977. Minneapolis, MN: Author.
GLICK, P. (1984) "How American families are changing." American Demographics 6: 21-25.
GOETTING, A. (1981) "Divorce outcome research." Journal of Family Issues 2, 3: 350-378.
HETHERINGTON, E. M. (1979) "Divorce: A child's perspective." American Psychologist 14, 10: 851-858.
———M. COX, and R. COX (1978) "The aftermath of divorce," in J. H. Stevens Jr. and M. Mathews (eds.) Mother/Child Father/Child Relationships. Washington, DC: NAEYC.
KALTER, N. (1983) "How children perceive divorce." Medical Aspects of Human Sexuality 17, 11: 18-45.
KELLY, J. B. and J. S. WALLERSTEIN (1976) "The effects of parental divorce. Experiences of the child in early latency." American Journal of Orthopsychiatry 46, 1: 20-32.
KULKA, R. A. and H. WEINGARTEN (1979) "The long-term effects of parental divorce in childhood on adult adjustment." Journal of Social Issues 38, 4: 50-78.
LANDIS, J. T. (1960) "The trauma of children when parents divorce." Marriage and Family Living 22, 2: 7-16.

LEVITAN, T. E. (1979) "Children of divorce: an introduction." Journal of Social Issues 35, 4: 1-25.

LONGFELLOW, C. (1979) "Divorce in context: Its impact on children," in G. Levinger and O. C. Moles (eds.) Divorce and Separation. New York: Basic Books.

MOTT, F. L. and S. E. MOORE (1979) "The causes of marital disruption among young women: an inter-disciplinary perspective." Journal of Marriage and the Family 41, 2: 355-365.

MUELLER, C. W. and H. POPE (1977) "Marital instability: a study of its transmission between generations." Journal of Marriage and the Family 39, 1: 83-93.

NYE, F. I. (1957) "Child adjustment in broken and in unhappy unbroken homes." Marriage and Family Living 19: 356-361.

RASCHKE, H. J. and V. J. RASCHKE (1979) "Family conflict and children's self-concepts: a comparison of intact and single-parent families." Journal of Marriage and the Family 41, 2: 367-374.

SPICER, J. W. and G. D. HAMPE (1975) "Kinship interaction after divorce." Journal of Marriage and the Family. 37, 1: 113-119.

SPRENKLE, D. H. and C. L. CYRUS (1983) "Abandonment: the stress of sudden divorce," in C. Figley and H. I. McCubbin (eds.) Stress and the Family, vol. 2. New York: Brunner/Mazel.

TESSMAN, L. H. (1978) Children of Parting Parents. New York: Jason Aronson.

WALLERSTEIN, J. S. (1984) "Effects of divorce on children and adolescents." Presented at the Dubo-Rabinovitch Lecture Series, Hawthorn Center, Northville, MI, April 12.

———and J. B. KELLY (1980) Surviving the Breakup. New York: Basic Books.

———(1976) "The effects of parental divorce: experiences of the child in later latency." American Journal of Orthopsychiatry 46, 2: 256-269.

———(1974) "The effects of parental divorce: the adolescent experience," in G. Anthony and C. Koupernik (eds.) The Child in His Family: Children at Psychiatric Risk, vol. 3. New York: Wiley.

DIVORCE

Couples Have a Right to Divorce Even If They Have Children

MATTI K. GERSHENFELD

Like others, I was raised to believe that marriage is forever, and when a couple makes a decision to marry, there should be no escape hatches or extenuating circumstances. They should prepare for marriage by dating and knowing each other; they are of age when they marry. They should know who they are and what they want, because marriage is a lifetime decision.

With time I, like others, have modified that initial position. I think many of us would agree that people will live a long time, and that if a couple marry, do not have children, and decide they have made a mistake, perhaps under those conditions divorce is acceptable. Perhaps they married for the wrong reasons, were immature, and needed the sobering experience. They can cut their losses, like in a business when you recognize that the results will be disastrous. In marriage too, you can think in terms of cutting your losses, rather than putting more energy, money, and resources into what will inevitably be a losing proposition. I think we have come to recognize that divorce, where there are no children, may have some validity. We understand that it may be a hurting, disastrous experience, but out of it will come maturity, a new understanding of what marriage means, and the behaviors needed to have a future relationship succeed.

But, what if there are children? The children did not ask to be born. When a couple brings a child into the world, don't they have a responsibility to set aside their own gratuitous pleasures and think of the child first? Don't they need to accept the responsibility for raising that child to the best of their of their ability? Don't they have a responsibility to their child to do the best that they can in raising that child? Who can say that a mother raising a child is sufficient? Who can say that having only one parent, be it a mother or a father, allows a child the role identification necessary to relate to the same sex and the other sex (or for psychoanalytic types to overcome their oedipal complexes)? Who would say that squabbling divorced parents, divisive and constantly one-upping each other to exert their control, is a way for a child to live—and is a model of good problem solving? Who would say that a divorce situation—Mom talking against Dad, and Dad talking against Mom—allows a child to build trust and a feeling of family?

Each of us knows horrendous instances in which children of divorce feel rejected, abandoned, and unloved. We think life becomes more complicated as they have to relate to two households, two sets of rules, and comings and goings in different environments. Is it not hard enough to be a child today, without having parents behave selfishly and exacerbating the already difficult tasks of childhood?

I, like others, have felt that I understand the justification for divorce and know that it is essential in certain circumstances. However, can divorce be justified when there are young children? Can divorce be justified when there are children depending on their parents for stability, guidance, and as role models? Should not a couple, as parents, be setting aside their own differences to remember that they have a prime responsibility to their children? They are that child's only parents. Maybe they need to focus beyond the "me generation" and focus on the needs of their children. It is not a perfect world; they brought their children into the world. The least that they can do is to provide a household and an atmosphere with two parents who love their children and put their parenting responsibilities in the forefront of their lives.

I really believe that when there are children, the couple need to give prime consideration to their children in contemplating divorce. I have been a marriage and family therapist for more than fifteen years. I do not believe that there is such a thing as value-free therapy; I tell my clients some of my values and tell them that I will be working with them in accord with my value system. I tell them this in the first session. And, I explain, if my value system is not compatible with theirs, they should not be seeing me. Some of what I tell them is that I am religious and believe that marriage is to be taken seriously, that it is not to be viewed as a whim or a short-term experience, and, especially, that a successful marrriage does not happen by itself. It takes commitment, ongoing work, and the desire to have a good life within a marriage. Problems are not scary; all marriages have problems. The real question is, how do we resolve the problems? My orientation is, how do I help you create a good marriage? My emphasis is definitely in the direction of how we can make this marriage work for you. It may take work, but if we want to succeed, it can be done. When people have children all of this is emphasized even more. I believe that two parents are better than one, one household is better than two, and a loving household with a mother and a father gives a child a real experience with two parents resolving differences. That is my orientation. I have been married to the same husband for over thirty years; it has not been easy. I have four sons. With this as my orientation, let me now present some cases from my clinical practice. The cases are real. The names have been changed for obvious reasons of privacy and ethical responsibility.

CASE 1—
HE MARRIED TOO YOUNG

Karen married late—at 31—and she married a man who was younger than she—25. She was a teacher, he had a business he was starting. They met around an interest in sports. She was a jogger and a bicycler. He believed in conditioning, was a weight lifter, and played racquetball. She knew that she wanted to get married. The biological clock was running out. At 31, if she wanted to have children, she needed to marry before she was too much older. He liked her company. She had a job, had bought a house, was organized with bills, was structured, had a bank account and savings, and even offered to help him pay off some of his debts. They got married and in less than two years had two daughters.

With the birth of the first child, he was around less and less. He had great difficulty sharing attention with the baby, being expected to help care for the child and coping with the additional bills. He was clearly annoyed that there was not the time to do things together, and worse that there were expectations for his being around and helping. He was inept and felt like a dumb mother's helper needing to be constantly corrected. By the time the second child was born, the pattern that had evolved was overwhelmingly clear. He was in no way interested in going anywhere with the children or her. She continued teaching and making all arrangements for the children. He was home less and less; saying that he had paperwork for his business which involved extra hours. He stopped paying his share of the bills for the household, saying he needed the money for his business, or it would go under. His business was going badly, and he discovered that it boosted his ego to be with other women. Karen found tickets for two in his pants pocket when she was taking them to the cleaners. Friends reported seeing him out with other women. Each time she confronted him, and forgave him. The children, two and four, needed a father. Any father was better than no father; she reasoned. She thought, maybe, therapy could be helpful to help him understand that he had a responsibility to the children both financially and emotionally; he felt therapy was a waste of time and would not come.

Further, he said he did not love her, and did not want to live in a household in which two babies consumed all the time. He hated this life. He felt that he was becoming middle-aged and overwhelmed with responsibilities. It was enough that the business was difficult and he had responsibilities there. He did not need all this additional pressure at home. And, if she did not like it, she could leave. But she did not. She was going to stick it out.

She became a walking skeleton. Her weight dropped from 125 pounds to 92 pounds. She was always crying. She had less and less energy. It was hard for her to wake up in the morning, to take care of the children, to go to work. Her principal called her in to ask what the problem was. She had always had energy, a spark, and had been unusually creative as a teacher. Now she seemed to be functioning on automatic—uninvolved, uncaring, spaced. She decided she needed therapy. She cried through the entire first session. She couldn't continue, she couldn't function. She decided to separate and, later, to get divorced. It is better. He sees the children sometimes and recently kept them overnight.

She is building a new life. She has activities and friends. She sees the responsibility for helping her children have a happy life now that she understands that she can have a happy life. There are alternatives to the powerlessness of depression. Life at 34 need not be over. He is running, dating a new woman every other week, and being moderately responsible for paying child support. Each month, given the limited contacts and the fact that the children are growing older, he is willing to do more and more with them.

SOME QUESTIONS TO CONSIDER

The children were two and four. Should Karen have continued to stay in the marriage for them? What was the effect of her depression and constant crying on them? What was the effect of her anger that she was paying all of the bills and doing all of the work of rearing children while he escapaded as a way of life? Let us hypothesize: What would be the identification children would form from their mother, and what would they see as a man's role based on their family? Should this couple have stayed together for the sake of the children?

CASE 2—
A BRILLIANT DOCTOR, BUT . . .

Janis was a beautiful woman and a nurse. She met a doctor in his last year of residency. They were viewed as a perfect couple. He was brilliant, she was beautiful, and both were interested in medicine. They would marry and live happily ever after—of course. They had two children, who were three and fourteen months.

Every day Janis was more unhappy. She kept thinking, what is the matter with me? She had two beautiful children, and while they were a lot of work, she was happy being with the children, watching their new "tricks," and enjoying every minute of the pleasures of having these children. There was sufficient money. His parents were wealthy and had been generous in providing them with a down payment for a house. She had household help. She kept telling herself she should be happy. What was the matter with her? She entered therapy to explore what was the matter with her that she was not happy.

It became increasingly clear that she did not have two children; she had three. As she put it,

> He is thirty, going on twelve at an emotional level. He cannot make a decision on anything—not where to live; nor how to furnish; nor how to keep a budget. He does not talk to me. He is unresponsive sexually. Typically, he comes home and walls himself in with journals. He says he loves the children, but he does *nothing*. He doesn't want children or a wife as living entities.

He had married because it was part of his image of success. A beautiful wife, two beautiful children. He was proudest of the image they portrayed in the photograph on his desk. She became aware that she could not live like that—to be always alone; to have to take care of him even to putting his clothes out in the morning and picking them up from where he dropped them on the floor. He was annoyed at having her parents over, or his. And, if she invited them to visit, he went to the study and read. Holidays were viewed as days to catch up on his sleep. Vacations were out of the question. Janis said,

> I lived with it for five years. I need companionship, a person to be with, a person to parent children with. It would be easy to stay in for the money, the house, the maid. I am sure, later, fur coats and diamonds. But I cannot live alone. I pleaded, I begged, I cried. He kept telling me there was something wrong with me, that perhaps what I needed was more household help, and that the children were getting to me.

Janis said, as much as she felt guilty about doing this to her children, she could not survive the present situation which would only deteriorate more as his practice expanded and he was busier. He, like the movie *Scenes from a Marriage*, was focused on work, and hard work, and the satisfactions from a career.

Since the divorce, things are much better. He often takes the children for limited times and is very generous with money. He really needs to be alone. "I never thought I would be 26, raising two children; but, I know it is better than living another 50 years like this."

SOME QUESTIONS TO CONSIDER

Should Janis have stayed? Are reasons like money, domestic help, status in the community (based on her husband's career) sufficient for a life? Is she expecting too much? Perhaps if life is a trade-off, companionship can be traded off. At 26, with two small children living with her, what are the chances of her remarrying? Would she have been better off to stay in the marriage and devote herself to raising her children? What would be the long-term outcomes of such a decision? How do her needs get met—only through parenting? In a different era, there would not have been a problem. Being married to a physician would have been ultimate happiness. At 26, is it enough? Is the solution that she create a hobby, become interested in horticulture, or take up tennis? Will that do it?

CASE 3—CRAZY

John and Maureen are devout Catholics who are committed to the teachings of their church. They met in college, where John was a business major and Maureen a music major. They both sang in the choir, attended concerts. John was hard working and expected to do well in a business career for a large industrial firm. Maureen taught music in school; she was very talented, sensitive, and creative. Prior to the birth of their first child, she retired from teaching to stay home to raise their children—Valerie, Chris, and Johnny.

Sometime after Johnny's birth, there was a drastic shift in Maureen's mood. She was frequently depressed, had difficulty sleeping, and smoked incessantly. Her care of the children became sporadic. Often she seemed in a trance, and did not know what was happening. Maureen said there was nothing wrong; she was fine.

John tried a variety of solutions. He had a woman come live in the house and take care of the children. Although financially it was impossible, he got a loan from his parents; he had no choice. He felt that he had to go to work knowing his children were being cared for. Maureen would have none of it. She screamed at the woman, and said she was taking her children away from her. She accused her husband of trying to supplant her. She literally beat the woman up. Next, John invited her mother to come live with them and help care for the children with some part-time help. Maureen screamed, ranted, raved. Her mother left, saying she could not take living there any longer.

John continued to beg, bribe, and cajole her to go into therapy; to no avail. One day in a bizarre moment, she thought she would have watermelon for dinner and ordered a truckload of watermelons delivered and deposited on her lawn. That incident was the basis for his committing her for treatment. She was furious at this ultimate humiliation. She was in treatment and returned home.

The household was still too much for her. There were other bizarre incidents and ways of "disciplining" the children. One time when Valerie was fourteen, on the phone, as usual, talking to her girlfriends about boys and clothes, her mother retaliated. After Valerie had taken a shower, her mother pushed her out the door while she was naked, and locked the door. This occurred when there were about ten children out on the street playing. Valerie, naked and humiliated, had to go to a neighbor's to be taken in. One day Maureen was smoking in the garage and after lighting her cigarette, threw the match on a stack of papers. Little Johnny, being punished by being made to stand in the garage, raced around stamping out the fires as quickly as she created them. After that day, he had nightmares about being killed in a fire. And, whenever he saw her smoke he stood terrified, in a place beside her, ready to put out possible fires. The children were doing very badly in school. When John now tried to bring them to his parents' home after school, where they would be less anxious, Maureen accused him of destroying her and taking her children from her.

The therapy continued sporadically with little outward change. John was a good Catholic, he stayed. Eventually exasperated, John moved out with the children. She filed for a court order, saying that she loved the children and that her husband was taking them from her. John, on the verge of collapse with trying to be there for the children, not having a home, and keeping his job, returned the children to Maureen and moved in with his parents.

There ensued a difficult divorce. It took all of John's money and put him in debt for at least the next ten years. He has custody of the children and they live in the house with his parents. The oldest and youngest children are in therapy.

John is a proud man. The children do not tell anyone that their parents are divorced. John tells no one. Divorce is the ultimate disgrace. John is trying to salvage his life.

SOME QUESTIONS TO CONSIDER

How long do you stay in a marriage that is destructive to your children? Should John have spent years exhausting the alternatives before he acted? Should he have continuously sought help for Maureen without considering termination of the marriage and protecting his children earlier? What was the quality of John's life in the ten years after the birth of Johnny?

In return for the divorce, Maureen wanted the house, all their savings, a guaranteed income for life, and half of his salary. Should he have acquiesced to get the divorce, or should he have continued to stay married? Even in this situation, consider his shame in getting a divorce, and the fact that neither he nor the children acknowledge it.

CASE 4—
HE TRIED AND TRIED AND TRIED

Cass was in her senior year in college. Dean was finishing law school. They met on a blind date arranged by their parents, who had known each other. They had common backgrounds, religion, and interests. They were both intelligent and enjoyed living in Washington.

Dean, with some of the other brightest and best young lawyers, was working in the Justice Department. There were a group of young couples, with babies, who enjoyed each other, had stimulating conversation, and reveled in their access to power. After two years they moved back to their hometown. Dean started practice and Cass taught reading. They had two children. Dean worked hard and achieved. His income tripled in ten years. Dean had a dream of some day becoming a federal judge. There was no way he could live on that salary and so he wanted to save money so that, should the appointment come, he could take it knowing that there was supplemental income. Cass felt that she contributed to their financial well-being; she was not a parasitic wife. She had survived a severe illness in her early childhood and had come to the conclusion that life was to be enjoyed. She convinced Dean to buy a big house with a pool, and to send their two children to private schools. She and the children had extensive wardrobes and they took the children on magnificent vacations at Christmastime and in the summer.

Cass would agree that sex was not important in her life, but that she would acquiesce sexually as part of her wifely duties.

Dean was becoming angrier and angrier. Cass did not seem to care. Each year they spent just a little over what he made. Since he earned more the next year that was covered; but there was not a penny saved. He was strongly committed to family life and loved his children more than anything.

Dean asked Cass to watch what she spent. He explained that he wanted a federal judgeship, should it be offered. She countered that he was not a consumer, and did not know how much things cost and that the price of things had gone up. She claimed that she was watching their money and that in no way was she excessive. In the sexual area, he suggested sex therapy; he suggested that they read erotic material together; he suggested that they watch a porno film together. He suggested, and suggested, and suggested. Cass felt it was all very juvenile and silly.

Dean thought about his great loneliness and found himself crying each night as he lay in bed. Nothing worked. His way of coping with tremendous anger was to speak less and less at home, to be more withdrawn, to be focused on watching TV or reading a book. It bothered Cass somewhat and she wished he were more social. He sought companionship with his children. They wondered, why was he so cold to their mother; why was he so withdrawn; why was there no laughter in the house? Cass was jealous that the children spent time with him. She pointed out to them how withdrawn he was and how uninvolved he was in the family. The older daughter took the role of family mediator; constantly saying to her father, "Dad, be nice to Mom," and to her mother she said, "Mom, try to understand Dad." In college, although she was bright and beautiful, she had great difficulty dating. When boys were cold to her, she got along well; when they acted warm and affectionate, she ended the relationship. The younger child, the son, handled the hostility by withdrawing to his room and closing the door; by separating himself. He had difficulty in speaking to anyone and was described as a "loner."

When the son left to go to college, Dean decided he could not live such a life any longer, and he left. Although Cass was devastated, she agreed that a life in silence, without any affection, with constant hostile comments, and with angry frequent stares was not a quality of life for her either. Both are in therapy—Dean to overcome his guilt at leaving his family, and Cass to try to survive being rejected by Dean and his leaving. She never thought it would happen. In fact, she thinks he needs psychoanalysis, that there are serious things wrong with him.

SOME QUESTIONS TO CONSIDER

What is the effect of Dean's having stayed in a family all those years when he was angry and unhappy, and where no affection was shown?

Cass is angry. She feels she was used to raise his children. He should have left earlier when, at least, the children would be there with her. Now she is all alone. Should he have left earlier?

What was the model of a family to the children, and what is the impact on their lives?

In the end, Dean and Cass were divorced. It will still affect their children. Would it not have been wiser for both of them to acknowledge their own needs earlier? Can it be that a couple have much in common at an early stage in their lives, and twenty years later have very different value systems and desired lifestyles? How do we reconcile that?

What happens when good people value their children and stay together for the children? Is it a good situation for them? For their children?

SUMMARY

It seems that we need to revise some basic assumptions—for instance, that divorce is usually a catastrophe, and when it involves children it is definitely proof of the parents' selfishness. We need to revise the idea that a two-parent home, no matter what kind, is superior to a home where a child lives with one parent. We need to revise the assumption that with a couple who have children divorce occurs because they put gratification of their own needs ahead of their basic responsibilities as parents. We need to revise the assumption that a couple can sublimate their needs and be what their children desire from them. We need to understand that couples can be divorced and that it does not mean selfishness or neglect of their children. These assumptions must be revised, understood from both the complexity of couples' relationships and our understanding of what children need from their parents.

Margaret Mead put it well:

> Every time we emphasize the importance of a happy, secure home for children, we are emphasizing implicitly the rightfulness of ending marriages when homes become unhappy and insecure.

Couples do have a right to their own happiness, especially when they have children.

SUPPLEMENTARY READINGS

BANE, M. J. (1979) "Marital disruption and the lives of children," in G. Levinger and O. C. Moles (eds.) Divorce and Separation. New York: Basic Books.

DANIELS, V. and L. J. HOROWITZ (1976) Being and Caring. New York: Simon and Schuster.

FISHER, E. (1974) Divorce: The New Freedom. New York: Harper & Row.

GARDNER, R. (1976) Psychotherapy with Children of Divorce. New York: Jason Aronson.

GETTLEMAN, S. and MARKOWITZ, J. (1974) The Courage to Divorce. New York: Ballantine.

GOLDMAN, J. (1981) "Can family relationships be maintained after divorce?" Journal of Divorce 5, 1/2: 141-158.

Journal of Divorce (1981) "Impact of divorce on the extended family." Special issue, vol. 5, 1/2.

KESSLER, S. and S. BOSTWICK (1977) "Beyond divorce: coping skills for children." Journal of Clinical Child Psychology 6: 38-41.

KRANTZLER, M. (1974) Creative Divorce. New York: M. Evans.

McCARY, J. L. (1980) Freedom and Growth in Marriage. New York: John Wiley.

RICE, D. (1979) Dual Career Marriage: Conflict and Treatment. New York: Macmillan.

ROSENBERG, M. (1972) "The broken family and self-esteem," in I. Reiss (ed.) Readings on the Family System. New York: Holt, Rinehart and Winston.

STEINZOR, B. (1969) When Parents Divorce: A New Approach to New Relationships. New York: Random House.

III. Parenthood

At issue in this section is the question of society's interest in the production of children to replenish the population. The first chapter opposes pronatalist pressures for childbearing, while the second indicates that society's interest in the quality of the children is so great that having children should be limited to those qualified.

The abortion question is a second issue in which there are societal pressures and controversies. The essays make the case for the rights of each of the three parties in the dilemma: the unborn child, the mother, and the somewhat unusual alternative—the rights of the putative father.

DISCUSSION QUESTIONS

(1) Drs. Abbott and Walters suggest that there are pressures on married couples both to have and not have children. Discuss the similarities and differences of their arguments about both of these pressures.

(2) If you could make the decision, what criteria would you use to decide who should be a parent?

(3) Some say it is the duty of all married couples to have children. Discuss this from the point of view of two chapters from this section.

(4) How important do you think the age of "personhood" is to the right to have an abortion?

(5) Why should rape be singled out as a reason many will use to allow an abortion? How do these arguments apply more generally?

(6) Indicate how parenthood affects the male over his adult life span. Indicate how some of these effects relate to his having equal rights to decide if his partner should carry a pregnancy to term.

(7) Is there any commonality in these three positions? Seek comparisons and alternatives including preventive measures.

(8) If persons are not qualified for parenthood, should that be an adequate reason for allowing abortion?

CLASS ACTIVITIES

(1) Have students bring in examples of pro- and antinatalist art and advertisements. Have an exhibit and discuss the messages of the art in terms of the issues.

(2) Have a commission discuss how they would set up a procedure for deciding who should become parents. Assume that any procedure is possible and acceptable, including birth control procedures.

(3) Have a role-taking exercise with persons taking the parts of husband and wife discussing why they should have a child. Have an alter ego who stands behind each person and presents the opposite point of view.

(4) Have someone take the role of an unborn baby doing a soliloquy on whether it seems wiser to be or not to be born and the conditions for each.

(5) Have class members write a brochure requesting funds for an abortion clinic.

(6) Have a male do a soliloquy about whether to have a child and how it will affect his life both positively and negatively.

(7) As a politician running for public office, develop a policy about both abortions and free choice about parenthood. What are the commonalities?

Parenthood Is a Question of Free Choice, and There Should Be No Societal Pressure

DOUGLAS A. ABBOTT
JAMES WALTERS

In the United States, as in many countries of the world, societal pressures—including formal governmental controls—are applied to regulate the fertility of married couples (Griffith, 1973). Pressures are applied in an effort to decrease fertility rates (e.g., providing easy access to inexpensive contraceptives) and to encourage fertility (e.g., through providing tax incentives and support for dependent families).

More subtle forces are evident, as well. For example, some leaders of the feminist movement discourage women from marrying, and others discourage women from thinking that homemaking and parenting are worthwhile occupations. Increasingly, the traditional role embraced by women is portrayed as embodying demeaning activities that fail to satisfy the achievement needs of women. Homemaking is viewed as including tasks that no one wants to do. The fewer the tasks of homemaking, the better the lifestyle. From the popular literature it would appear that an increasing number of highly educated women are minimizing the importance of homemaking and are questioning the desirability of parenthood.

The level of living promoted in our nation leads many couples to delay marriage and to embrace values that necessitate the gainful employment of both husband and wife. Both of these forces—that is, the rejection of traditional roles and the need for greater economic resources—tend to result in lower birth rates (Schulz, 1982).

Population specialists increasingly emphasize the necessity of examining the effects of family size in relation to dwindling resources and increasing pollution (Population Crisis Committee, 1976). Too, many of the data from the social sciences contribute to the development of attitudes that discourage childbearing by emphasizing (a) the costs of children, (b) the limited rewards of parenthood, and (c) the marital disruption and disharmony in families where children are present (Glenn and McLanahan, 1982).

On the other hand, friends, parents, and grandparents encourage couples to have children, and the media provide constant reminders of this expectation (LeMasters, 1977). The Judeo-Christian tradition affirms this expectation as well, for the admonition to be fruitful and multiply is often interpreted as a God-given command to marry and procreate (Levitan and Belous, 1981). Catholics and Mormons, for example, are encouraged to have large families and are condemned for using abortion as a contraceptive method. A more subtle force to procreate has been recognized by sociobiologists, the inclination to reproduce that is a function of our genetic heritage (Wilson, 1975).

Although it is clear that many forces influence our fertility choices, there are good reasons to support freedom of choice in fertility matters. However, the decision should be an informed choice based upon a couple's awareness of the many advantages and disadvantages of parenthood.

ECOLOGICAL PRESSURES

In 1983 the world's population grew to nearly 4.8 billion. This is double the number of people on earth at the end of World War II. If the increase continues at an annual rate of 1.7 percent, the world population will reach 6 billion by the year 2000. Concern has been expressed about high birthrates in Third World countries. Women in less-developed countries average about 5 children each, compared with 2 or fewer in more developed countries. Youth predominate in the Third World. More than 40 percent of the population is under 15 years of age (Kent and Haub, 1984). Even in China, where population control efforts exceed those of every other nation in the world, it is anticipated that their one billion people will continue to proliferate: One-third of that nation is 14 years of age or younger. From the foregoing context, it is clear that concern whether given couples will not have children cannot rationally be based on fears that the world's future is threatened by efforts to limit population growth. The foregoing figures support the increasing concerns related to overpopulation: social-psychological stresses of crowding, depletion of natural resources, and increases in environmental pollution.

Although the world's population continues to increase, when one considers the Western world, and the United States in particular, there appears to be less cause for alarm about overpopulation. Over the past 100 years there has been a continual decrease in the fertility rates of American women (Glick, 1983), and we are now below the replacement level and approaching zero population growth (Reiss, 1980). Some believe that the United States has no foreseeable overpopulation problem and that our contribution to world population growth is negligible and declining (Kando, 1978). It should be noted that in some countries—Sweden, France, Luxembourg, West Germany—there is actual concern with *low* fertility and the *declining* population (McIntosh, 1983).

When examining problems related to overpopulation of the world, one of the primary concerns is whether enough food can be produced. It has been maintained, however, that the problem is not whether we can feed an overpopulated world but what to do with the excessive food production (Kando, 1978; Levitan and Belous, 1981). A substantial argument is made that the world's food supply is adequate and that it is the mismanagement and poor distribution of food that is the real problem—not the growing number of people to feed (Bouvier, 1984; Revelle, 1976).

Others, though confirming the decline in fertility rates, still propose some type of control or restriction on fertility because the steadily increasing total population of new Americans will consume much of the world's resources and add greatly to world problems

(Gilland, 1983; Schulz, 1982). Clayton (1979) has predicted that the decision to reproduce will be taken out of the hands of married couples in the future and that governmental permission may be required to conceive more than one or two children.

INTERFAMILIAL AND INTRAFAMILIAL PRESSURES

As stated before, because motherhood is still seen as a central role by many women and an important ingredient to marriage, some couples perceive pressure from friends and family to have children (Lamanna and Reidmann, 1981). A problem also arises when one partner desires more or less children than the spouse. Thus, peers, parents, and partners can exert powerful influences upon spouses to have children or to curtail childbearing. These "in-house" forces may cause a couple to make an unwise fertility choice. Attempts to deal with these pressures might begin with the realization that nontraditional family forms will be given increasingly wider acceptance throughout our society. It may also help if couples discuss some of their values and life goals in regard to childbearing with family members. This openness may foster support from these significant others.

OTHER SOCIAL PRESSURES

Should singles have children? Persons who are familiar with the Cornell studies (Walker, 1973; Walker and Woods, 1976) of the amount of time spent within a day on child-related activities can only conclude that it is far easier for a mother and a father to meet the caretaking needs of children than for either a mother or a father alone. These findings have been confirmed in subsequent research. It is no surprise to those who have been faced with the care of children without a spouse that rearing children alone is a demanding, if rewarding, task. Although most children reared by one parent function well, there is little doubt that when the day-to-day requirements of child rearing are considered, it is far easier if there are two parents who take child rearing seriously. Singles who consider having children should be as aware of the pros and cons as married couples who consider childbearing.

EDUCATIONAL INFORMATION

Some couples will decide not to have children as the result of the influence of social science researchers who have concluded that children alter marital functioning in a way that reduces marital satisfaction (Abbott and Brody, 1984; Bell et al., 1980; Belsky et al., 1983; Feldman, 1981; Glenn and McLanahan, 1982; Houseknecht, 1979; Ryder, 1973; Waldron and Routh, 1981). Specifically, Feldman (1981) found that childless couples had more fun away from home, exchanged stimulating ideas more, talked with each other more, and reported working together more frequently on projects than did couples with children. Ryder (1973) found that couples with children were less satisfied with their marriages than were childless couples, and mothers reported more frequently than childless females that their husbands did not pay enough attention to them. Houseknecht (1979) reported less cohesion among couples with children than couples who were childless. Abbott (1984) found that among mothers of young male children less satisfying marital adjustment was evident than among a similar group of childless wives. Interestingly, mothers with female children and especially with female infants reported no notable differences from childless wives.

In a review of the literature (Bell et al., 1980) on the effects of children on the marital dyad, evidence has been provided that an increasing number of children within the family is related to

  (a) lower morale of their parents;
  (b) less satisfying marital communication;
  (c) less egalitarianism;
  (d) an increase in the number of rules mothers expect children to follow although, interestingly, the number of rules diminished in families of five or more;
  (e) a decrease in parental attention;

(f) an increase in family tensions;
(g) less parental interest in the school progress of children;
(h) a decrease in parent-child closeness (except for later-born children);
(i) an increase in parental authoritarianism; and
(j) a decrease in maternal energy.

Single mothers (and mothers with three or more children under age six) reflected less nurturance and less friendliness toward their children and were more dominating. As Bell et al. (1980) have noted, however, few answers to cause and effect questions can be found in the literature.

The depletion of financial resources as a result of having children has clearly been emphasized, and the personal freedom of childlessness has been extolled. Women who have children are viewed as being unable to pursue educational and career opportunities. They must resign themselves to playing a secondary role in the family because their daily sacrifices require them to forgo achieving their full potential and, thus, the great satisfaction that supposedly comes with career success. The fact that the majority of women who enjoy a high level of career success are also parents does not keep this myth from persisting. In the minds of many, one cannot attain extraordinary success in a career and extraordinary success as a mother, however untrue this belief is. If a mother undertakes a career, it is believed by many couples that it should be secondary to her role as a mother. The belief that excellence cannot be attained in two roles in life serves as a self-fulfilling prophecy, and leads many women into unsatisfying, residual employment that does little to contribute to their success as mothers.

An important factor in an examination of the impacts of children on parents is the gender of the parent: wives perceive less satisfaction in marital quality than husbands. As Abbott (1984) has observed, this gender effect could be related to the fact that the presence of a child may move the couple toward a more traditional role orientation. As relationships between spouses become traditional and equality is subordinated, the wife may lose power and sustain an increased work load. Many women are likely to perceive such a shift in role functioning as undesirable and will experience less happiness in their marriages.

It appears that there is an increasing number of professionally oriented women who are postponing childbearing in order to complete advanced degrees and start their careers. A common question among better-educated couples is, "How long should we wait?" Data provided by the 1976 National Survey of Family Growth (Bongaarts, 1982) made it possible to calculate the proportion of couples who used no contraception and who did not conceive during the twelve months preceding the time of the interview. Those not conceiving after one year, by age: 20-24, 6.7 percent, 25-29, 10.8 percent, 30-34, 16.1 percent; 35-39, 22.9 percent. Stated conversely, over three-fourths of those in the oldest group became pregnant. Keeping in mind that one would expect declines in coital frequency with age, the declines in conception rates with age are modest. As Bongaarts (1982: 78) concluded,

> For the majority of women who want to postpone childbearing until they have completed their education and established themselves in a career, the risks they are running may well be quite small compared with the benefits.

Ryder (1973) has found that among 6752 women who used contraception, 26 percent reported that within their first year of exposure to risk of unintended conception they failed to delay a pregnancy they wanted to have at a later time, and 14 percent of contraceptive users who did not ever intend to become pregnant became pregnant. It is clear that those who have no intention of ever having children are more successful at conception control than those who merely wish to delay conception. Over a 5-year period, however, 34 percent of those who never intended to become pregnant did so.

The group that experienced the greatest failure rate was the young group, with a 56 percent failure rate. In a similar study (Schirm et al., 1982) of contraceptive failure, based on data from the 1973 and 1976 National Surveys of Family Growth, conducted by the National Center for Health Statistics, additional data were obtained. Those with the highest rates of contraceptive failure are the young poor (birth control pill, 8 percent; IUD, 15.5 percent; condom, 37 percent; spermicides, 50 percent; diaphragm, 52 percent; rhythm, 62 percent). It is important to note that these high failure rates are for a twelve-month period. Those with incomes over $15,000 annually and who are 30 years of age and older reflect substantially different rates of failure (pill, 2.3 percent; IUD, 4.4 percent; condom, 2.5 percent;

spermicide, 17 percent; diaphragm, 18 percent; rhythm, 23 percent). Although it is clear that those who are older are less vulnerable to failure, when one examines the failure rates of the young at all income levels, it is apparent that the success rates of various forms of contraceptives are less than is commonly believed.

Within the last generation, limiting family size to that which is desired has become a possibility. The evidence indicates, however, that problems still remain in the timing of births, with many couples finding themselves involved in childbearing before they are ready.

CONCLUSION: FREEDOM TO CHOOSE

The right to bear and rear children has always been considered an inalienable right of Americans. Legislation and the courts have upheld these rights in most cases. Marriage and family are integral parts of almost all religious tradition, doctrine, and practice, and Judeo-Christian tradition also supports the couple's right to determine their own fertility. Any attempts to legislate this privilege of procreation endangers a most fundamental freedom. It is hoped that a pattern of noninterference by society will be accepted and that couples will take upon themselves the responsibility to make wise fertility choices.

REFERENCES

ABBOTT, D. A. (1984) "Children's influence on parents' marriage: strengthening the husband-wife relationship." Presented at the National Symposium on Building Family Strengths, Lincoln, NE.
———and G. H. BRODY (1984) "The relation of child age, gender, and number of children to the marital adjustment of wives." Journal of Marriage and the Family.
BELL, C. S., J. E. JOHNSON, A. V. McGILLICUDDY-DELISI, and I. E. SIGEL. (1980) "Normative stress and young families." Family Relations 29: 453-458.
BELSKY, J., G. B. SPANIER, and M. ROVINE (1983) "Stability and change in marriage across the transition to parenthood." Journal of Marriage and the Family 45: 567-577.
BONGAARTS, J. (1982) "Infertility after age 30: a false alarm." Family Planning Perspectives 14: 75-78.

BOUVIER, L. F. (1984) "Planet Earth 1984-2034: a demographic vision." Population Bulletin 39, 1: 1-44.

CAMPION, M. A. (1984) "The state has no right to interfere with sexual expression within the family," in H. Feldman and A. Parrot (eds.) Human Sexuality: Contemporary Controversies. Beverly Hills, CA: Sage.

CLAYTON, R. R. (1979) The Family, Marriage and Social Change. Lexington, MA: D. C. Heath.

CODY, S. S. (1984) "Delayed first-time childbearing: is later better?" Presented at the National symposium on Building Family Strengths, Lincoln, NE.

COLEMAN, J. C. (1984) Intimate Relationships, Marriage and the Family. Indianapolis, IN: Bobbs-Merrill.

ESPENSHADE, T. J. (1983) "Paths to zero population growth." Family Planning Perspectives 15, 3: 148-149.

FELDMAN, H. (1981) "A comparison of intentional parents and intentionally childless couples." Journal of Marriage and the Family 43: 63-72.

GILLAND, B. (1983) "Population and the food supply." Population and Development Review 9, 2: 2-3, 212.

GLENN, N. D. and S. McLANAHAN (1982) "Children and marital happiness: a further specification of the relationship." Journal of Marriage and the Family 44: 63-72.

GLICK, P. C. (1983) "The future of the American family," in J. G. Wells (ed.) Current Issues in Marriage and the Family. New York: Macmillan.

GRIFFITH, J. (1973) "Social pressures on family size intentions." Family Planning Perspectives 5: 237-242.

HOFFMAN, L. W. and J. D. MANIS (1982) "The value of children in the United States," in F. I. Nye (ed.) Family Relationships, Rewards and Costs. Beverly Hills, CA: Sage.

———(1979) "The value of children in the United States: a new approach to the study of fertility." Journal of Marriage and the Family 41: 597-603.

HOUSEKNECHT, S. K. (1979) "Childlessness and marital adjustment." Journal of Marriage and the Family 41: 259-265.

KANDO, T. M. (1978) "Sexual Behavior and Family Life in Transition. New York: Elsevier North-Holland.

KENT, M. and C. HAUB (1984) 1984 World Population Data Sheet. Washington, DC: Population Reference Bureau.

LAMANNA, M. A. and A. RIEDMAN (1981) Marriages and Families. Belmont, CA: Wadsworth.

LASSWELL, M. and T. LASSWELL (1982) Marriage and the Family. lexington, MA: D.C. Heath.

LeMASTERS, E. E. (1977) Parents in Modern America. Homewood, IL: Dorsey.

LEVITAN, S. A. and R. S. BELOUS (1981) What's Happening to the American Family? Baltimore, MD: Johns Hopkins University Press.

McINTOSH, C. A. (1983) Population Policy in Western Europe. Armonk, NY: M. E. Sharpe.

Population Crisis Committee (1976) Mankind's Greatest Need: Population Research. Washington, DC: Population Crisis Committee.

REISS, I. L. (1980) Family Systems in America. New York: Holt, Rinehart & Winston.

REVELLE, R. (1976) "The resources available for agriculture." Scientific American 235: 177-184.

RYDER, N. B. (1973) "Contraceptive failure in the United States." Family Planning Perspectives 5: 133-142.

SCHIRM, A. L., J. TRUSSELL, J. MENKEN, and W. R. GRADY, (1982) "Contraceptive failure in the United States: the impact of social, economic and demographic factors." Family Planning Perspectives 14: 68-74.

SCHULZ, D. A. (1982) The Changing Family: Its Function and Future. Englewood Cliffs, NJ: Prentice-Hall.

SOLLIE, D. L. and B. C. MILLER (1980) "Normal stress during the transition to parenthood." Family Relations 29: 459-465.

WALDRON, H. and D. D. ROUTH (1981) "The effect of the first child on marital relations." Journal of Marriage and the Family 43: 785-788.

WALKER, K. E. (1973) "Household work time: its implications for family decisions." Journal of Home Economics 65: 7-11.

———and M. F. WOODS (1976) Time Use: A Measure of Household Production of Family Goods and Services. Washington, DC: American Home Economics Association.

WILSON, E. O. (1975) Sociobiology: The New Synthesis. Cambridge: Harvard University Press.

Only Qualified Persons Should Be Parents

GAIL ANN THOEN

I can be silent no longer. To come to terms with one's highly controversial beliefs and to take a stand on them publicly—when you know that you will be ostracized and misunderstood and branded as a heretic—is perhaps the most painful and difficult psychological task a human being can be called on to face. Yet, I know the time has come for me to do just that.

Something must be done to ensure that only qualified people have children, and it must be done by those people who are most competent to do it! Otherwise, I am convinced that there will be an ultimate Armageddon.

Author's Note: Gail Ann Thoen is on sabbatical leave from her duties as Assistant Professor of Social and Behavioral Sciences at the University of Minnesota. She is currently a postdoctoral fellow in the Department of Psychiatry at the University of Minnesota Medical School. The author would like to thank Leonard L. Heston, M.D., Professor and Director of Adult Psychiatry, and Paula Clayton, M.D., Professor and Chair, Department of Psychiatry, University of Minnesota Medical School, for their support and encouragement during preparation of this manuscript.

A first step toward preventing social breakdown is for all of us to give up the myth that The Family is the strength of this nation. How can it be a happy place for children when parents, who are supposed to nurture and protect them, neglect or batter them instead? In 1982, according to the National Center on Child Abuse, more than a million cases were reported (Pogrebin, 1983: 16).

The family is not a happy place for children when the arguments of incompatible parents become the children's nightly lullaby, or when frictions and jealousies of (step) family life embitter everyone involved. The family is not a happy place when irrational parents beat sense into children by beating them senseless, when fanatical parents exorcise the devil by torturing the child, when parents refuse a child lifesaving medical treatment, or when perverted parents pollute the family trust with the crime of incest (Pogrebin, 1983: 17-18).

The worst thing about family violence is its reproduction of itself by people who should not become parents. Most sex offenders were preyed upon sexually as children, and children of battered women become battered wives and battering husbands. Parents who were abused as children often become child abusers toward their own children.

Today it would be hard to find a group or institution in American society in which violence is more of an everyday occurrence than it is within the family. One-fifth of all murders committed are of a family member. It is thought that over four million women are beaten each year by their husbands. Over one million cases of child abuse are reported to local or state authorities each year. It was recently reported that at least 45,000 children are sexually abused each year in incidents ranging from fondling to various forms of intercourse (Latts, 1984).

As abused children become adults, more and more are openly discussing their pasts both to conquer their emotional problems and to help others deal with theirs. Private and government agencies are forming to aid victims. At the same time public awareness of the depth and breadth of the problems of family violence has greatly increased. In 1976, for example, polls showed that only about 10 percent of Americans considered it a serious national problem. A recent Louis Harris survey placed that concern at 90 percent (Latts, 1984). Yet, as a society, we fall painfully short of altering the course of destiny, even though the means are well known to many who have kept silent.

Perhaps the Chinese have a solution for us? Let us face facts: The freedom to allow anybody who wants to have children to do so is an outdated luxury of postindustrial Western affluence.

In a recent review of how people engage in making fertility decisions, Skovolt and Thoen (1984) note that most of the world's people do not choose what they will become, where they will live, who they will marry, what job they will take, or whether they will have children. They note that China utilizes psychological, financial, and peer group pressure to persuade all newly married Chinese couples to limit their family size to one child. But more to the point, *the government also mandates that the couple must apply for permission when, and if they are qualified, to try and conceive the solitary child.* Severe sanctions are inflicted in the name of the welfare of the state to those who try to defy the policy (Eberstadt, 1984).

I will agree that the Chinese example is an extreme solution. At other times and places, parenthood and marriage were not separate entities. For example, in years past in rural villages of Turkey, many young brides were pregnant at the time of marriage. Conceptualized in the framework of American views in the 1980s, this suggests active sexual fertility and, therefore, justified marriage. In such a place, marriage was for children. Without the possibility of children, there was no reason for marriage (Skovolt and Thoen, 1984).

In Western postindustrialized societies, the knot between marriage and children and family influence has loosened. Two major reasons for this change involve decreased fertility and the exercise of greater personal choice. Decreased fertility is a function of such changes as contraception, which enables women greatly to reduce involuntary pregnancies; children, once an economic asset, are now an economic liability; older adults no longer rely exclusively on younger family members for their economic welfare; an enlarged road map for women now permits routes other than mothering during adulthood (Hoffman, 1974; Sheehy, 1976; Scott, 1979).

> Indeed, Montagu (1969) ranks the significance of the "pill" with that of the discovery of fire, learning how to make tools, the development of urbanism, the growth of scientific medicine, and the harnessing of nuclear energy [Scott, 1979: 5].

In the current affluence of the West, the freedom to have children whenever one wishes is now thought of as a natural right. Without children, a person often feels deprived and betrayed. Yet freedom to choose can itself be psychologically stressful because freedom brings confusion, and great freedom may result in great confusion. When everything is possible, the act of choice may absorb tremendous amounts of time and anxiety and may ultimately result in the birth of children who are unwanted and uncared for.

SHALL I BECOME A PARENT OR NOT BECOME A PARENT?

Until now this question has seldom been asked in human history. At present, however, this question is repeatedly asked by many young adults in the United States and in other countries.

Little is known in general about how people voluntarily and pragmatically decide whether or not to have children. In the past decade, however, a scientific body of information about a self-selected group of the population has appeared in the literature and popular media. Numerous studies (Veevers, 1973; Bram, 1974; Thoen, 1979; Scott, 1979) are in accord that whenever self-help therapy and/or educational groups to explore the parenthood option are offered by a university, public agency, or private practitioner, a consistent type of population emerges: caucasian, upwardly mobile, highly educated, professional men or women, often in couples, mean age in the early 30s. While patterns differ, Thoen's work (1979, 1984) suggests a general profile of indecision about whether or not to become a parent—an indecision that the couple or person can no longer tolerate. This often occurs after about five years of committed relationship. Often the delay in deciding to have a child is related to these factors: an increasing divorce/remarriage and/or cohabitation rate may delay a person's decision; increasing job opportunities for women in the 1970s and 1980s made possible by enforcement of affirmative action laws; abortion on demand; effective birth control; and the economic recession of recent years.

THE NEED FOR PROFESSIONAL EXPERTISE[1]

In less than one decade, books (e.g., Peck, 1974), self-help inventories (e.g., Peck, 1974), films (e.g., Russell, 1982), and a national organization supporting nonparenthood as a "sane choice in a pronatal world" (NAOP, 1972) have "sprung up" throughout the United

States, Europe, and Australia. An award-winning film produced by PBS, *A Baby Maybe,* was recently shown nationally (PBS, 1984). Is any of this really necessary? Yes, I think so. On the following pages I would like to suggest some general areas in which professionals can help to develop these much-needed services.

MANDATORY COUNSELING FOR ALL POTENTIAL PARENTS

I believe that genetic and psychological counseling for all potential parents must ultimately be required, and that these types of counseling offer one possible solution as to who should become parents in this society. I will never be ready for—nor would I stand by and tolerate—any government-imposed solutions to fertility such as those used in China. But self-help programs such as those just cited might serve as prototypes for more sophisticated models yet to be developed. Teachers and professionals in the mental health field can and must help prevent the birth of unwanted children.

When the great freedom of life becomes questions with no answers, a person may turn to a teacher or therapist for help. Such is the case with the question of parenthood. I am a professor and marriage and family therapist and have conducted workshops and prepared a manual to increase the effectiveness of parenthood choices (Russell et al., 1973; Thoen, 1979). During the course of my work on parenting issues in recent years, I have come to believe that fantasy and daydream therapy, which has escaped the interest and framework of counseling and psychology until recently, offers an area for discovery of a solution to who should become parents in our society. (While human beings have continuously engaged in these processes, psychology has only recently discovered the obvious: People do daydream and have fantasies.) How does it work? How would professionals use this technique?

AN EXAMPLE OF GUIDED FANTASY

Thoen (1979) has described the exact procedure used in a parenthood option fantasy involving an awards banquet, which could be readily adapted for genetic and psychological counseling and educational models. In this guided fantasy participants are asked to consider (a) potential conflicts between a focus on career achievements and a focus on parental responsibilities and (b) their own hopes for the future. After a period of relaxation training a la Jacobson (1938), the participants are asked to imagine an elaboration of the following:

> I want you to imagine receiving an award at a banquet. Imagine that it is five years from now. I want you to imagine that you are sitting at a banquet award dinner. You have remained childfree in order to pursue your career goals. . . . During the meal you think about the award, what you've done to get it, whether it was worth it, whether you are thrilled by it all. . . . Your name is being called for a special honor. . . . What are you being praised for? . . . Did you want it very badly, moderately, or just a little bit? Enough to have remained childfree? So you receive congratulations, you receive the public acknowledgement, and you proceed back to your table. On the way back you think about it. You think as you're moving in slow motion whether it was worth it, to give up children, to grow older without having a family [Thoen, 1979: VI-4, 5].

PROCESSING A GUIDED FANTASY

Benefits of a guided fantasy exercise seem to multiply when there is a skillful teacher or therapist to help process the experience (Lange, 1982). Why? A core reason is that individuals seek out therapy, counseling, and educational workshops when they feel alone and do not know how others handle a particular situation. Often a feeling of relief occurs when a person hears another person express formerly private sentiments that are the same as one's own. For example, as a reason for joining a parenthood option group, one of Kimball and McCabe's (1981: 153) group members said, "I'm tired of going over and over the question in my own mind. Perhaps talking to others will help me gain perspective." This seeking and finding of "social comparison information" may lead to increased levels of self-esteem (Brothen and Skovolt, 1981) and other desirable results. Yalom (1975) calls this the "universality of experience" dimension and describes it as an essential curative factor in group work.

Occasionally, a guided fantasy experience will evoke an intense, unexpected affective response from a client. If this happens it is important that the client/student receive at the time, and on a follow-up basis, properly monitored intensive counseling and therapy services. Guided fantasy is a powerful tool for helping people decide whether or not to become parents. It is imperative, however, that the teacher/therapist perform with excellence and be alert to his or her subject's reaction to this provocative experience.

DELIVERING EDUCATION AND COUNSELING IN THE CLASSROOM

In the preceding section of this chapter, I made a strong recommendation that mental health professionals and educators use creative methods when working with individuals facing parenthood decisions. I also suggested the guided fantasy experience as one example of a technique that could be readily adopted in a number of settings for delivery of services to potential parents.

If I had my way, we would start requiring all ninth-graders to complete successfully a required course on parenthood decisions. This course would be required in the core curriculum just as we now require students to take credits in English and math and science. The class would be both didactic and experiential; all students would also be required to spend some time in individual counseling with a qualified and empathic therapist to explore on a one-to-one basis what they are learning in the classroom about their potential qualities and skills as parents. Actual child-care experience in nurseries and home life situations would be required in the form of an internship. Although this course would be an educational experience for all students, the ultimate decision as to whether or not to become a parent over the life cycle must remain with the individual. No coercion, overt or covert, must ever be applied.

In designing this ideal course, the curriculum must be broad-based enough to give students all the necessary cognitive and emotional data they need to be well informed about decision making. Thus, the latest information on such traditional topics as birth control, abortion, and parenting skills certainly must be included. However, lectures must go beyond the mechanics of human sexuality and basic child care. Students must also be taught about characteristics of high-risk families, family violence, and the incest epidemic rampant in this country. Frankly, they must learn if they are at risk to become child abusers or to marry a child abuser before they have children.

Given that most experts agree that causes of family violence are frequently multidimensional and not totally understood, education for parenthood must involve many diverse elements and resources in the community. The teacher, who is ideally well trained and compassionate, cannot and should not be expected to do it all. The size and location of the geographic community and the number of available speakers and services in a given educational district will vary greatly. Nonetheless, dedicated educators and mental health professionals can join together to build a curriculum that reflects respect for individual rights and differences in parenting decisions, yet makes it clear that having children should not be taken for granted or done without prior preparation for parenthood.

In closing, I wish the reader to rest assured that I am aware that this sketchy overview of a potential curriculum for parenthood decisions poses many practical and ethical problems that cannot be addressed in this brief essay. Nonetheless, I hope that this piece will provoke the reader to think and act about what substantial penalties to individuals, families, and society will be incurred if we do not begin somewhere in insisting that only qualified people should become parents. And we must do it soon—before Armageddon is upon us.

NOTE

1. The following section is heavily influenced by a manuscript written by Skovolt and Thoen (1984). No collaboration or endorsement by Skovolt in the current essay is implied.

REFERENCES

BRAM, S. (1974) "To have or have not: a social psychological study of voluntarily childless couples, parents-to-be, and parents." Ph.D. dissertation, University of Michigan, Ann Arbor.
BROTHEN, T. and T. M. SKOVOLT (1981) "Social comparison theory and the universality of experience." Psychological Reports 48: 114.
DESOILLE, R. (1938) Exploration de l'affectivite subconsciente par la methode du reveille. Paris: D'Autry.

EBERSTADT, N. (1984) "A profamily president meets Peking's population planning." Minneapolis Star and Tribune (April 26): 29A.

HOFFMAN, L. W. (1974) "The employment of women and fertility," in L. W. Hoffman and F. I. Nye, The Employed Mother and the Family. San Francisco: Jossey-Bass.

JACOBSON, E. (1938) Progressive Relaxation. Chicago: University of Chicago Press.

KIMBALL, K. (1982) Personal communication (June).

———and M. E. McCABE (1981) "Should we have children? A decision-making group for couples." Personnel and Guidance Journal 60: 153-156.

LANG, P. (1977) "Imagery in therapy: an information processing analysis of fear." Behavior Therapy 8: 862-886.

LANGE, S. (1982) "A realistic look at guided fantasy." Presented at the annual meeting of the American Psychological Association, Washington, DC, August.

LATTS, S. (1984) "Family violence: a course proposal." (unpublished)

LAZARUS, A. (1971) Behavior Therapy and Beyond. New York: McGraw-Hill.

MONTAGUE, A. (1969) Sex, Man and Society. New York: Tower.

POGREBIN, L. C. (1983) Family Politics. New York: McGraw-Hill.

NAOP (1972) PLEASE PROVIDE REFERENCE INFO.

PECK (1974) PLEASE PROVIDE REFERENCE INFO.

Public Broadcasting System [PBS] (1984) A Baby Maybe. Summer, Houston, Texas.

RUSSELL, M. G., R. N. REY, G. A. THOEN, and T. WALZ (1973) "The choice of childlessness: a workshop model." Family Coordinator: 179-183.

SCOTT, L. (1979) "Intentionally childless women: An exploration of psychosocial and psychosexual factors." (unpublished)

SHEEHY, G. (1976) Passages. New York: Dutton.

SIMON-GRUEN, B. (1979) Personal communication (May).

SKOVOLT, T. M. and G. A. THOEN (1984) "Mental imagery and parenthood decision-making: concepts and techniques for counseling and therapy practitioners." (unpublished)

THOEN, G. A. (1984) "Factors in childlessness." (unpublished)

———(1979) The Parenthood Option: A Manual for Professionals Helping People Decide Whether to Have Children or Remain Childfree. Washington, DC: National Alliance for Optional Parenthood.

VEEVERS, J. (1973) "Voluntary childless wives: an exploratory study." Sociology and Social Research 57: 356-366.

YALOM, I. (1975) The Theory and Practice of Group Psychotherapy. New York: Basic Books.

ABORTION

Once Conceived, a Child Has the Right to Be Born

CONNAUGHT MARSHNER

Modern man's capacity to suppress the uncomfortable seems infinite. In the 1930s and 1940s, Germans chose not to think about the appalling things that were happening in their country, and thus allowed the evils to grow and flourish. So it is with abortion in our country today. There is bitter irony in our refusal to look at abortion's stark realities. The United States is history's greatest experiment in individual freedoms. But our enviable experiment seems to have run aground on the rocks of the ultimate selfishness of abortion. Americans' cavalier attitude toward abortion is a classic example of freedom abuse, of liberty becoming license.

Yet perhaps it bodes well for a return to responsible exercises of freedom that a significant proportion of our society, perhaps even a growing proportion, is unwilling to give silent consent to the American holocaust. When the abolitionist movement was first born in New England in the 1820s and 1830s, abolitionists were highly unpopular. It took forty years to raise the nation's consciousness to the point that the country was willing to reject human slavery. Already, 15 million children have been killed in the last thirteen years, at the request of their mothers and with the willing consent of their doctors. How many more must die before the nation says, "Enough!"?

The issue this chapter addresses—the humanity of the unborn—is not really open to doubt. Those who feel a loyalty to the notion of "a woman's right to choose" avoid thinking too deeply about what it is that is growing steadily within the woman's womb. Many converts to the right-to-life viewpoint will report that their minds were changed when they had to acknowledge precisely this fact—that the unborn child is, indeed, a human. If he is human, he is a brother. And if he is a brother, he is entitled to protection.

These are people who, if they saw a toddler wandering onto a highway, would stop their cars and take the child by the hand to find its parent or caretaker. These are people in whom human instinct runs strong: A primeval voice deep within them speaks insistently, "That child is one of us, we must protect it." It is not to those who hear this primeval protective force that this chapter is addressed.

Rather, this chapter is addressed to a different and, one hopes, less numerous audience: namely, those who, on seeing the toddler wandering along the roadside, would continue to drive along saying to themselves, "What is that child doing along the highway? Curious, I wonder if there's a playground near," and would otherwise ignore the child, seeing no cause for alarm in its proximity to death.

The unborn child's humanity is not really open to doubt. The critical question is this: Assuming the unborn child *is* human, what do we do about it? That is the uncomfortable question the pro-choice movement seeks to obscure. Pro-abortionists obscure the fact of humanity and strenuously avoid the question of personal responsibility for a life that is demonstrably human. Those who say, "OK, so abortion is life-destroying—so what?" are the people whose abuse of freedom will destroy it. Either that, or they will destroy humanity as we know it.

But first, the first step. Consider your own situation, your own dependence. You, the reader, a student in college, are alive, and unless you are clinically depressed, you feel that you have a right to be. No one has a right to take your life, although, of course, someday you must die because you are not immortal. Yet, while you live, you are dependent. You are dependent because you must eat: that means others provide you with food. You must be clothed lest you freeze; you must be sheltered lest you die of exposure. All of these things are provided by others, on whom you are dependent. Perhaps they are given to you as gifts, by your parents; perhaps you pay for them. Either way, you are dependent on them. Even if you were a noble savage, a Robinson Crusoe, you would be dependent on the availability of fresh water, fruits to eat, and a cave to shelter you. And so on. In society, you are dependent on the continuing goodwill of your fellow men.

But go back yet another step. You are dependent in still a deeper way. You did not create your life. You were dependent on a man and a woman to create it for you. So the creation of your existence and the continuation of your existence are dependent on others. You, then, are dependent.

But does your dependence detract from your right to life? Not at all—on the contrary, your very dependence on others is the reason your right to live exists. Were you the only human being alive, you would have no need for rights; who would there be to affront or endanger you? It is because you are a social being, because you are dependent, that you have rights enunciated on your behalf by society, as a safeguard to you and every other member of society.

There is no stage of your life during which you are not dependent. The degree of your dependency may change—and, indeed, will—throughout the course of your life. In infancy you are dependent on others for everything: food, shelter, warmth, and the more subtle but nonetheless essential interactions that develop your personality. Lucky for you that somebody felt an obligation to protect your right to be fed, sheltered, clothed, educated, loved. As you grew out of infancy you became less dependent: you could, for instance, pull your own covers up on a cold night, kick them off on a warm night. Later, you could fix yourself a meal. Perhaps you can learn to build yourself a house. But the tide of life will ebb away. You will become old; you may be too ill to work and earn money. Your fingers may be too stiff to button your own coat. You will again be more dependent. The degree of dependency will vary; the greater your dependency, the greater your need for the safeguard of rights guaranteed to you by society.

A body of laws that withdraws the safeguards of any person's rights interrupts the flow of protection to everyone. Once the principle of interpretation is introduced, it cannot logically be prevented from being applied to any other person or group. For instance, the law says you shall not drive over 55 miles an hour. (If you happen to break that law, and are not caught, it is not the law's fault; it is your own luck). If you are caught going 65, and you offer as rationalization that you are on your way to meet an airplane, the policeman does not step aside and say, "Oh, well, in that case, go right ahead; the 55 mile limit does not apply to people meeting planes." Because if airplane meeters were exempted from the speed limit, next it would be people meeting a bus who would demand it, and the next might be people hurrying to a doctor's appointment, or businessmen hurrying to an important meeting. Where would it end? Either the law means the same thing to everybody, or it means nothing to anybody.

Yes, of course, people will always break laws, and they will bend them. Human nature is such that we will always try to get around things that obstruct us. Your rights under the law are still safe, however, so long as it is not the law that bends itself. Suppose you were a millionaire. There are laws against embezzling money from bank accounts. How would you feel if a bank clerk stole $100,000 from your bank account? You would be angry, and you would say your rights had been violated. Correctly so. But how would you feel if the courts said, "Oh, we won't prosecute the bank clerk. He only stole from you, and you already have a million dollars, so you could afford to lose a mere hundred thousand." In that case, the law would have bent itself—in such a way as to exclude you from its protection. Obviously, nobody is going to make a law like that. Either everybody's money in a savings account is safe from embezzlement, or nobody's is. Either the law means the same thing to everybody, or it means nothing to anybody.

Well, it is the same with human lives. There are laws against murder. If an unknown assailant guns down an old lady while stealing her purse, he is charged with murder. If a burglar happens to kill the homeowner while in the process of robbing the house, he is charged with murder. It doesn't matter if the old lady is a bank president or the homeowner a welfare recipient. It is as much murder to kill the bank president as to kill the welfare recipient. Why? Because both are human beings. The protection of the law extends equally to them.

Suppose the murderer on trial for killing the welfare recipient argued that he was really doing society a favor by killing the person. "After all," the murderer may argue, "His welfare checks come to about $800 a month, that's $9600 a year. Instead of prosecuting me, you should thank me!" Would any lawyer make such a case? What do you think the judge would say to that? Do you think the jury would nod its assent, and agree that the murderer was, indeed, doing society a favor? Of course not.

Suppose that the murderer who killed the bank president tried a different tack. "Listen," this accused may argue, "that bank president had cancer. She wouldn't have lived a year. All I did was hurry up the process, and save her a lot of pain and suffering and expense in the process. I'm the angel of mercy, and her family should thank me for putting her out of her misery." Do you suppose the family would be very sympathetic to that approach? Again, what would the judge say? What would the jury think?

It is hoped that the jury would put themselves in the position of the welfare recipient and the bank president. Maybe I do cost the state $800 a month, maybe I do have cancer, but who's this character deciding he has the right to knock us off? I have a right to life, liberty, property, and the pursuit of happiness. Maybe I am an old lady bank president with cancer, but that doesn't mean I am not enjoying my life. Who are they to say I have no right to live? Maybe the state can argue that it should not pay me so much welfare—I will be happy to argue that—but the fact that I cost the state money does not mean anybody has a right to kill me.

Fifty-five mile an hour speed limits. Embezzlers. Little old lady bank presidents. Welfare recipients. Do you see where I am going? Because now we come to little babies.

Suppose when you were born, your parents had said, "Oh, no, it's a girl. We did so want a boy. Let's just smother her." Or suppose one day your mom was tired when you, a toddler, had been running and yelling all day, and she said, "I just can't stand another minute of this," and threw you into the deep end of the pool, and drove away. You would have been dead in either case. Did your parents have a right to do that to you? No. Why didn't they? If you had been a member of a litter of kittens, they could have. What was different about you?

You are human, that's what. That makes all the difference.

The question is sometimes put concerning human babies several months before birth: Are they really human? Well, if they are not human, what are they? They do exist, after all. After conception, something exists in the mother's uterus. What is it?

Its stage of growth does not define it, as stage of growth does not define a child, teenager, adult, or senior citizen as human. You are a human being in your childhood, your prime, and your senility. For someone to take your life at *any* of those stages is to take away your humanness—to change you from being a person to being a corpse, to change you from a living, changing being to a disintegrating mass of chemical elements.

To deprive you of your talents or attributes—to amputate an arm, to blind you, to do specific brain trauma which causes permanent depression—all these would be evil, but they still would not have deprived you of your humanness. You would still be one living, human being. The ultimate injustice would not have been perpetrated. You would still be alive.

Your potential is in your humanness. For example, you do not have the ability to sleep and to think rationally at the same time. Some people argue that because a prenatal baby is not yet thinking, it is not human. Well, if that were true, a sleeping adult would not be human either. Yet to kill an adult in his sleep is to deprive him of his humanness as much as if it were done when he is awake. Should people decide to sleep for an hour, a night, a week, or nine months, it does not detract from the evil of killing them in their sleep.

So a child exists. His essence, his "is" ness (the sort of thing a fetus is) is human, an organized dynamic unit.

The baby's development is astonishingly fast when you think about it. By 18 days after the sperm joins the egg, the baby has a heart. His mother probably does not even dream he exists yet. By 45 days, electrocardiogram (EKG) waves are emanating. By 9 weeks the thyroid gland is functioning. By 12 weeks, unique fingerprints are there, should the FBI want them. Talk about developing your potential! The child is dependent, yes, but dependent only for the conditions of growth—not for the "is-ness," not for humanness, not for potential. All of that is his and his alone.

The baby's mother could not give her her humanity. That took two, a mother and a father. And this humanness can be taken away only by a natural death or a killing. The baby is dependent on her mother for the conditions to grow, and all these conditions are in her womb. But how does that make her any less human? Even after birth, the child will be dependent on adults for food, shelter, and affection for many years. A healthy 12-month old baby is completely dependent. This dependency does not take away from the baby's humanness.

To yield on the inviolability of human life for any one group is to yield for all, including all groupings of which we are members, or potential members. At some point or other in history, tyrants have said, "It's okay to kill Catholics," or "It's okay to kill Protestants," or "It's okay to kill Jews." Right now in America we're saying, "It's okay to kill somebody who has no friends," and "It's OK to kill somebody who is going to cost a lot of money to care for." Isn't that what most abortions come down to? Either the mother does not want to carry the baby for nine months, in which case that baby is utterly friendless—more friendless than we would wish any living human being to be. Or the parents believe the baby will be deformed, retarded, handicapped, or sick, any one of which will cost lots of money that the parents would rather spend on a trip to Europe, a new car, or a healthy child.

"I have a right to my body," the woman argues. Yes, she does. But she does not have a right to everything in her body. If you and a friend were walking down a dark street, and you saw somebody coming who was sure to rob you, you might take off your diamond engagement ring, saying, "Where can I hide it?" and your quick-thinking friend swallows it before you can say jack robinson. Then you get robbed, and all your cash and credit cards are stolen. A few days later you ask your friend, "Say, can I have my diamond back?" Suppose she says, "What diamond? You mean the one I swallowed? Well, that's part of my body. That belongs to me now. You have no rights over it." Would you be so quick to agree that that woman has a "right to her own body?" It all depends on how you define "her own body," doesn't it? The baby who arrives in her arms 42 weeks after conception is obviously not "her own body."

Another common pro-abortion argument is this: "I don't want a baby." It's not helpful, when someone is comtemplating abortion, to tell them that the time to think of that was a certain while ago. The statistics of pregnancies that result from rape are such that you could say hardly any pregnancies per year result from genuine rape, including incest. The fact is that most pregnancies are begun by a voluntary act of copulation. So, though it is not helpful, it is true to point out that the time to decide whether or not you want a baby is before you have sex, not after.

Be that as it may, is the fact that the woman "doesn't want a baby" sufficient reason to destroy the baby? Hitler didn't want the Jews, after all. Was that sufficient reason to destroy them? Once a human life is created, another human being does not have the right to deprive the world of that life's potential. The unborn life does not belong to the woman in whose body it temporarily resides. The fact that the woman who conceived the child does not want to raise the child is not a justification for killing it. The Centers for Disease Control have estimated that one-fourth of American couples have a fertility problem; that is, they cannot become pregnant when they want to. With that kind of figure increasing steadily, you can be sure there are plenty of people who would be thrilled to have someone else's birth baby to adopt and raise.

Some people still think they are doing a baby a favor by killing it if they think they would be poor or that the baby would be sick or a less than perfect specimen. Remember, first, we are talking about people, not about Siamese cats. A purebred cat with a congenital defect may be a less than perfect specimen and, thus, cannot bring a good price to its owner because it would not win ribbons at the cat show. Human beings are not in any such contests. Heaven help us if we start saying that in order to be a citizen with full rights, you have to have two eyes, ears that work fine, two arms and legs that function, and a brain that meets someone's definition of "adequate." Where would the lines be drawn? Or, more seriously, who would be drawing them?

Is it "merciful" to kill someone who sees the world differently than you do? One's appreciation of life is entirely subjective. Down's syndrome children and adults enjoy life to a rare degree—perhaps more than more ordinarily endowed children. Yet abortion of them is often justified on the grounds that their quality of life is not likely to be very good. Indeed, allowing retarded babies to die of starvation is frequently allowed for the same reason. People who say somebody else's quality of life will be lacking usually mean the person is not, to them, worth the cost, inconvenience, or effort of raising them. They're using a materialistic scale of some kind to measure love and human worth. If materialistic scales were to be a valid basis for assessing whether a human being should be allowed to live or die, we might as well build gas chambers for anyone who is out of work any length of time. Think about it: Isn't that the logical conclusion of the premise that "only those beings with a good quality of life should be allowed to live?"

Right now, that logic is being extended only to helpless little babies. A few years ago it applied only to those in the womb, now it is routinely applied to what reporters term "defective newborns." You must ask the question, who's next? Accident victims? Sick old people?

Then why not psychiatric inmates? Their quality of life can be pretty low, after all.

Where are you going to draw the line? Who is going to decide how to bend the law? You? That's okay as long as you are the one in power—the woman with the pregnancy, the parent of the handicapped infant. But suppose you are on the receiving end of someone else's tender mercies? Suppose you are the paralyzed accident victim that everyone wishes was not around to need care anymore? Suppose you are the one whose quality of life seems sort of dismal to those who are not in a wheelchair? How would you feel then? Safe, in the knowledge that your rights are protected, or fearful, that it might be too easy to "put you out of your misery"? Remember, either the law means the same thing to everyone, or it means nothing to anyone.

ABORTION

Only the Pregnant Woman Should Have the Right to Decide

ANDREA BALIS

There can clearly be no argument as to which of the potential parents of a child will have to go through the pregnancy, should that child be carried to term. It is the woman who will have to suffer the physical discomforts and dangers of pregnancy. If the fetus is aborted, it is the woman who will have to go through the pain, emotional and physical, of the abortion no matter how supportive her partner may be. Regardless of the amount of discussion there may be between the couple concerning either choice, it is the woman's body that will bear the brunt of the decision.

Certainly no woman should be compelled to have an abortion, either by the state or by the father of the fetus. The prospect is horrifying, and there is no question that the woman would suffer greatly. Few people argue that such a situation should occur (although in cases of forced sterilization that is basically what happens). It is equally appalling that a woman should be forced to bear a child that she does not want. The idea that the state could intervene in such a personal decision would threaten a major area of freedom of choice. To legislate that the father should have such a right is a clear case of sexual discrimination, implying as it does that men have the right to decide what a woman can or cannot do with her body. Again, it is as upsetting a possibility as that of a man forcing a woman to have an abortion.

To compel a woman to carry a child to term is to force her to take a physical risk far greater than that of an abortion. According to a recent article in the *Journal of the American Medical Association* (LeBolt et al., 1982) the risk of maternal death is seven times greater in childbirth than it is from abortion, and that figure includes late abortions. With increased facilities, the number of late abortions is dropping and the procedure becomes even safer. Under no other circumstances would we compel a citizen to risk his or her health to such an extent. There are 12.5 maternal deaths for every 100,000 live births (LeBolt et al., 1982). Obviously the health risk is the woman's alone. On that basis alone, pregnancy must be a voluntary choice.

Since it is solely the mother's responsibility to nurture the child during her pregnancy—and, in realistic terms, her primary respon-sibility after its birth—logically the decision must ultimately be hers.

Obviously the decision about whether or not to have a child is a difficult one. Nobody enjoys considering the possibility of having to have an abortion, but there are times when that may seem like the best choice. The question of the fetus's personhood is a difficult one, and is essentially a personal, moral, ethical and religious decision. If abortion is to a pregnant woman an unacceptable choice, then of course she will go ahead and bear the child. But she, not the state, must decide. The state has no business legislating morality.

The father may, obviously have some stake in the decision, but this may not necessarily be the case. For one thing, we live in a society that does not insist on monogamy—not for men, and not for women. Giving fathers a legal right to participate in the decision assumes that the relationship is a monogamous one, which may not be the case. In any case, no woman should be required to bear any man's child if she does not wish to do so. Any other arrangement makes her a breeding device, a kind of chattel. Certainly the state should not be legislating what kind of relationship two people should have.

In addition, the fact remains that in most cases in which a marriage or relationship dissolves, it is still the woman who remains respon-sible for the children. Although the father is generally expected to assume at least part of the financial responsibility of raising his children, frequently that responsibility is not met. In practical terms, women far too often wind up with the cares of parenthood, and must be permitted to make the choice about whether or not to assume them in the first place.

In the best of all possible worlds there would be perfectly safe, totally effective forms of birth control that all sexually active persons would responsibly use when they did not wish to have a child, and the issue of whether or not to terminate a pregnancy would arise only in cases in which the fetus was known to have severe deformities or the mother's life was endangered by the pregnancy. Alternatively, we could hope for a world in which all relationships were sufficiently open and trusting that an unwanted pregnancy could be considered by both partners, and the decision about what to do and the consequences of that decision were shared by both partners equally. Unfortunately we do not live in such a perfect world.

Women are left with the responsibility and, therefore, must make the decisions. Pregnant women must have the same rights to control over their own bodies that the rest of us have. The Supreme Court of the United States has agreed with that position through a series of decisions.

In its 1973 landmark case, Roe v. Wade, the Supreme Court established that a woman had a constitutionally guaranteed right to choose whether or not she would carry a pregnancy to term. The Court divided a pregnancy into three trimesters and stated that in the first trimester the decision was that of the woman in consultation with her doctor. In the second trimester the state had the right to intervene to protect the mother's health. In the third trimester the state could intervene to protect the life of the unborn fetus (Roe v. Wade, 1973).

The Court based its decision on the woman's right to privacy, which it called a fundamental right that could not be restricted unless the state could show a compelling reason for doing so. Until the fetus could be considered viable (capable of living outside of the mother's body), the state's interest in protecting potential life was not as strong as that of the mother's right to privacy.

The right to privacy is not a new concept in constitutional law. In cases going as far back as 1891 the Court has recognized that right, even if it is not explicitly stated in the Constitution. In its decision in Roe v. Wade the Court stated that the right to privacy, which included the right to choose whether or not to have an abortion was included in the right to liberty guaranteed by the due process clause of the Fourteenth Amendment.

In several of its decisions the Court has made it clear that one of the liberties protected by the Fourteenth Amendment includes the right to make personal choices in matters of marriage, the use of contraceptives, the right to bear children and the right to control family life. All of this is covered by the concept of personal privacy.

The Court stated in its decision in the case of Eisenstadt v. Baird (1972),

> If the right of privacy means anything, it is the right of the individual, married or single, to be free from unwarranted governmental intrusion into matters so fundamentally affecting a person as the decision whether to bear or beget a child.

The idea that the state should have the right to intervene in such a private matter is an appalling one. It was Justice Brandeis who wrote in a dissenting opinion (Olmstead v. U.S., 1928) that the right to be left alone by the government was one of the most comprehensive and most valued rights of a civilized society.

The question of when life begins is a complex one, which biologists, theologians, and philosophers have pondered for centuries. They have come up with many different answers, and most of them are contradictory. There is no general consensus as to what exactly can be considered the beginning of life. The debate continues to rage, affecting the abortion issue as well as many kinds of popularly used birth control devices, such as intrauterine devices and many forms of oral contraceptives, all of which prevent a fertilized ovum from implanting itself in the uterus. What we can agree on is a definition of viability. The fetus cannot survive outside of the mother's womb before it has reached the age of 24 weeks. Its lungs are not sufficiently well developed until that point. It would take the creation of an artificial womb to change that medical fact, and such an invention will raise many more issues than that of abortion.

The Court did not attempt to claim to know when life begins, but they were able to state that personhood—and, therefore, the full protection of the Constitution—begins with viability. Before that point, the fetus is not a person, but the mother is. The Court's decision basically asserts that until the fetus can be considered a separate viable life, its rights do not supersede the rights of the mother.

There is no question that whatever decision a woman makes, it will affect the lives of other people around her—her partner; in the case of a young woman, her parents; and other members of the family and community. But the fact that her choice will touch other people cannot be used as an excuse to deprive her of the right to choose. Many of the life decisions that we make affect other people, but we are still permitted to make them. The way in which we deal with the interrelationships in our lives creates the context of our society. These things certainly should not be eliminated just because they are difficult.

Every tradition of our society leads us to believe that ideally the decision about whether or not to have a child should be made by the two biological parents, but that may not be possible or even desirable in every case. Even allowing for the obvious exceptions (e.g., cases of incest or rape), there are many other circumstances in which it may not be appropriate for anyone but the potential mother to decide. Lifestyles change, and many people choose not to live within the nuclear family structure with which we are all so familiar. While we may deplore some or all of those changes, legislating personal morality or family structure is a dangerous idea.

It may be ideal, whenever possible, that the choice about whether or not to bear a child should be a voluntary, mutual decision made by two loving partners, but the state cannot force that situation to occur, and neither can the rigid adherents of any particular morality or religion. A woman must have the right to control her own body. It is a fundamental freedom that should belong to every citizen. Our history is made up of the struggle to preserve that freedom, and a woman's right to choose is an essential part of that struggle; it is a right which cannot be subverted. The only parties who could interfere with that right would be the state, the father, or in the case of a minor, the parents.

Any of those alternatives would be depriving a pregnant woman of her basic rights as described in the Constitution and would clearly be discriminatory. Women bear children, they take the risks to their own health that pregnancy and childbirth involve, and they alone have the right to make decisions about whether or not they wish to undertake those risks. Biology may not be destiny, but it is a physical reality; unless that changes, it has to remain a woman's right to choose.

REFERENCES

LeBOLT, S. A., D. A. GRIMES, and W. CATES, Jr. (1982) "Mortality from abortion and childbirth," Journal of the American Medical Association 248 (July).
Eisenstadt v. Baird (1972) 405 U.S. 438
Olmstead v. U.S. (1928) 277 U.S. 438
Roe v. Wade (1973) 410 U.S. 113

ABORTION

The Putative Father Should Have Equal Rights to Decide

MARIE COLES CALDWELL
ADRIAN SOLOMON

Decision making about an unplanned, unanticipated, or unwanted pregnancy, under the best of circumstances, is perhaps one of the most difficult dilemmas a woman may have to face during her lifetime. Dealing with the dilemma has been made more arduous by the struggles women have had with the state regarding legal sanctions and with family and friends regarding social sanctions. As pointed out by Gil (1976: 60), "American society tends to be ambiguous in defining the scope of parental and societal roles and responsibilities for the rearing of children." The emphasis on the conflict between women and the state has led to a focus on the issues of women's rights with respect to privacy and to women's rights of control over their own bodies.

Women have promulgated the argument that abortion should be the sole decision of women. It is their position that there are many consequences of childbearing that are related to women only. These include the commonly raised consequences of the planned use of the woman's body and her right to decide about its use by herself. Added to this argument is the issue of health and abuse of the body. Maternal mortality was a serious health problem in this country at one time. There is evidence now that the risks to the mother's life are less in abortion than in childbirth (Frohock, 1983: 102). This fact played a part in the Supreme Court decision of Roe v. Wade (1973), the historic case in which the Supreme Court supported women's rights to privacy on the basis of the Ninth and Fourteenth Amendments. These amendments guarantee rights to the people and protect personal liberty. The Court ruled in support of women's argument that the woman's decision whether or not to terminate her pregnancy was hers alone.

As women have pushed for equal opportunities and rights for themselves, they have systematically excluded men or any considerations of their points of view regarding abortion. In some measure, they can be accused of reverse discrimination. The legal and political struggles for women's rights in these areas also have led to a relative neglect of the role of the co-participant in the conception and in the decision-making process. It is our position that as co-participants men should be equal partners in the decision-making process for several reasons: They share equally in the act of conception; roles of men and women have undergone significant changes over the years; relations between women and men have been altered; during the time of decision making and after, both parties can benefit from support provided by the other; and there are advances in medical technology that may relieve women of some earlier consequences of carrying fertilized ova to term.

Why have the lines about the differences in women's and men's rights been so stringently drawn? What are some of the issues and concerns that provide the basis for the exclusion of men in the decision regarding abortion?

Society has adopted a double standard with respect to female sexuality. While it has been generally accepted that men, married or not, might have affairs, women were held responsible for the consequences of sexual behavior. Unmarried pregnant women and unmarried mothers have been viewed negatively and socially ostracized. Paternity has frequently been denied and the woman abandoned. Children of these unions tend to be devalued and not accepted.

The term "illegitimate" epitomizes the negative judgment of society toward these children. Before abortion became a legal procedure, pregnant unmarried women were forced to choose between engaging secretly in an illegal procedure or to go public with their "shame" by remaining pregnant and giving birth. Illegitimate children have been the burdens of their mothers, and the accompanying shame attached to their mothers. Devalued by society and abandoned by men, women were left with no choice but to make decisions without the co-participants in pregnancy.

It has been deemed that mothers have the right to decide if they will carry pregnancies to term. These society postures are reflected in conflicting policies that demand only child support from the putative father and estranged and former husbands (Leashore, 1979), that chide mothers for being recipients of public assistance by virtue of their dependent children, and that resist provision of funds for family planning and abortion. These policies reinforce women's attitudes that men should be excluded from involvement in decision making regarding unexpected pregnancies.

A woman's decision to give birth can affect the life of the potential father and his behavior, especially in terms of legal and financial obligations. Upon her decision, he may be expected to be supportive emotionally, offer marriage (if not already married), take care of medical expenses, and of course, financially support the child to adulthood. If the male denies paternity, he can be taken to court to establish paternity and financial support. Similarly, a woman's unilateral decision to abort can affect the emotional well-being of the man who desires to be a father and to assume responsibilities of fatherhood. By contrast, the potential father has no comparable impact on the life or behavior of the woman. Is it not ironic that both the male and the female are co-participants in the process of conception, but the woman has virtually total control of the man's destiny in relation to fatherhood? This imbalance in the decision-making powers is a manifestation of gender inequality.

There are many women in the work force; career opportunities have increased for them. There have been changes in sex roles for both men and women, and there have been movements toward more egalitarian relationships between women and men. Career choices have influenced family choices (Newman and Newman, 1981). The increasing numbers of women in nontraditional occupations and career advancement may mean postponement of family either through conscientious use of contraception or even abortion (Glick, 1977).

The changing roles of men and women have led to alternative styles of couple relationships (Weiten, 1983). Among these have emerged two divergent relationship patterns, one based on egalitarism and one based on gender separatism. In egalitarian relationships, decision making is shared and is based upon the particular knowledge and skills with respect to the issue in question. This is in contrast to those couple relationships characterized by gender-referenced power struggles over new roles and decision-making authority.

Women's struggle for equality may have produced or perpetuated the image of men as the enemy, holder or occupier of power. The liberation concerns of women often involve power issues between women and men. Abortion may well be one of these issues. We believe that the egalitarian method for decision making is best for both parties and that men should have an equal role in the decision regarding abortion when they are involved in relationships with women who become pregnant.

Will equal rights for the father in consideration of abortion result in denial of the mother's rights? What if the father wants an abortion and the other doesn't? Should the father be absolved of all financial support and responsibility? Or, if the father does not want abortion and the mother does, can the father appeal and accept full responsibility for the infant at the time of delivery?

Technological advances also will have significant implications for decision-making options with regard to undesired pregnancies. These have been sharply highlighted in the following statement by Luker (1984: 244):

Although it is safe to predict that women's roles will continue to change, in all probability the long-term trend is that women will continue to combine work and motherhood in increasing numbers. It is also probably safe to predict that technological forces, which have historically triggered new debates about abortion, will continue to confront us with new social, political and ethical dilemmas. We must soon consider the implications of a new technology in abortions so that they can be accomplished at home, the ability to transplant one woman's fertilized egg to another woman's womb, and even artificial uteruses that can support an embryo outside the body from the earliest days of pregnancy. These developments are all closer to reality than to science fiction.

The already-demonstrated procedure in which the fertilized ovum can be removed from the body of one woman, frozen, and later implanted in the uterus of another and successfully brought to term strengthens the male partner's rights to participate in the couple's decision about unanticipated pregnancies. As in adoption, the woman in this case who does not desire motherhood at this time can be relieved of the fertilized ovum and of the responsibility of child rearing, emotionally and financially. If the male wishes to assume responsibility for the child after birth, should he not be allowed to do so, if a carrier for the fertilized ovum is found? Men may wish to make this decision for various reasons, such as religion, family continuity, or personal fulfillment. This option grants men the right to a decision regarding parenthood, a right that should be guaranteed to them as it is to women.

Decision making about pregnancy must be made in consideration of the social-psychological factors affecting both partners. Pregnancy is laden with physical, psychological, and social consequences. It is unlike any other human state in that it is considered a normal state of development—accompanied by happiness under some circumstances and, under other conditions, considered a problem, a burden, or a disgrace. Although not an illness, it has some of the earmarks of incapacity. Social approval and recognition are shown to both parties when pregnancy occurs within socially sanctioned contexts. Two persons equally contribute to the pregnancy, although only one of the parties delivers or carries the product. Not only are the lives of the two persons affected, but there is often a rippling effect on the family, others, and of course, the unborn child.

The potential mother has to deal with her own feelings regarding the pregnancy as well as relate to the feelings of her mate and other significant persons. If the pregnancy is unplanned or unanticipated, there is much stress that may be manifested by feelings of resentment, fear, guilt, and ambivalence. The exclusion of the male from the decision-making process may represent an attempt to reduce a source of added stress and complications.

What is the emotional impact on male partners in abortions that occur without their consent or consideration or against their desire?

Studies have shown that in such circumstances men report a variety of emotional responses, which include feelings of guilt, anger, loss, mourning, and bad dreams, some of which are of long duration (Shostak, 1979). In caring relationships one would expect that women would be concerned about the impact of abortion upon their partners. The pride in fatherhood is amply demonstrated in hospitals at the time of delivery and at numerous other times throughout the life of the offspring. The deliberate exclusion of the male from the decision-making process deprives the woman of a significant support base. Women require a great deal of support at the time of pregnancy. Being able to utilize the support provided by a loving, caring partner is of great value. Men need support also in the decision that involves their potential for fatherhood. Since exclusion serves to deprive both women and men of a basis for much needed support, this approach is detrimental to the needs of both persons.

A satisfactory outcome of a mutual involvement in the decision-making process is dependent on how effectively parties communicate with each other and how they handle conflicts. In instances of agreement, there is no conflict to resolve. In sharing, however, there is a great deal of support for each partner about the correctness and appropriateness of the decision for them. In those instances in which there is conflict, the method of conflict resolution most likely will be dependent upon the nature of the relationship in its totality. For example, in those relationships that can be characterized as egalitarian, the resolution of this would come about in the manner in which this couple has handled other important conflicts—presumably through exchange and equal participation. In contrast to this approach, when the relationship has been characterized by gender separatism, there are likely to be struggles, which may be gender-referenced power issues rather than collaborative problem solving. In nonegalitarian relationships, adversarial positions may be assumed rather than one in which partners look at the problem together and try to respond to each other's needs.

In summary, therefore, the method by which couples approach these scenarios reflects the nature of the relationship in the past. If other aspects of the relationship have been adversarial, the methods of resolving may be a resort to authority in terms of ultimate or relative rights of one over the other. With the egalitarian approach, the focus would not be on rights but in terms of settling conflicting needs and desires. Each takes into account the other's needs, wishes, and desires.

By so doing, there is less risk of one person reluctantly deferring to the other.

Abortion can no longer be viewed as a woman's issue only. Yes, the fertilized ovum does reside in her body and is under her care until time for delivery. But attitudes, roles of women and men, and medical science have moved to new levels, making it necessary and possible to consider other alternatives. Single parenting is no longer uncommon; women work outside of the home in almost every profession and position; some men remain at home by plan as househusbands, doing chores and taking major responsibility for child rearing; artificial insemination is more common; science has advanced to fertilization or conception outside of the body; and more recently a technique has been perfected to permit removal of the fertilized ovum early in the pregnancy and freezing it for preservation for later implantation and development. The arguments put forth regarding women's exclusive right to the decision regarding abortion cannot stand in light of these developments. The position of men as co-participants and necessary and equal actors in the conception process must be respected. This respect, which is already granted to women, should be extended to men. The decision about each abortion should be individual, made by the couples together (where possible) and taking into account the things that affect their lives, their needs, and their desires.

REFERENCES

FROHOCK, F. M. (1983) Abortion: A Case Study in Law and Morale. Westport, CT: Greenwood Press.

Gerstein v. Coe (1976) 428 U.S. 901

GIL, D. G. (1976) Unravelling Social Policy. Cambridge, MA: Schenkman.

GLICK, P. C. (1977) "Updating the life cycle of the family." Journal of Marriage and the Family 39, 1: 5-114.

LEASHORE, B. A. (1979) "Human services and the unmarried father: the 'forgotten half.' " Family Coordinator (October): 529-533.

LUKER, K. (1984) Abortion and the Politics of Motherhood. Berkeley: University of California Press.

NEWMAN, P. and B. NEWMAN (1981) Living. Homewood, IL: Dorsey Press.

Planned Parenthood v. Danforth (1976) 428 U.S. 52

Roe v. Wade (1973) 410 U.S. 113

WEDDINGTON, S. R. (1982) "The woman's right of privacy," in E. Batchelor (ed.) Abortion: The Moral Issues. New York: Pilgrim Press.

WEITEN, W. (1983) Psychology Applied to Modern Life: Adjustment in the 80's. Belmont, CA: Brooks/Cole.

IV. Nontraditional Family Forms

This section has four major topics: long-term cohabitation versus conventional marriage, long-term fidelity in marriage versus alternatives, couple-created contracts versus the Bible as a contract, and whether homosexuals should have the same family rights as non-homosexuals. This comprises a wide range of controversial issues about families and one where many persons have strong feelings that are being played out on the national scene.

DISCUSSION QUESTIONS

(1) How would our society be different if legal marriage were prohibited?

(2) Why do parents tend to be more negative to cohabitation than students? Which of their objections seem valid to you?

(3) Under what conditions would you recommend marriage or long-term cohabitation?

(4) Discuss the need for perfectability of marriage. To what extent are these same methods applicable to couples with other forms of relationships?

(5) Why do you think persons engage in other than lifetime exclusive marital relationships?

(6) How do you feel that other than lifetime exclusive relationships influence marriage?

(7) Is the notion of love, honor, and obey sufficient? Should it mean that if one of these is broken the marriage could be legally ended?

(8) Why do some people feel that spelling out marriage contracts has a negative effect on marriage?

(9) Discuss some of the limitations and advantages of the biblical and the personal procedures for marriage contracts. Try to synthesize the two.

(10) Since most homosexuals come from heterosexual parents, shouldn't we insist that only homosexuals be allowed to have children?

(11) How is objection to legal homosexual marriage an example of homophobia?

(12) Discuss homosexual parenthood from the child's perspective. Present both advantages and disadvantages.

(13) Should a legal marriage contract be a socially acceptable way to deal with nontraditional marriages, including homosexuality and cohabitation?

CLASS ACTIVITIES

(1) Plan a marriage ceremony that includes traditional features. Discuss why you include whatever you do.

(2) Plan a nontraditional ceremony for a cohabitating couple. Why did you include what you did?

(3) Invite to your class a minister who believes strongly in marriage and a couple who have been cohabiting without marriage. Their task is to try to find ways to incorporate the point of view of the other and find a new synthesis after they have explained their position.

(4) Have students discuss and practice some of the methods of marriage enrichment. Try to find a trained leader.

(5) Have a TV talk show with persons advocating multiple marriage, swinging, adultery, and open marriage.

(6) Invite a dance group on campus to portray each alternative form of marriage. Then have the class try to do "body sculpturing" in which each individual or couple takes a fixed body pose to represent the idea of one of the marriage forms.

(7) Have a traditional minister come to class and discuss the advantages of a biblically based marriage.

(8) Have students pair up and work out a marriage contract. Have the class discuss some of the similarities and differences within the class noting areas of incompatibility within couples.

(9) Divide the class into small groups and have them work up a marriage contract for homosexuals, swingers, cohabiters, adulterers, and those having an open marriage. In what ways would it be different, if any, from a marriage contract for those contemplating a lifetime exclusive marriage?

(10) Invite someone to class who is opposed to homosexuals becoming parents or getting married. Have the class find reasons they agree with and those they do not.

(11) Ask some gay men and women to discuss why marriage and parenthood should be allowed for them.

(12) Have a debate between those who are pro- and anti-homosexuality. Try to get them to agree on some of the conditions under which they would allow homosexual marriage and parenthood. If they find this difficult, speculate as to why.

(13) Have a debate with those who take the more traditional approach of a legal lifetime exclusive heterosexual marriage with those who are committed to a less traditional relationship. What are some of the similarities in goals for the two groups?

Legal Marriage Is the Most Satisfying Method of Pairing Couples with a Long-Term Commitment to Each Other

NED L. GAYLIN

Marriage may be defined as the public and conscious taking of a member of the opposite sex for a life partner. No other social institution is either so indigenous to us or so defining of us as a unique species. Although cross-cultural comparisons reveal all manner of variations (including homosexuality) of the typical monogamous unit we have come to know, marriage remains the most basic of all human institutions. For all cultures, marriage serves the universal function of maintaining responsible intimacy. Thus marriage continues to be one of the few bastions of interpersonal security—a safe house for love, trust, and faith.

In the present period of rapid social change, there is much conjecture about the viability of the institution of marriage. Figures abound to highlight the plight of the modern marriage: Two out of every five marriages now end in divorce; illegitimate births have nearly tripled since 1960; 15 percent of American children live in single-parent homes (twice that of 25 years ago), and so on (Glick and Norton, 1977). Certainly one might conclude that the future of marriage is at best uncertain. However, the other half of the story might well lead to some different conclusions. Of the 40 percent of divorced individuals, over three-fourths remarry. Furthermore, the two-thirds of our population who marry for life stay married far longer because of the increase in our life spans. Despite what recently appeared to be a declining marriage rate (but which actually proved to be a delayed-age-for-marriage trend), America is still the most marrying country in the world (Gaylin, 1980).

Thus, to question the viability of marriage is tantamount to questioning the viability of civilization as we know it. The real issue facing us is how the institution of marriage is being modified and employed to help us as a species adapt to our modern world. It is not that we are not marrying; we are marrying, divorcing more frequently, and remarrying. We are continuously seeking the right relationship, the eternal match. The underlying impelling force—the romantic quest for the ideal state between man and woman—surely speaks to who we are and where we are going.

All mammalian species mate for sexual reproduction, and it belabors the obvious to note that this biological imperative is requisite for species continuance. While some infrahuman species have analogues to monogamous marriage (e.g., certain species of birds tend to mate for life) there is little evidence that any have the special consciousness of the future that the bonds of matrimony imply. Thus, marriage is palpably different from any analogous mating behavior in other animals. Marriage is a conscious contract that has an explicit past as well as an implicit future. Marriage transtemporally bridges the past by recognizing ancestry, the present by joining individuals and families, and the future by anticipating and producing heirs. Marriage, because of its link with the past and its projection into the future, is in fact humankind's attempt to overcome the limitations of the life span. By marrying, one establishes a relationship with ramifications far greater than either partner's individual longevity. Thus, conscious transtemporality and generativity enable marriage to bridge and connect individuals, generations, families, communities, even empires. Marriage and its inevitable sequel, the family, are the social paradigm, the keystone in the arch of civilization. Therefore, marriage may also be conceptualized as the civilizing of sexuality.

BASIC ELEMENTS

There are two basic elements to a workable, satisfying, and lasting marriage: love and trust. How these elements articulate within a given cultural context determines the effectiveness of marriage as an institution for the people of that culture.

The conceptualization and understanding of love have been grappled with by poets, philosophers, and scientists with most concluding that love is the language of the arts, not the sciences (Kaufman, 1958; Levi-Strauss, 1969). Love is a word, an abstraction and, like all words, its meaning is derived from complex memories of myriad sensations: smells, touches, sounds, images—all stored in our individual and collective histories. Thus, while there is a timeless and universal quality to our common understanding of love, there is also a mutable quality that can subtly modify our view of it both as members of groups with common histories and as individuals with unique histories. Our collective histories are perhaps best embodied and crystallized by our artists, musicians, and poets, who project on a recognizable screen before us our universal experiences and remembered feelings. Thus, for most Westerners, David's love for Bathsheba, Tristan's for Isolde, and Romeo's for Juliet, all conjure up a form of common experience with personal overtones (as might also a given painting, sculpture, or concerto).

The sexual aspect of love—the biological imperative—is part of the initial attraction of male and female and is, by its very nature, fleeting and limited. Although none would deny the impelling quality of the sensual pleasure of the arousal state or the ecstasy experienced in the orgasmic moment, this momentary exultation cannot wholly account for the continuous concern, tender tactile attentiveness, nostalgic bittersweet reverie of separation, and the anticipated joyous reunion of human lovers. Neither does the biological imperative explain the conscious desire of those in love to actualize their love for each other through the creation of children. Our awareness of these differences between biological and nurturant love tends to affect all human sexuality, and particularly love in the context of marriage.

Thus, while sex may be the basis on which species survival exists, it is the parental bond on which civilization rests. The nature of the parent-child bond is the crucial ingredient in the transcendence of love over sex. The two uniquely human qualities of transtemporal consciousness and the protracted dependency of the young, enable Homo sapiens to experience and know kinship ties well beyond the bonding period. Memories of comfort, sustenance, and caring by parents are carried with the human organism throughout life. It is the awareness of past nurturance and an anticipation of future giving and receiving of pleasure that make love a far more complex phenomenon than sex.

Trust (in contrast to love) is an interpersonal construct that has virtually escaped or eluded attempts at scrutiny. Yet, ironically, throughout history we are aware of loveless marriages arranged for the purposes of establishing trust between families, clans, or nations. Few have had much to say with respect to the issue of trust in marriage. Yet, without trust, marriage is at best a fragile contract of questionable viability. Perhaps because trust is so basic to human interaction and to society in general, its necessity and existence simply have been assumed and taken for granted.

Trust has often been equated with confidence (e.g., Lederer and Jackson, 1968). Confidence tends to be a more specific and transitory feeling, whereas trust is more encompassing and comprehensive: It implies a greater permanence. For example, one may have little confidence in a spouse's driving skills yet still maintain a basically trusting intimate relationship. Not a simple feeling state, trust rests on the accretion of confidence-building past experiences, and projects itself into the future as faith. Thus, it falls somewhere between the concreteness of confidence and the less tangible elements of faith. Trust has both a retrospective base and a projective thrust.

The most dramatic breach of trust in a marriage is adultery, which strikes at the very heart of the union. For this offense there is even special terminology—infidelity, unfaithfulness. On the other hand, one may tolerate in one's partner monetary extravagance, alcoholism, neglect, differences about child rearing, or difficult extended family relationships—problems that may be associated with insensitivities, broken promises, even lying—stretching the confidence aspects of trust. Such stretching, if extreme, could eventually strain the marriage to the point of dissolution. But there is often much wider latitude in these problem areas than in that of infidelity.

The faith extension of trust is what makes marriage the ultimate contract. Faith does not require proof or logic; it is there and, like love, it tends to be blind. Virtually no one enters into marriage today without faith that the union will be permanent; otherwise he or she would not marry. Modern marriage vows have evolved over time, but the nature of the marriage contract, the assumptions of its permanence, and the necessity of making it a public affair (i.e., witnessed) seem to have remained roughly similar throughout history and across widely varying cultures. It is the sanctification of pledging troth publicly that gives the union life.

CEREMONY AND SIGNIFICANCE

All societies have ceremonies to mark passages through life, although some have more than others. Those subcultures in our own society that have retained more ritual practice tend to demonstrate greater family cohesion, better individual adaptation, and less propensity to social deviance. Traditionally, the Chinese, Japanese, and Jewish ethnic groups are noted for maintaining greater family integration and reduced rates of alcoholism, delinquency, and divorce. These same subcultures tend to surround birth, marriage, and death with rich ceremony. While it might be countered that these groups have generations of religious tradition on which to draw, one of the few studies of secular traditions of nonethnic American families (Bossard and Ball, 1950: 203) demonstrated similar findings: that secular (as well as sacred) "ritual is a relatively reliable index of family integration."

The marriage ceremony is one of the few ceremonies still retained by most Americans, although even this practice appears to be diminishing somewhat. Indeed, marriage seems to be the last rite of passage that we continue to ceremonialize to any real degree. It remains the one step in our biological and social development that American culture at large recognizes and marks by ritual embellishment from the prenuptial arrangements, to the exchanging of vows and rings, to the honeymoon. Few young first-marrieds and their families seem inclined to dispense with the choreography involved in such rituals, and with good reason. Marriage, in our society as in most others, demarcates the leaving of childhood and the entering into the adult world. Furthermore, the public witnessing of marriage has the impact of affirming and renewing the marriages of those who witness; their vicarious participation in the vows engenders a sense of community.

By and large our society has dispensed with the ceremonializing of the premarital developmental passage common to most cultures, including the biological coming of age. Ironically, the closest thing we have to such a rite of passage is the obtaining of a driver's license. (Indeed, we might have more responsible drivers if we were to celebrate more richly the adolescent's initiation into independence via physical mobility, although it might contrarily be argued that marriage licenses do not guarantee success, despite all of their ritual accompaniment.) Thus, marriage has become a heavily loaded fulcrum with few structural supports to aid it in its work of gracefully moving both the individuals and the culture through the life-span journey.

Nearly one-half century ago, Ruth Benedict (1938) explicated an American dilemma that she called our "discontinuities in cultural conditioning." In all cultures Benedict noted discontinuities surrounding various turning points in the life span. She explained the importance of these normative crises and the need for all cultures to facilitate their members' recognition, anticipation, and preparation for the impact of these crises. She observed that those cultures that did this best demonstrated smoother functioning, and their members experienced greater well-being. Cultures with disjunctive turning points often accomplished the transitions effectively by attending them with elaborate ceremony.

In discussing American culture of the time Benedict (1938: 163) noted three major discontinuities between childhood and adulthood: "responsible-non-responsible status role, (2) dominance-submission, and (3) contrasted sexual role." Thus we expect childhood to be a time of play and relative irresponsibility ("the best years of our lives"), a time of submission to adult authority (the power struggles we lament with our adolescent children), and a time of asexuality (despite high heterosexual social contact). Benedict depicted American culture as one with great discontinuities and few sources of mitigation. That is, our transitions were abrupt and painful; we had little preparation for them, and little celebration of them.

It is not suggested here that we develop a more ritualized society as the only appropriate method for dealing with our discontinuities. Indeed, ceremony and ritual could appear to be somewhat disjunctive to our scientifically oriented culture. Benedict's point was that if a society does not adopt the means with which to mollify normative crises inherent in life transitions (especially if the society demands radical change during those transitions), enormous strains will be placed on both the individual and society. This is particularly true of the transition from child to adult status. For several decades, many have advocated family-life education as a way to moderate through preparation the rather difficult child-to-adult passage. However, by and large, such programs have not received the support of either our educational institutions or the public at large (Gaylin, 1981). This notwithstanding, the social indicators of our time all validate Benedict's premise. Our inability to ease the transition, even as we protract adolescence well beyond its biological years, may well account for the recent increase in rates of adolescent drug abuse, crime, suicide, and other social barometers. With little or no role preparation, and few ceremonies with which to ameliorate cultural discontinuities, the burden of expectation we place on our children to become overnight successes as spouses, breadwinners, and parents may be too great for some of our fledglings to bear.

STRAINS AND STRESS

In the adult years, marriage is the bulwark that serves as a buffer for the normative and aberrant crises and stresses of life. Marriage is also the ultimate form of intimacy between adult members of society. As such, it is a primary counteragent to loneliness and isolation—states anathematic to the human condition. However, marriage is also a responsive institution that may be positively or negatively affected by life's predictable and unpredictable vicissitudes.

No exposition of modern marriage would be comprehensive without some elaboration of changing gender role delineations and the marital strains that often result. In previous times men have, by and large, known what was expected of them and what they might, in turn, expect of women (and vice versa). Because of basic irrefutable biological differences, premodern mankind left women those tasks relating to child care and the home, but relegated to men the more physically strenuous and demanding tasks of maintaining the mother and child units via gathering, farming, and hunting (later, industry and politics). Thus, despite the widely varying distribution of labor in various cultures throughout time, "Two features of gender roles in all cultures then, are (1) female ties to child rearing and (2) male ties to economic power" (Reiss, 1980).

Today we are in the process of discarding operating procedures that are centuries old and gender specific. Men and women no longer know what to expect of each other, and this too is a cultural discontinuity that has a direct and powerful impact on the institution of marriage. If we are to move on successfully we will have to find new roles and rules to replace the old.

One of the first and more dramatic accommodations for the newly married is sexual reciprocation. Marital sexual activity can be mutually satisfying and a major source of joy when successful, and correspondingly a source of anguish when unsuccessful. At the same time, the most pleasurable sexual life may be affected adversely when the couple is under stress in other areas. As a result, the other problems may then be exacerbated rather than resolved (Belliveau and Richter, 1970). While our society affords our maturing members few preparations for marriage, both nature and society do offer some time for the newlyweds to accommodate to each other sexually. Furthermore, although greater numbers of young people are entering marriage with some sexual experience, a large percentage are virtually inexperienced in this most crucial aspect of the marital relationship.

A more subtle and long-term potential stressor on marriage per se is the adaptation the newlyweds must make to each other. Within each person's response to the mundanities of life there will be behaviors to which the other of the newly married pair must learn to accommodate. Often individuals are attracted to each other because their differences and styles are complementary. A relaxed person often finds an intense person interesting, a loquacious person may find a taciturn individual fascinating, and vice versa. However, common life stressors can turn healthy complementarity into conflictual polarization. Those attributes considered charming, attractive, or humorous during courtship and even through early marriage, may prove to be sources of irritation and conflict later when the pressures of daily living mount. Even though conflict is inevitable in intimate personal relationships, we are neither educated in its understanding nor trained in its resolution (Bach, 1968). However, with a mutually engendered intimate and loving relationship and a willingness to confront and resolve conflict, most marriages are capable not only of withstanding but also of mitigating the expectable and unexpectable stresses and crises that are inevitable in life.

Some crises are both inevitable and therefore expectable. Those anticipatable nodes in the branches of growth that mark our development through the life span are also commonly stressful; they are often termed normative crises. The impact of crisis and stress upon the institution of marriage, and the manner in which the institution and its members respond and cope with these events have received increasing attention by theorists and researchers (Figley and McCubbin, 1983). Reviewing the investigations of stress and coping during the decade of the 1970s, McCubbin and his associates (1980: 858) summarized the major life events considered sources of stress:

(1) transition to parenthood, (2) child launching, (3) post parental transition (i.e., 'empty nest'), (4) retirement, (5) widowhood, (6) relocation and institutionalization.

Another stressor with more insidious erosive qualities is that of economic insecurity. In our highly monetized society, economic insecurity as a form of stress does not refer just to those experiencing poverty. Any abrupt change in living standards or any event that is likely to cause the anticipation of such a change (e.g., change of job, temporary or long-term unemployment, or illness) can impose strain severe enough to have deleterious effects on the marital relationship. This tends to be particularly true of men, for whom self-esteem is highly dependent upon the ability to provide for their wives and children. Ironically, in its most severe form such strain can lead to aggression and physical abuse of loved ones within the family (Prescott and Letko, 1977).

Catastrophic events are rarely anticipated, hardly ever prepared for, and usually devastating to those directly involved. Such events include those indigenous to society (some tragically so, like war or murder) or to life on this planet (like natural disasters, severely debilitating illness, or untimely death). Regardless of origin, when a catastrophe affects one individual in a marriage, the catastrophe also assaults the marriage itself. Paradoxically, marriage, family, and society as a whole are the individual's best source of protection, support, and comfort against catastrophe. One might even go so far as to say that it is in response to such adversity that marriage and society, in general, came into being.

DIVORCE AND REMARRIAGE

While marriage is the most basic and perhaps the most resilient of all social institutions, it is not immune to failure. Historically, divorce, the dissolution of the "eternal" bonds of matrimony, has always been recognized as an option, if an unhappy one. Because of the importance we place upon marriage (even to the point of divine approbation), heavy sanctions have generally been levied against divorce. Even today, as divorce becomes a more common occurrence, it is nevertheless looked upon with considerable disfavor and heavily imbued with the notion of both personal and interpersonal failure.

Divorce, by nearly any standard, must be viewed as a highly negatively charged life event. It certainly qualifies as a discontinuity of cultural conditioning. Although we have cultural tools for facilitating an appropriate entry into marriage (i.e., ceremony, social witnessing, etc.), we have none for easing our exit. If we are to address divorce as a necessary cultural phenomenon, we must comprehend both its rational and nonrational aspects. From an emotional perspective, divorce typically represents an extreme form of personal loss. Like any other such loss, divorce may also require a grieving and mourning period before rehabilitation can be anticipated.

Finally, in a discussion of divorce there is also the possibility of remarriage. The increase in the divorce rate seems to have done little to disenchant us with the idea that marriage is the best way for man and woman to live together. Nearly 90 percent of all divorced men and women remarry (Cartier and Glick, 1970), and recent figures indicate that nearly one-third of our annual marriage rates consist of remarriages for either one or both partners (Price-Bonham and Balswick, 1980). These figures seem to suggest that it is not the institution of marriage we consider a failure, but rather our abilities and preparations for it.

CONCLUSION

The debate with regard to the universality and viability of marriage and family will undoubtedly continue among social scientists and social critics. These are truly academic issues. Suffice it to say that for all intents and purposes, marriage—even in cultures in which sexual permissiveness is accepted and pervasive—is indigenous to the human species. Living together without both the personal and public commitment of marriage is at best a pale alternative, but not a substitute for marriage. Marriage is perhaps the most satisfactory institution we have fallen heir to, and far more functional than any other we have as yet devised.

REFERENCES

BACH, G. R. (1983) The Intimate Enemy. New York: Avon.

BELLIVEAU, F. and L. RICHTER (1970) Understanding Human Sexual Inadequacy. New York: Bantam.

BENEDICT, R. (1938) "Continuities and discontinuities in cultural conditioning." Psychiatry 1: 161-167.

BOSSARD, J. and E. BALL (1950) Ritual in Family Living. Philadelphia: University of Pennsylvania Press.

CARTER, H. and P. C. GLICK (1970) Marriage and Divorce: A Social and Economic Study. Cambridge, MA: Harvard University Press.

FIGLEY, C. R. and H. I. McCUBBIN (1983a) Stress and the Family, Vol. 1: Coping with Normative Transitions. New York: Brunner/Mazel.

———(1983b) Stress and the Family, Vol. 2: Coping with Catastrophe. New York: Brunner/Mazel.

GAYLIN, N. (1981) "Family life education: behavioral science wonderbread?" Family Relations 30: 511-516.

———(1980) "Rediscovering the family," in N. Stinett et al. (eds.) Family Strengths: Positive Models for Family Life. Lincoln: University of Nebraska Press.

GLICK, P. and A. NORTON (1977) "Marrying, divorcing and living together in the U.S. today." Population Bulletin 32, 5. Washington, DC: Population Reference Bureau.

KAUFMANN, W. (1958) Critique of Religion and Philosophy. New York: Harper & Row.

LEDERER, W. J. and D. D. JACKSON (1968) The Mirages of Marriage. New York: Norton.

LEVI-STRAUSS, C. (1969) The Raw and the Cooked: Introduction to a Science of Mythology. (J. Weightman and D. Weightman, trans.). New York: Harper & Row.

McCUBBIN, H. I., C. B. JOY, A. E. CAUBLE, J. K. COMEAU, J. M. PATTERSON, and R. H. NEEDLE (1980) "Family stress and coping: a decade review." Journal of Marriage and the Family 42: 855-871.

PRESCOTT, S. and C. LETKO (1977) "Battered women: a social psychological perspective," in M. Roy (ed.) Battered Women: A Psychological Study of Domestic Violence. New York: Van Nostrand Reinhold.

PRICE-BONHAM, S. and J. O. BALSWICK (1980) "The noninstitutions: divorce, desertion, and remarriage." Journal of Marriage and the Family 42: 959-972.

REISS, I. L. (1980) Family Systems in America. New York: Holt, Rinehart and Winston.

COHABITATION

Long-Term Cohabitation Without a Legal Ceremony Is Equally Valid and Desirable

LYNN ATWATER

"If people really cared for each other, they would get married instead of living together." Nonsense. Living together, or cohabitation as it is more formally known, is as valid a way for a couple to relate intimately as is marriage. People both get married and live together to fill personal needs. As long as their needs are being met by the particular arrangement they choose, and as long as their arrangement is not socially harmful, both marriage and cohabitation should be equally acceptable. The choice should depend on whether the couple prefers a traditional or contemporary lifestyle, and not on some unquestioned allegiance to a norm that marriage is the only appropriate way for a couple to relate on an intimate, daily, and long-term basis.

As a sociologist, I feel that long-term cohabitation is a practice that is not only appropriate for many couples but also has the potential to make a positive contribution to the American family system. The underlying reasons many do not recognize this possibility, I believe, are that the practice of cohabitation is relatively new, it is not yet institutionalized, and it is not yet well studied or understood. Let us consider each of these reasons for the objection to cohabitation in more depth.

Cohabitation as a new lifestyle burst into our consciousness during the cultural revolution of the 1960s and 1970s, owing to a combination of various social changes.[1] On college campuses, administrators relaxed rules against opposite-sex visitors in response to student demands. Students also increasingly took advantage of new options to rent off-campus apartments. During this same period, young adults began to liberalize their sexual attitudes and behaviors, making premarital sex more openly acceptable. These changes fell upon the fertile ground of a particularly large cohort of college students, products of the post-World War II baby-boom years (Reiss, 1980).

It is likely that cohabitation began at first among the more radical members of the student subculture and then spread to other more conventional students. What attracted both kinds of students to living together was not only the opportunity for premarital sexuality, but the chance to reduce the artificial aspects of dating and to enhance the daily intimacy of relationships without making it necessary to marry before one was ready. During the two decades of the sixties and seventies, the median age at first marriage increased by a year and a half for both women and men compared to the 1950s (Reiss, 1980: 222). Cohabitation no doubt helped some young people to delay first marriage by giving them an alternative path to intimacy.

Since its inception in the late 1960s, the popularity of cohabitation has grown. On the basis of various studies, it is estimated that 25 percent of college students have cohabited at some point (Macklin, 1978) and that another 50 percent would like to (Bower and Christopherson, 1977; Henze and Hudson, 1974). Living together has also spread to other segments of the population. In a random sample of young men who registered for the draft between 1962 and 1972, 18 percent had cohabited for at least six months, with rates higher for blacks (29 percent) than for whites (16 percent), according to Clayton and Voss (1977). Other population groups who find cohabitation meets their needs are people who have divorced and are not yet ready to step back into legal marriage. Older people, especially those who are widowed and/or retired, often will cohabit in order to avoid loss of Social Security benefits or to keep their finances separate.

Cohabitation has, in fact, grown remarkably during the last several years, more than tripling in the 1970-1982 period to a total of 1.9 million unmarried couples, according to Census Bureau data.[2] The number of married couples grew during that same period (from 44.7 million to 49.6 million), but at a much slower rate. Unmarried couples now represent about 44 percent of all couples (both married and unmarried). Although this is still a small percentage, the expectation is that cohabitation will continue to increase. One prediction is that we are following the path of Sweden in changing our family and living styles. In 1977 it was estimated that approximately 15 percent of Swedish couples who maintained a home together were cohabiting (Reiss, 1980: 445).

From these data about the rise in age at marriage and the growing popularity of cohabitation, it may appear to some that cohabitation is a threat to marriage. This is not so, however, for the percentage of people who marry today is still higher than it was during most of our history. What is happening in our era is that young people, as in the sixties and seventies, are delaying marriage and changing the atypical marriage age pattern that was established in the 1950s. In terms of age at first marriage, young brides today are more like their grandmothers than their mothers. The continuing high marriage rate suggests that when we fully understand cohabitation, we will see that it is not a challenge to marriage, but that it actually supports and encourages the system of legal marriage. This is not yet clear to us because cohabitation, as a relatively new practice, is not yet fully institutionalized.

What do we mean by cohabitation becoming institutionalized? Institutionalization, a process of much interest to sociologists, means that a particular social behavior keeps occurring and comes to follow an orderly pattern or structure. This structure becomes apparent over time as more and more people live out the behavior and do it in similar ways. Eventually the pattern of the behavior is accepted by enough people for it is to be recognized as part of a larger related system of behavior. This is what is now happening with cohabitation.

To understand this process further, especially as it relates to our courtship and marriage system, it is worthwhile to look back in history to trace how our premarriage, or dating, customs arose. Our society has featured, from its very beginnings, a courtship structure that was relatively free from parental control. This fit in directly with the ideology of the first settlers, who, after all, came here because they wished to practice their own beliefs. Added to this initial American emphasis on independence was a very high rate of mobility of all kinds. There was geographic mobility from east to west and from rural to urban areas, as well as social mobility from lower to middle classes. Mobility had the effect of increasing an individual's freedom from parental controls because of the geographic or social separation. Thus, young people have always largely defined and invented the courtship system for themselves.

For example, during the nineteenth and especially the twentieth century, the custom of casual dating arose to supplement the serious dating that had always existed as a prelude to marriage. In response to increased contact between the sexes at work and in schools, casual dating arose to provide a structure of roles and norms within which young men and women could interact before they were ready seriously to contemplate marriage. Similarly, the custom of going steady arose later in the twentieth century to enable people to narrow down the field of eligibles they met through casual dating and to test out a relationship with a prospective spouse (Reiss, 1980).

Both customs of casual and steady dating were social inventions designed to meet the changing personal needs of women and men in a modernizing society. Both customs were initially criticized by many segments of society who foresaw various dangers in allowing young men and women to interact so freely before marriage. Both have obviously become institutionalized and accepted as part of courtship as the decades have passed. So it is with cohabitation. It is a custom that has arisen to meet the changed personal needs of people in ways that traditional legal marriage cannot. It is a social invention that has come to us through the same historical process that has given us other well-accepted features of our courtship and marriage system. People may be reluctant to accept cohabitation as a valid lifestyle because they do not see it as part of this ongoing process of institutional-ization. The family system, like all elements in society, is constantly undergoing a process of change. As changes occur, there are always difficulties in adjusting to and accepting them. It is the nature of people to resist change; yet, placing changes in historical perspective can help to reassure us about the continuity we all desire.

Let us consider now what is known about cohabitation in an effort to understand it better and to see its place in contemporary courtship and marriage.[3] Researchers generally agree that one distinct type of living together is what is known as courtship cohabitation (Macklin, 1978). This occurs between young adults who have never married.

Living together is not expected to be a permanent arrangement, nor is there a desire for children to be born of the relationship. Because the participants have defined themselves as not yet ready for marriage, they may be living together for reasons that are different from those for getting married. Their reasons may include convenience, economy, or that they just gradually fell into the habit of not going home to their own places of residence. This form of cohabitation typically lasts for only a few months and is best understood as an extension of the courtship stage, as a variation on steady dating but one that openly acknowledges sexual intimacy.

On the other hand, long-term premarital cohabitation lasting for a year or more can be validly compared to young marriages, especially those that end in divorce. Half of all legal divorces occur before the seventh year of marriage, which means that the actual breakup occurred even earlier (Cherlin, 1981). From a couple's perspective, the major difference between cohabitants and young couples who divorce is that cohabitants realize ahead of time they are not yet ready for marriage. From a societal perspective, the major difference is that the cohabiting couple does not produce children. Cohabitors do not see their relationship as suitable for children, and so they are very efficient contraceptors. Early divorces, on the other hand, increasingly involve young children (Cherlin, 1981).

The pattern that is being established in long-term premarital cohabitation is remarkably similar to first marriage without children. Long-term cohabitation fills the need for young adults to test out their ability to relate intimately to another person, a necessary skill for survival in legal marriage. It enables couples to combine love and work and sex in a setting that is relatively independent of their parents' control. It gives them the opportunity to continue to grow and change during their twenties, as people increasingly do in contemporary society, without forcing them to make a permanent commitment to another person before they are developmentally ready. Because they have not made a permanent commitment that they later find they cannot keep, they are free to separate without the burden of failure and guilt associated with divorce. Nor, of course, do they face the herculean task of becoming one-parent families after divorce. From this perspective, long-term cohabitants are making a very wise choice.

Premarital cohabitation, as it is practiced, seems increasingly to be precisely the idea Margaret Mead had in mind when nearly twenty years ago (1966) she recommended two-stage marriages. Stage one was to be an individual marriage for the benefit of the couple; stage two, which might be with a different partner, was to form a union to produce and nurture children. Stage-two marriage would require a previously satisfactory individual marriage and would be more difficult to break by divorce than today's legal marriage (Mead, 1966). Cohabitation certainly seems to be the social invention Mead was looking for, and it is certainly preferable to premature marriages that fail. Young couples may succumb to social pressure to marry before they are ready because they do not perceive any other socially acceptable pattern to extend their intimacy. Given the increasing divorce rate, it may now be in society's best interest to recommend that young couples uniformly consider cohabitation as a stage to live through before engaging in a marriage with children. This policy might reduce the growing number of child victims of divorce. This type of cohabitation can never be tested as social policy, however, as long as our attitudes remain negative and we do not consider it as valid as marriage.

A second major type of long-term cohabitation is that in which one or both partners have been previously married. Typically, these cohabitants are considerably older than the college age population. About half of all cohabitants are in this group (Macklin, 1978).

Some older cohabitants may have children from a previous marriage living with them, but this is not the usual case. Nor is it usual for these cohabitants to have a new baby while they are cohabiting. We know the least about this group, as most studies of cohabitants have focused on younger adults, especially college students. Accordingly, I did several in-depth interviews of my own with cohabitants of this type to supplement the existing research (Yllo, 1978; Weitzman et al., 1978; Blumstein and Schwartz, 1983). Typically, with previously married cohabitants, the pain and sense of failure from divorce left them reluctant to step into remarriage without first testing their ability to sustain a relationship. Most felt that, after a while, cohabitation was exactly like marriage without the legal ties. They felt as emotionally committed to their partner as if they were married, and somewhat ruefully admitted that in the event of a breakup they would suffer as much as they did in their divorce. To some extent, then, not getting married in order to protect themselves was self-deceptive.

However, all stressed that living together, rather than getting married, provided a greater sense of independence at the same time that they were emotionally connected. This independence manifested itself in keeping their financial affairs at least partially separated, in using their own names, in both partners working and taking responsibility for their own support, and in spending some of their free time away from each other in different activities. Women felt more strongly than men about retaining their independence and separate identity, a reaction to their previous experience in more traditional marriage.

There is less agreement in research data over whether cohabitants actually succeed in carrying out nontraditional roles in other areas of their cohabitation, specifically in the division of household duties and in whether men and women share equal power in their relationships. Early reports indicated these roles tended to be just as traditional as in marriage (Macklin, 1978), but the most recent and extensive survey concludes that cohabitors are uniformly more successful than marrieds in establishing and living out egalitarian couple roles (Blumstein and Schwartz, 1983).

Perhaps these cohabitors, with marriage experience before they live together, may be looked upon as social pioneers testing out a new pattern of intimacy that they feel is an improvement over legal marriage. They are, in a sense, people who are designing their own marriage rather than accepting the more traditional model that has been handed down to us. The individual choices they are living now may well set the structure for marriage in the future, continuing the process of innovation and autonomy that has been a feature of the American marriage system since it began.

Some may object to the argument that cohabitation is a testing ground for future patterns of marriage on the ground that marriage itself has changed so much today that you can do the same thing within marriage as within cohabitation—that you can design it in any way you want. Indeed, there is more freedom today to do that within marriage. There are two-career marriages, two-location marriages, child free marriages, open marriages, househusband marriages, and the like. But the institution of marriage is still *legally* based "on outmoded assumptions about the family, assumptions often contradicted by the reality of the [couple's] own experience but nevertheless applied to them by law" (Weitzman, 1981: xvii). Even if a couple tries to write their own personal contract for marriage, provisions "that seem just and fair to them are invalid and unenforceable in a court of law." Unfortunately, a couple may not discover these facts about marriage until they are in the divorce court, when the shortcomings of the legal contract they made at marriage become painfully obvious.[4]

One goal the legal contract does achieve, however, is a relatively greater permanence for marriage. Research to date indicates that living-together relationships tend not to last as long as marriages. There are several possible explanations for this. Cohabitation may still be too new to measure adequately against marriage, or its shorter duration might not be found in more extensive research in the future on cohabitation. Another possibility is that many cohabiting couples may not end their relationships, but transform them into legal marriages. And the fact that cohabitation is not supported by society to the same degree as is marriage may serve to indeed make it less stable. This is an important question for which we do not as yet have a complete answer.

CONCLUSION

I have become convinced, while thinking and writing on the issue of cohabitation versus marriage, that this is a false issue. Cohabitation is not a challenge to marriage, it is not taking the place of marriage now nor will it in the future. Virtually all cohabitants go on to marriage at some point in their lives. What is happening is that as cohabitation develops and spreads to various age and class groups; it is becoming institutionalized and accepted as part of the marriage system, as a step on the way to legal marriage or remarriage. This process is exactly the same as that by which casual and steady dating were invented and accepted in the past. We do not all recognize this as yet because cohabitation is so new, and because there always tends to be in a fast-changing society an "emotional lag." That is, social and technological invention often outpaces people's ability to change their thinking and feelings about traditional ways of doing things.

We can best understand cohabitation by looking at its two major forms. Short-term cohabitation is an extension of courtship. Long-term cohabitation is a variation of couple marriage without children and, as I have suggested, may even be socially preferable to premature marriage for young adults.[5]

Cohabitation, finally, is an option. It is not something that all people should or will do, but it is valid and acceptable for many people at different points in the life cycle. Long-term cohabitation can help to meet the changing personal needs of both young and older adults in today's society which traditional legal marriage cannot. That is why it was invented, that is why it is becoming institutionalized, and that is why it will become a recognized part of our American marriage system.

NOTES

1. It is likely that some people have always cohabited in our society. The poor, for instance, have often not been able to afford legal marriage, and so have sometimes lived together in common law unions (Weitzman, 1981: 193). In fact, it is very possible that this association of unwed cohabitation with poverty is an unrecognized aspect of whatever current negative attitudes exist toward cohabitation. The cohabitation I am discussing in this article is that which occurs through free choice, and which involves two people who have an ongoing, emotionally and sexually intimate relationship.

2. This figure of 1.9 million couples cohabiting may include nonintimate arrangements such as a widow who rents a room to a college student. However, such situations account for only a small portion of unmarried couple households and are probably far fewer than those cohabitants who have not been counted for one reason or another.

3. Since research on cohabitation is still in the early stages, it is incomplete and sometimes contradictory. There is not even agreement on the definition. What I have tried to present in this discussion is a general overview, stressing those points with which most researchers agree. See Macklin (1978) for a review of the literature to that date.

4. It is true that the state is beginning to regulate cohabitation, as in the famous Marvin v. Marvin case. However, there are only a few, mostly ambiguous legal norms as yet regarding cohabitation, and there certainly are far fewer and much less powerful social norms. A common report from cohabiting couples who later marry is that everything changed when they married. They slipped into more traditional roles and even started taking each other for granted.

5. I liked the pronouncement of one woman I interviewed, who stated, "The real issue is not marriage versus cohabitation, but whether you will be a couple with or without children."

REFERENCES

BLUMSTEIN, P. and P. SCHWARTZ (1983) American Couples. New York: Morrow.

BOWER, D. W. and V. A. CHRISTOPHERSON (1977) "University student cohabitation: a regional comparison of selected attitudes and behavior." Journal of Marriage and the Family 39 (August): 447-453.

CHERLIN, A. J. (1981) Marriage, Divorce, Remarriage. Cambridge, MA: Harvard University Press.

CLAYTON, R. R. and H. L. VOSS (1977) "Shacking up: cohabitation in the 1970's." Journal of Marriage and the Family 39 (May): 273-283.

HENZE, L. F. and J. W. HUDSON (1974) "Personal and family characteristics of cohabiting and noncohabiting college students." Journal of Marriage and the Family 36 (November): 722-737.

MACKLIN, E. D. (1978) "Review of research on nonmarried cohabitation in the United States," pp. 197-243 in B. I. Murstein (ed.) Exploring Intimate Lifestyles. New York: Springer.

MEAD, M. (1966) "Marriage in two steps." Redbook (July): 48-49, 84-86.

REISS, I. L. (1980) Family Systems in America. New York: Holt, Rinehart and Winston.

U.S. Bureau of the Census (1982) "Marital status and living arrangements." Current Population Reports, Series P-20, No. 380. Washington, DC: Government Printing Office.

WEITZMAN, L. J. (1981) The Marriage Contract. New York: Free Press.

———C. M. DIXON, J. A. BIRD, N. McGINN, and D. M. ROBERTSON (1978) "Contracts for intimate relationships." Alternative Lifestyles 1 (August): 303-378.

YLLO, K. A. (1978) "Nonmarital cohabitation beyond the college campus." Alternative Lifestyles 1 (February): 37-54.

Lifetime Monogamy Is the Preferred Form of Marital Relationship

DAVID MACE
VERA MACE

Our preference is for lifetime marriage, both for ourselves and for others. Our thesis is that by improving marriage there is less need for extramarital relationships and more gratification for the couple involved. This does not mean that we are opposed to divorce and remarriage. We are well aware that in our culture there are persons who, not necessarily through any fault of their own, must be described as "unmarriageable" in terms of the reasonable expectations in today's culture. Lederer and Jackson (1968: 129), estimate that such persons may be found in from 5 to 10 percent of all marriages; they add that in these marriages sometimes one person is unmarriageable, and sometimes both are. We would regard this as a fair estimate.

On this basis, therefore, it would seem reasonable to assume that divorces in about the same proportion would also be reasonable; and we would uphold the right of divorce in our culture today, and deplore the fact that in Western society in the past that right was often denied.

Having made this clear, however, we would go on to say that the current high rate of divorce and extramarital activity in our culture is in our opinion excessive and disturbing. In our view these high rates do not represent the inability of the persons concerned to achieve a reasonably satisfying interpersonal relationship; rather they reflect an irresponsible failure in our culture as a whole to provide the necessary understanding of the marriage relationship, and the skills and tools required for its successful accomplishment. What we mean by this will appear more clearly as we proceed.

THE NATURE OF MARRIAGE

For an adequate understanding of marriage, we must go back to the subhuman species. The famous dictum of Edward Westermarck (1925: 72) that "marriage is rooted in the family, and not the family in marriage" provides us with a good starting point.

The continuity of any and every species is secured by the process of reproduction. As we ascend the evolutionary ladder, we pass from the state where the young start life independently to states of increasing dependency extending over increasing time spans. In some lower forms, this requires only one-parent care, and this is possible for humans. But two-parent care provides much greater security; and throughout human history this has been recognized as the most desirable arrangement.

In order to provide for this, marriage in some form has become virtually a universal system; and it has been regulated by custom and law as a requirement for the preservation of social order. In some cultures the system has been regulated too strictly, in others too loosely; but it has on the whole fulfilled its function in providing a protective and supportive family system for children over the extended period now required for their growth to full maturity—

roughly estimated as about twenty years. No alternative system has yet emerged that is remotely comparable in its effectiveness.

However, over time marriage has also developed an auxiliary function. When two parents jointly care for the children they have jointly produced, their cooperative task inevitably unites them in action, and under good conditions this can lead them into a companionship relationship. They also provide each other with welcome services—sexual pleasure, assistance in difficult tasks, mutual support in illness and crisis. These mutual services bear no relation to their duties to their children, and can continue to be meaningful after the young have become independent and have departed. So, to care of children there is added the reward of mutual companionship, and marriage becomes a relationship of lifetime duration. The value of this is fortified by all the supports provided by the extended family system.

CHANGES IN MODERN MARRIAGE

During the present century our culture has undergone extensive changes, and many ancient customs and institutions have been shaken to their foundations. Marriage has been no exception.

The major change in our ways of looking at marriage has come from the extended application of the democratic ideal, based on the doctrine that all men are created equal. This first challenged the traditional class system by insisting on the doctrine of human rights, which led to a considerable extension of individual freedom. For many, this extended to a rationalization of extramarital relations. As women were also seen to be eligible for individual freedom, there was a further breakdown in traditional supports for fidelity.

Marriage until recent times had always followed the universal societal system of vertical relationships—dominance and submission—which had been found necessary for the avoidance or control of interpersonal conflicts. Also, marital conflict had been further avoided by the strict division of rights and duties within the family group. As these controls ceased to operate, conflict and competition disrupted the controlled peace of family relationships.

Although the immediate consequences of this disruption were disturbing, in reality the way was being opened to new and exciting possibilities for love and intimacy in couple relationships, which Ernest Burgess recognized as the "companionship" system. But the achievement and management of a companionship relationship, particularly when it replaces a former hierarchical relationship, can be very difficult, and the attempt can lead to explosive interactions. This is happening extensively in our present culture. Unsuccessful attempts to deal with conflict, lacking the necessary insights and skills to process it constructively, have led on a wide scale to the alienation of affection and extramarital relationships, often followed by termination of the relationship.

Now, however, as we make continuing progress in the study of close relationships, we are learning the necessary skills, and how to teach them to couples. This is not an easy task, because the learning must be acquired by both experientially and extended over time; and we are only beginning to develop the methods to make this possible. But the marriage enrichment movement is making steady if slow progress, and is producing highly gratifying results. It can now be confidently demonstrated that, at a time when many marriages are failing to an extent we have never known before, other marriages are succeeding to an extent we have never known before.

RELATIONSHIP ENHANCEMENT PROGRAMS

For a period of some twenty years, we have been involved in the marriage enrichment movement, and more recently the "family wellness" movement. We had previously been occupied in pioneering what is now called family therapy; but we reached a point at which we began to see clearly that we were starting at the wrong end. True, compassion demands that, when disruptive tensions develop in marriage and family relationships, it is our clear duty to offer help and, if possible, rehabilitation to those concerned. Yet to do only that is a fruitless policy, because it now can be clearly demonstrated that most relational crises develop over time, as a result of unskilled management in the first place. By applying what we have learned in family therapy and tracing it back to its origins, we can now guide couples and families in the development of constructive, instead of destructive, interaction patterns; and by doing this we can prevent much of the damage with which therapists are now having to deal at a later stage.

This is true theoretically; but we are only at the beginning of the task of changing our views and attitudes to enable these new concepts to be put into effective action. However, these changes offer very favorable promise for better marital and family relationships, and it now seems inevitable that they will be applied more and more widely over time. What follows is a brief consideration of how this could be done.

The removal of social controls over marriage, which is now nearly complete, has resulted in the freedom of the individual to choose a future partner, and also to terminate the partnership at will. Controls that remain have little more than nuisance value; marriages can now be entered or left at will. Indeed, the recent development of cohabitation reduces the process to an entirely private arrangement, with no public registration involved.

It might be imagined that this process, which gives the individual complete freedom to select a life partner on the basis of natural attraction and personal choice, would have made marriages more successful and durable than they have ever been before. Instead, the opposite has happened. Why?

In the process of working personally with hundreds, perhaps thousands, of couples over the years, it has become clear to us that the building of a successful marriage is a very complex task, for which most people are very poorly equipped. The views widely held about marriage consist of a confused assortment of muddled misconceptions; and because of what we have called the "intermarital taboo," there is little chance of letting in the light until our new insights become more widely understood and accepted.

To begin with, partner choice is commonly based on romantic sentiment, with sex attraction as a major component; and these emotional determinants have little or no enduring power once the couple settle down to a shared life. Often there turn out to be quite radical differences in emotional attitudes, value systems, and personal habits, which simply shatter their romantic dream.

We have found also that, in the early days of marriage, communication systems are deplorably ineffective, and the couple soon find themselves in a tangled web of misunderstandings. This provides no means of facing and resolving the long series of disagreements and conflicts that we now know are normal and inevitable in the early development of all close relationships, and which continue until they are processed and resolved. But all this is simply not comprehended by the average couple, who generally have not even made a specific commitment to work together on the complex task of building a companionship relationship. Depending on the facile assumption that "because we are in love, it will all work out," they find themselves increasingly alienated and disillusioned. Ironically, our culture, in order to respect their privacy, then imposes on them the assumption that they should be enjoying an extended honeymoon, and that to need help implies that they must be abnormally dumb and incompetent.

It is now our considered conclusion that achieving real success in building a companionship marriage is a task equivalent to achieving success in a high-level career; and that we need to make provision for this as soon as possible. Further, we take the view that the best way to provide this help is to guide the couple through their first year together so that their interaction patterns can be healthily established from the beginning. A major British study of couples who divorced across the life cycle found that one-third of them admitted to having been in real trouble by the time they reached their first wedding anniversary.

Under the circumstances we have described above, is it any wonder that the Bureau of the Census now predicts that about half of all couples being married today will ultimately divorce? And when they do, most of them within a few years will marry again, on the assumption that what they need in order to be happy is a change of partners. Some of them, it may be supposed, will now have come to their senses, realizing that marriages do not descend from heaven, but have to be built by the cooperative use of the proper skills. This does happen to some divorced couples—but only for some. The sad truth is that the failure rate for second marriages is higher than for the first. This has led Mel Krantzler (1981) to declare that if your marriage is in trouble, you will have a better chance of happiness by working seriously, with help if necessary, to repair it than you would have by divorcing and trying again with another partner.

THE CASE FOR
LIFETIME MONOGAMY

We are now ready to state the case for the position we are defending—lifetime monogamy. It will probably be best for us at this point to focus on our personal attitudes.

We have now been married for fifty years, which is good measure for a marital lifetime. As we look back briefly on our personal experience, we shall try to identify the reasons we favored extended monogamy in the first place, and why we continued to favor this option as the years passed. Here they are.

1. Respect for the established tradition. When we were in England in 1933, divorce and remarriage were relatively rare events. The divorce laws offered very limited options, and public opinion took an unfavorable view of divorced persons. The outstanding example was the high-level crisis that occurred when King Edward VIII had to surrender his title to the throne because of his determination to marry a divorced woman. But we can also recall a small town in which the bank manager divorced his wife to marry another woman and found the public disapproval so strong that he had to leave the community.

The general attitude at that time was expressed by a public figure who stated that to break your marriage was an act that "unsettled the foundations of human society." This reflected the concept that individual needs must be sacrificed to our major duty to maintain social order. It is this concept that has been almost totally jettisoned in American society in recent years.

We would defend the concept. To interpret democracy as the unlimited freedom to meet individual needs is a grave error. It can lead only to the point where we exchange the tyranny of one major dictator for the equally harmful tyranny of a host of petty dictators. True democracy is a fair balance between individual needs and the welfare of the wider society. We therefore see the development of no-fault divorce as a tragic surrender of duty and principle by the leaders of our communities.

2. Fulfillment of parental duties. We ourselves have always taken the view that the foundation of any system of human rights must be the right of every child to be cared for in the critical period of early development by the two parents who gave him or her life in the first place. The fact that during World War II our family endured an unavoidable period of separation was seen by us as a tragic violation of our rights and duties. It is therefore hard for us to understand how so many parents today plan such family disruption as a matter of personal convenience.

Before divorce became so common that it was simply taken for granted, many couples desiring to separate felt it to be their duty first to raise their children to an age at which they could understand what was happening and had developed enough self-confidence to adjust to the dissolution of the family. They postponed the upheaval in order to discharge what they felt to be their parental obligations.

3. *Cumulative benefits of lifelong companionship.* If there is one thing that has been proven again and again in recent years, it is our deep and fundamental need for at least one dependable close relationship, to support us as we confront the changes and chances of the human life cycle. Probably the major finding of the recently published eight-year study of American couples (Blumstein and Schwartz, 1983) is that what people are looking for most of all, in their relationships with others, is one durable established companionship that will continue across the years. According to Blumstein and Schwartz, "When Americans marry, they hope they are making a lifetime commitment . . . people would like their relationship to be permanent" (p. 11).

We are not really surprised, however, given all the circumstances, that so many marriages today are failing; because we now realize that the average marriage, when it is launched, is desperately ill-equipped for the journey before it. By contrast we, and many other couples in the marriage enrichment movement, have found our experience to be the opposite. And this is not because we were necessarily superior persons, or better matched. It was simply our good fortune to have access to, and to be able to make practical use of, the new insights the behavioral sciences are now making available.

On the day on which we celebrated our fiftieth wedding anniversary, we chose not to have a party to which our many friends would be invited. Instead, we made a trip together to the summit of Mt. Mitchell, the highest U.S. peak east of the Rocky Mountains. There we looked back across the years, affirmed each other, and gave thanks for a multitude of shared experiences. We also tried to determine what had been the decisive factors in our years of happiness together.

We arrived at an interesting and unexpected conclusion. In our attempt to assess the favorable and unfavorable factors with which we had started out, and how we had made use of them, we reached the agreement that, on balance, the differences between us, and the challenge of working through them in the consequent growth process, had contributed more to our eventual happiness than the similarities that had seemed at first to constitute the promise of success!

We may in this respect be different from others. But it does at least suggest that the resources with which you begin may be much less important to marital success and duration than the commitment you make to each other, and the cumulative effectiveness of a shared life over many years. In other words, your marriage is what you make it; but if you want a really good one, the job takes a lifetime!

REFERENCES

BLUMSTEIN, P. and P. SCHWARTZ (1983) American Couples. New York: Morrow.
BURGESS, E. W. and P. WALLIN (1953) Engagement and Marriage. Chicago: Lippincott.
KRANTZLER, M. (1981) Creative Marriage. New York: McGraw-Hill.
LEDERER, W. J. and D. JACKSON (1968) The Mirages of Marriage. New York: Norton.
WESTERMARCK, E. (1925) The History of Human Marriage, vol. 1. London: Macmillan.

ALTERNATIVES TO MONOGAMY

There Are a Number of Equally Valid Forms of Marriage, Such as Multiple Marriage, Swinging, Adultery, and Open Marriage

ROBERT N. WHITEHURST

The basic argument to be elaborated here involves the notion that the concept of "valid" in the title of this chapter is not one that is fixed in history, religion, or law, but is a notion that is subject to constant though often subtle and imperceptible change. The reason that many persons erroneously have thought that there is basically one, and only one, form of marriage rests in misunderstanding the historical, economic, and religious forces and their powers to define and control the beliefs of the past.

There have always been sexual undergrounds (Whitehurst and Booth, 1980) that have provided people with choices of lifestyle and alternative sexuality. Social changes and coverage by mass media have made alternatives today much more visible on the one hand, and on the other have set the stage for negative sanctions becoming either inoperative or weakened. Neither the community, religion, nor family/kin groups have the same power of control over lives of most people as once was true, Instead, we have expanded choices because some of us do not perceive the negative sanctions to be so strong as to outweigh the perceived advantages or rewards. Thus, in a more real sense today, "validity" of relationship forms rests with individual choice and reference group support, not some absolute standards set by the state, religion, or the community.

Sociologists and others have long chronicled the social changes that have affected lifestyle choices; some of the major ones include increased longevity, lowered fertility, mobility (both geographic and vertical), rampant individualism, the industrialization of the household (Eichler, 1983), changes in occupational structures and the labor force, divorce made easy (and nonstigmatized) and dramatically altered roles of women, children, and men. Technology has added a number of freedoms (and placed limits on certain kinds of behavior as well) and been instrumental, if not causal in making for changed social arrangements. One way to view the problem of validity of relationship forms is to see the current problem of relationships as one of cultural lag: We have the means and will to engage in a variety of lifestyle adaptations, but the mores of contemporary society have not entirely bought into the necessary adaptive normative set, which might be called pluralistic (Whitehurst and Booth, 1980). Many people tend to insist there is still only one valid lifestyle form of relationship when there is evidence to the contrary all about us. To arrive at that narrowly legitimized view of relationship validity, one must exercise not only historical, but also contemporary, selective perceptions of relationships.

A sociological explanation of why multiple forms of relationships arose when they did in our century might involve aspects of sociological functionalism. Functionalists believe that when social organization fails to meet human needs under changing conditions, then new forms will arise to fill the gaps and meet these needs. It is obvious from the above discussion that times have changed; thus new social forms arose to meet these needs. Under conditions of more equality, gays tended to try to legitimize their needs by having homosexuality relabeled as a lifestyle choice, not a disease or perversion. When male shortages appear (because of wars, unbalanced sex ratios, or geographic dispersion) women and men make arrangements with what they have that may deny tradition but be the best they can arrange at the time when and where they are. Given the directions and amount of changes in the above listing, it is naive not to expect change in the social arrangements of persons in an increasingly open and free-choice kind of society, especially with fewer sanctions opposing such forms, mobility making for anonymity, and the stress on equality and individualism continuing. This does not mean that newer choices are easy; they are not, since some negative sanctions still remain. It merely means that some people will opt for them since this is the choice they make and perceive rewards to outweigh punishments.

In order to assess validity, we must define and make relative the concept to some standard or baseline view of what it means. In my view, validity depends on support and continuation in the population for the behavior or acts in question. Thus, if monogamous marriage were truly valid, there would be virtually no one practicing a kind of relationship other than this style of marriage. Insofar as there is support and encouragement for other forms, then there is validity. Of course, we do not have legal validity for other forms of marriage, but it may not be long before recognition is given to gay marriages, legitimizing of cohabitation, and perhaps plural spouses for at least older persons. All of this presupposes some continuation of rational governments and liberal social and political trends over the long run. This prediction of pluralistic democracy may be far from a correct appraisal, given current trends, and may be far afield from actual futures.

To summarize the argument thus far: Social changes, technology and a rapidly changing world have in some measure failed to respond to some persons' needs. Alternative forms thus arise to fill gaps and we have the beginnings of a newer, more democratic, pluralistic society. Validity of new or old social forms rests upon support of the people. Although there is still lip-service support for lifelong monogamy, it is as obvious that there are many variants of monogamy now being practiced, and many of these tend to gain legitimacy (thus support and ultimately validity) as time goes on. For example, few now raise eyebrows about unmarrieds living together, as was true only a short generation ago. Adultery, though still punishable by law, is widely practiced by both sexes. No longer does it maintain quite the power in terms of divorce as it once did, though clearly it has not lost all its former status as a primary rationale for divorce. Gay persons no longer are so willing to suffer "in the closet" and now often prefer to fight for their human rights and will likely continue to be active on political and job-related fronts. Swinging has gone essentially commercial, and national conventions are held without fear of intrusion by the law.

The above discussion involves a sociological view of reality and has little to do with morality. Whether the reality is a reasonably correct perception of the real world is the problem, not whether this is the way it ought to be or not. It also has little to do with what one chooses to actively work for in terms of choice in lifestyle or marital arrangement. Since a variety of forms is now coming to be legitimized (and validated at least by some persons and groups), then democratic pluralism by intent and design would allow persons freely to choose lifetime monogamy and feel as good about that as a gay couple might in seeking a valid marriage.

If we use only the legal criterion to verify validity, then we indeed conclude that monogamous marriage is the only form. If we follow the notion that social support creates legitimacy and thus a level of validity, then we must be more cautious in our interpretation of what is valid. In the rest of this article an attempt will be made to rank order some of the more visible extant forms of relationships and assess their present and potential future validity as compared with monogamous marriages. In some respects then, since my criteria are social support and longevity of form to judge validity, the options listed below will be ranked in order of their frequency and their social supports. These tend to give them a sort of legitimacy, if not in law, then in mores or by virtue of numbers, who may prevail against tradition to avoid being stigmatized and/or eradicated. The bottom line is power; persons or groups who have power to redefine situations, to make or change laws, and to constrain or restrain persons who violate them are at the crux of this discussion. Throughout the remaining discussion, it will become clear that some choices may become more or less frequent depending on ways in which power is used.

RELATIONSHIP OPTIONS

LIFETIME MONOGAMY

Although few people go into marriage believing they will get a divorce, increasing numbers have that experience, and in the near future it may become a norm to have experienced two marriages (one that might be chalked up to inexperience, or perhaps we will come to allow one marriage period to be for personal growth and the next for stability). Whether monogamous marriage in fact continues to dominate the relationship scene (or if it even does today) is a matter of some debate. The ideal is one to which most persons still adhere when they marry. What they do in later years is another problem, but the increased tenuousness of long-term marriages makes it problematic as a future dominant form. Traditional monogamous marriage has the most strength of custom, law, religion, and community supports to prop it up; thus we might speculate that it remains in part as a perseverance of an older form that in some respects simply does not provide people with clear options and will only decline when more options are open and available.

ADULTERY

This form of marital violation is obviously as old as man/woman, since it is generously mentioned in the Bible. In terms of modern practices, we ought to recognize variations in the dimension of openness and permission related to nonmonogamy. All couples have rules, whether written or not, spoken or not, and clearly understood or not. Some partners maintain nonverbal rules that, in essence, admonish the person sexually active outside the marriage to act as though it does not happen or to otherwise protect the other from this knowledge. Therapists relate many tales of spouses who in fact "know" that their spouses have affairs. They are thus many complications in comprehending the nature of "monogamy," unless both partners in fact declare and adhere to its ideals and in fact practice monogamy. If we had clear statistics showing how many did this, it is quite likely that monogamy would not be the most usual form of marriage, even though it is still held as the ideal one.

If we persist in selectively seeing only that which upholds our own preferred view of reality, we will continue to have a situation of uneasy pluralism. If we are able to comprehend the complexity, ambivalence, and mixed nature of life about us, we stand more chance of accepting and adapting more peacefully to pluralism. For example, the media give us not only messages of free-choice and open sexuality, but messages of hoped-for permanence in relationships too. It is possible to support virtually any belief or lifestyle by being highly selective in use of materials. There are without doubt a number of sources to support adultery as a lifestyle choice if one were so inclined to find these. In second place as most popular lifestyle adaptation, we must recognize that the rules of affairs have been well codified, even in writing; thus, conducting these becomes simpler as more people gain personal freedoms and the know-how to create and sustain them without severe consequences (Hunt, 1969; Ellis, 1972).

Perhaps the best way to characterize adultery as a lifestyle is to suggest that its supports are informal, rather than inhering within accepted institutions, and that its constituency lies somewhat outside the pale of the conventional, but not really very far, since most practitioners are also legitimate members of the establishment. Since such extramarital behavior shows no signs of abating, it may be safe to conclude that adultery will continue to be a very popular (at least part-time) added feature to otherwise normal marriages. Since recent experience with sexually open marriages has suggested generally that such arrangements are fluid and explosive (if not ephemeral), then what many find positive and useful in their marriages (stability) will not normally be endangered by extramarital sexual affairs. Thus, my conclusion is that such affairs will not only continue, but will proliferate. The vagaries of love, however, will continue to take their toll in divorce and create a larger remarriage pool, which in all likelihood will not be materially happier (nor more sexually satisfied) than other persons (Cargan et al., 1984).

NONMARITAL COHABITATION

In the United States most cohabiting relationships are still at the courtship phase of their relationship (Macklin, 1983: 60). It is likely that in the early 1980s most persons who cohabit do so with the intent of getting married at some time (to someone), if not in the immediate future. It is not difficult at the same time to find couples who have lived together for long periods of time (either after being divorced or before their first marriage) and still not contemplate marriage. Also, people sometimes get married for various reasons after highly varied periods of cohabitation.

Macklin distinguishes five types of cohabitation, each varying in seriousness of intent and meaning to the participants (Macklin, 1983:

56). If we lump together all of these five types, it is easy to conclude that cohabitation is popular. It is not so often seen as an alternative to legal conventional marriage; it thus has rather limited validity in this respect in terms of our definition. It has somewhat more validity as a kind of semilegitimized relationship of convenience, trial, or comradeship. It may be proper to view cohabiting as a variable-term stop-gap, not as a permanent alternative. At the least, many persons will have had some experience with cohabiting in their life-cycle relationships. Whether some cohabiting experience implies liberalization for and further potential for other sexual experimentation is not well known. It may, at least for some persons mean that the wild-oats period is past and people are ready to settle down into conventional roles and lifestyles.

What we have been discussing so far by way of life-styles might be considered as relatively normal behaviors, given that the three adaptations above tend to approximate statistical (or social) normality in our society (Whitehurst and Booth, 1980). The remaining adaptations are less frequently found, even though densities in certain places (such as gay subcultures) may make this less frequent occurrence seem doubtful.

Except for the gay alternative to be described in the following, the reader might suppose that all of the adaptations are statistically insignificant and socially acceptable to only a very small minority of persons. This is true today, but it is unwise to be so certain about futures that we cannot envision circumstances that would change our view and potentials for other relationship futures. Anyone presently over five or six decades of age will attest to the dramatic and seemingly radical changes that have occurred in their lifetimes. Projecting technological and social changes forward is risky, but the point is worth noting that change continues, and may well do so at an even faster rate.

THE HOMOSEXUAL ADAPTATION

Even though there is still a large area of common concern and consensus among gay people with respect to human rights and political actions, there is no longer much of a monolithic gay community anywhere. It has become diversified, split, and pluralistic within its ranks. Gays have become more accepted into other parts of the community, and job discrimination is beginning to be seriously questioned where gays are involved. Many who formerly lived active and variety-filled sex lives now are monogamous and conventional in most respects other than their sexual choice of partner. The larger community has yielded to political pressures in some ways and has become liberalized and educated and more frequently find gays among their friends and acquaintances. All of this makes for easier assimilation of gays into the larger culture and may well make for more gays refusing to stay in the closet.

Popular thought is now divided as to whether homosexuality is an acquired choice deeply ingrained, perhaps at birth in some ways we poorly understand now. Depending on which view prevails in the future, we may see more rapid hastening of homosexuals' acceptance in the large community and therefore the potential legitimacy of gay marriages and couple relationships not unlike the variety that heterosexuals experience. Barring unforeseen political repression on a wide scale, the clear trend is for validity of gay lifestyles' enhancement and legitimization; when or how soon this might come to include legal gay marriages is speculative.

OPEN MARRIAGES

There is overlap between open marriages and adultery, since SOM (sexually open marriages) may involve consensual adultery. In another respect, ROM (role open marriages) are becoming in some circles the ideal. The latter imply the flexibility that accompanies gender-free activities, both inside and outside of the home. Although very few marriages persist for long with open sexual arrangements, they do sometimes persist and thrive in some contexts. Those that do persist without a great deal of support from networks of persons of similar persuasion are likely a very small number. For most, if interests in open sexuality persist beyond some experimentation phase, they will most likely turn to one of several adaptations: Nonsexual (or sexually clandestine) friendship in an intimate network, swinging, or a kind of adaptation fostered by the Kerista communities, in which several persons form a kind of group-marriage household. Marriages characterized by the SOM adaptation are likely to remain small in number, since it appears to take a pair of highly individualistic persons to make for the easing of strains of such complexity and potential feelings of being left out of many activities (Whitehurst, 1977: 323). Marriages that have elements of ROM, however, are likely to expand; whether or not this ultimately leads to the more open choice of more SOM potential is speculative.

MULTIPLE MARRIAGE

If we mean by multiple marriage the simultaneous bonding of two or more partners with one or more others, then the concept is not at all valid in our context of socialization system today. The relatively low level of familism (putting the group first, not the self) makes for a low probability of success in group or communal ventures in marriage. This may be why religious communities more often succeed where more secular organizations fail, since they are sometimes able to call forth loyalty to a higher power or more noble motives that supersede one's personal desires. Groups that stress doing your own thing and personal satisfaction are usually of short duration in terms of stability of membership. Depending on the exact definition of multiple marriage, we cannot expect this form to be visible on the scene in the foreseeable future.

SWINGING

This form of recreational (and generally uncommitted) sex involves consensus and a relatively high degree of solidarity between the partners as to goals and values. With high-volume turnover in marriages and divorces, it is possible that people with more similar values, such as swinging, may more likely find each other the second time around and be able to make swinging a slightly more long-term adaptation in their lives.

Swinging by its nature tends to have a short half-life. By this I mean that the male's fantasy of a candy-store freedom to grab all the sex one can from anyone nearby is rapidly replaced by a more discriminatory approach to such casual sex. Male appetites are notorious for being large in prospect but small in retrospect (wanting lots before the fact but becoming sated more easily than one had imagined). Thus, where women are more reluctant to begin swinging, men are more reluctant to continue such behavior. Fear of diseases also gives pause to many who otherwise might feel more free to participate.

The commercialization of swinging in the past decade has made for a mixed scene: some people like it because of the convenience, selectivity, and ease of access to parties and conventions. There are elements of festivals, Halloween, and other ritual escapes that make them popular. To others, it is too depersonalized, commercialized and—in short—Americanized. Those desiring discretion, friendship, and longevity of relations may try such swinging conventions but then revert to more informal networks of low-key activity.

In short, hothouse sex is seen as basically undesirable by many. The fact that these organizations have prospered in the recent past attests to something of the demand for them. One Midwest Organization regularly turns out 400 to 600 persons for weekends on occasion. Whatever its growth or decline, swinging likely attests to the advance of a pluralistic acceptance of variety in lifestyle.

SUMMARY, IMPLICATIONS, AND CONCLUSION

The concept of "valid" as used to describe various relationship forms has been relativized and used in terms of social acceptance and longevity of form. Since no statistical base is available that would empirically verify the numbers of persons practicing each form, we are left with estimates and are free to interpret what each might mean for life today and tomorrow. Depending on definition and context, we might well come to the conclusion that monogamous marriage is no longer the only way to practice an adult relationship style. Although monogamy is not the only form, it is still the most accepted, most visible, and simplest lifestyle. But many persons opt for complexity and novelty, not simplicity or tradition. These are likely to be found practicing a variety of other ways of being sexual and of carrying on relationships.

Some rationales were provided to suggest that our budding pluralism will support many lifestyles now and in the future; barring radical political and economic changes, current trends will likely be continued, ensuring some variety, but not the phasing out of the most popular forms of today. Some of the trends noted involve the increased use of clear contracts, networks, and commercialism (Whitehurst, 1984). The tendency to prepackage and commercialize many aspects of life may be accompanied by further development of more highly specialized networks, which will serve to make for easier access to and sustenance of variety lifestyles.

The dominant nature of the idea of monogamous lifetime commitment in traditional marriage is not likely to fade, even though it may increasingly become at least partly invalidated by more frequent violations. This may not keep people in such a position from holding it forth as an ideal simply on sentimental and symbolic grounds. The need for nostalgic ties remains strong and "monogamy" may coexist with more modern needs for self-expression, legitimized by a more immediately hedonistic society.

REFERENCES

CARGAN, L., R. N. WHITEHURST, and G. R. FRISCH (1984) "Social life and happiness: the differences among singles." Presented at the Popular Culture Association Annual Meeting, Toronto, Ontario, March 29.

EICHLER, M. (1983) Families in Canada Today. Agincourt, Ontario: Gage.

ELLIS, A. (1972) The Civilized Couple's Guide to Extramarital Adventure. New York: Peter Wyden.

HUNT, M. (1969) The Affair. New York: World.

MACKLIN, E. D. (1983) "Non-marital heterosexual cohabitation: an overview," pp. 49-76 in E. D. Macklin and R. H. Rubin (eds.) Contemporary Families and Alternative Lifestyles. Beverly Hills, CA: Sage.

WHITEHURST, R. N. (1984) "Alternatives to legal marriage and the nuclear family," in M. Baker (eds.) The Family: Changing Trends in Canada. Scarborough, Ontario: McGraw-Hill Ryerson.

———(1977) "Changing ground rules and emergent lifestyles," pp. 319-334 in R. W. Libby and R. N. Whitehurst (eds.) Marriage and Alternatives: Exploring Intimate Relationships. Glenview, IL: Scott, Foresman.

———and G. V. BOOTH (1980) The Sexes: Changing Relationships in a Pluralistic Society. Agincourt, Ontario: Gage.

The Model for Marriage Contracts Is Found in the Bible

VIRGINIA A. HEFFERNAN

Although Jews and Christians draw from the same well on the subject of marriage, namely, the book of Genesis, the interpretation of the biblical model of marriage expressed herein will be a Roman Catholic interpretation, as befits my own background. Scriptural citations are from the *Jerusalem Bible*.

SPECIFIC SCRIPTURE TEACHING

Two of the marriage passages from Genesis that are the beginning point for an understanding of Christian marriage are Genesis 1:27: "God created man in the image of himself, in the image of God he created them"; and in the second story of creation Genesis 2:23-24: "This at last is bone from my bones and flesh from my flesh! This is to be called woman for this was taken from man. This is why a man leaves his father and mother and joins himself to his wife, and they become one body."

Pope John Paul II (1981) discusses this passage as follows:

The text of Genesis 2:24 defines this character of the conjugal bond with reference to the first man and the first woman, but at the same time, it does so also in the perspective of the whole earthly future of man. . . . Formed in the image of God, also inasmuch as they form a true communion of persons, the first man and the first woman must constitute the beginning and the model of that communion for all men and women, who, in any period, are united so intimately as to be "one flesh."

The body, which through its own masculinity or femininity right from the beginning helps both to find themselves in communion of persons, becomes, in a particular way, the constituent element of their union, when they become husband and wife. This takes place, however, through a mutual choice. It is choice that establishes the conjugal pact between persons, who become "one flesh" only on this basis . . . when they both unite so closely as to become "one flesh" their conjugal union presupposes a mature consciousness of the body.

The marriage theme in Hosea links the Genesis passages with the New Testament passages. To summarize, Gomer, Hosea's wife, became an adulteress and ran off with her lovers. Hosea continued to love her and desire her return, even bringing her back in hopes of reconciliation. This story is a prophetic model of God's love for his people, so often unfaithful, and the insight works its way into the teaching of the Church as the bride of Christ (Peifer, 1982). The themes of people (Israel) and God constantly interweave with the personal model of marriage and cannot be separated without misunderstanding.

In the Gospels, Jesus repeats the traditions on marriage found in Genesis. For example, Matthew 19:3-6:

Some Pharisees approached him, and to test him they said, "Is it against the Law for a man to divorce his wife on any pretext whatsoever?" He answered, "Have you not read that the creator from the beginning made them male and female and that he said: This is why a man must leave father and mother and cling to his wife and the two become one body? They are no longer two, therefore, but one body. So then, what God has united man must not divide."

There are a number of passages in the Pauline letters that refer to marriage. One commonly used for weddings is Ephesians 5:21-31:

Give way to one another in obedience to Christ. Wives should regard their husbands as they regard the Lord, since as Christ is head of the Church and saves the whole body, so is a husband the head of his wife, and as the Church submits to Christ, so should wives to their husbands, in everything. Husbands should love their wives just as Christ loves the Church and sacrificed himself for her to make her holy—husbands must love their wives as they love their own bodies; for a man to love his wife is for him to love himself. A man never hates his own body, but he feeds it and looks after it; that is the way Christ treats the Church.

Please note that the directions to the husband are similar to Hosea's love of Gomer.

AN EXEGESIS FOR TODAY'S MARRIAGE

Having quoted some passages from the Bible to give the context to the main portion of the article, I shall proceed to analyze their meaning in the contemporary Western world. Where appropriate I will draw upon my own marital experience as data.

We have begun, in Catholic circles, to speak of marriage as covenant rather than as contract. Marriage as covenant is about making an irrevocable choice. The root meaning of covenant is to trust another and to entrust oneself wholly to the other. To marry then is to say, Here is my future, I trust you with it.

In the Old Testament passages, reference was made to the totality of the marriage commitment. The Old Testament itself is the slow unfolding of God's love, which creates His people. When Scripture says God spoke to Abraham or Moses or to the prophets, it has Him speaking in terms of His love and His commitment to be their God and to form them into His people. Scholars have labeled this relationship a covenant in which God freely and unconditionally committed Himself faithfully to love the people He made His own. The institution of marriage was frequently cited by the prophets as the visible sign and model of the covenant love with which God embraced His spouse Israel.

In the New Testament we find the themes repeated again—the marriage relationship and its presence in the Covenant.

What do all these words mean in terms of the lived reality of marriage? First of all, marriage is a call to intimacy, not only the intimacy of a total giving in sexual intercourse, but the intimacy of self-revelation. To tell each other of thoughts and feelings, of yearnings and worries, of joys and sorrows is to become naked before each other.

Today even the devout Christian woman looks warily at the commandment to obey or submit to her husband which appears in several of the Pauline letters. Many women will not permit these passages to be read at their weddings.

Several Catholic women sat in my living room recently and wrestled with the concept as it is lived in their own lives. The word "obey," the concept of servile submissiveness, was abhorrent to them. It becomes necessary to go beyond this to the mutuality of directive that appears in the Pauline remarks. It becomes then a mutual obedience in the Lord, a concern to come toward and yield to each other. There is an awareness that the woman who knows the right moment to yield may reap a greater harvest than the one who never stops naying. The word "obey" is drawn from a root word meaning to be attuned to. None of us was arguing against "obey" in that sense.

The Roman Catholic Church does not use a literal approach in her understanding of scripture. We are pressed to view scripture seriously but to seek to nuance the material in a way appropriate to contemporary life without losing the central meaning. The Word is a living word, which speaks to all time. The process described above took place in a scripture sharing group, a common lay activity in the post-Vatican II church.

It was popular at one time to say that marriage was a 50-50 proposition. The implication in that statement is that if one partner does not give his or her share, the contract is null and void. With a covenant, the partners are committed to give 100-100 to marriage. There is a gift of self, no holding back, no waiting for the other to come forward. The movement forward, toward the other, is implicit in the nature of sacramental marriage.

In concrete terms, this means that even if there is no specific resolution to a conflict, we are still open to the other, we continue to show affection, and we continue to work for compromise. Even in secular terms, research validates that partners in successful marriages are those who learn the art of compromise. Clinging rigidly to my ways and my wants is the antithesis of unity either in secular or sacred terms.

A Christian lifestyle calls for "dying of self." This phrase may well conjure up visions of self-negation and frighten someone raised in the era of "me first." Scripture compares this dying to that of a seed that dies that the plant may grow. The seed does not really die; it is transformed into the plant. Neither does the person die as he or she becomes transformed in the vocation of husband and wife. Joseph Martos (1981) has written that the transformation begins with the wedding: "They are being transformed, and they are going to be transformed even further. The wedding is a door through which they enter into that sacred transformation."

This marriage model then is a death to the me-first attitude. I retain myself as I express who I am to my partner, in dialogue and in deed, but I become more than self as I incorporate my spouse's being into my own.

Sexuality comes to its full meaning within the dynamics of marriage. The sexual component bears a special task in the irrevocable community of a man and a woman. The force that draws a man and a woman together to form this community possesses a special creative charge. This creativity is expressed not only in children but in the love that continues to nurture the relationship. The genital unity reflects what we are in other dimensions of our relationship. That is, there is a linking in and building element rather than competitiveness about the way we live our married life.

The man and woman who believe they have made an irrevocable covenant in partnership with the Lord seek to move in the direction of unity. Nowhere is this more true than in reconciliation. Reconciliation is far more than conflict resolution and goes far beyond the elements that might be present in a contractual marriage.

Reconciliation has a primary value in the Christian scheme. Scripture reminds us that we have no right to go unto the altar of God as long as our brother (or sister or spouse) has something against us. We are thus motivated not only to say we are sorry but to ask our loved one to forgive us, even as we ask God to forgive us. In our turn, we must forgive the other for what he or she has done against us even if he or she does not express remorse or has made no request for forgiveness. This facet is one of the most difficult aspects of living a Christian life, but it is probably one of the most essential qualities of the irrevocable covenant.

Forgiving in this manner is not being a doormat, but it does mean not harboring grievances or seeking to retaliate for presumed offenses. It means to continue to will the good of the other, to continue to act benevolently toward him or her, to pray for the other, and to presume in Christian hope that God's grace continues to operate in the other. Christian marriage is a calling that is part of the whole Christian lifestyle.

Life begins with a man and a woman. It does not begin with a baby. The basic nuclear unit, one man and one woman, is the beginning of family, the beginning of community, the beginning of a faith community. In a very real sense, all of human life depends upon what goes on between a man and a woman.

Research continues to reveal that the marriages of believers are more stable than the marriages of nonbelievers. It runs across the board and it does not seem to matter which faith community; it is the condition of believers who are part of a faith community that is significant (Dominion, 1982).

The need has increased to stress the unfolding process of healing and sustaining love in a framework of permanency. The newly married couple, often living far from relatives, need other couples to sustain them. Such couples are apt to be found within the faith community, sometimes as part of groups like Marriage Encounter or on an informal one couple to one couple basis. My husband and I have been a part of such groups for almost all of our marriage of thirty years. Where once we received encouragement from older couples, we are now the givers of it. We witness in our life together the reality of lived promises once made.

This article is being written for a secular audience, but I feel compelled to use some of the terminology peculiar to Christians, which does not translate readily into secular terminology or understanding.

One of the major Christian beliefs is that grace from God has become especially operative through Christ. All of the Christian sacraments are considered means of grace, as well as prayer. Grace is the power given by God to live by His teachings and draw closer to

Him. In other words, the Christian does not do, nor expect to do, what has been described here, under his or her own power.

An axiom of this teaching is that grace builds on grace. As the couple lives out a Christian life, the grace will come to ever greater fulfillment. Therefore, the couple is a real and effective sign of God's love.

The Catholic church calls the family the "domestic church."

It is the place in the Church where life is conceived, nourished, and loved. The domestic church is the school of love for the whole church— Without the domestic church there can be no Church, for it is within it that love, which is the nature of God, is kept alive and this is the reason why marriage is of such importance [Dominion, 1982].

Such a home provides a root place for its children. Children are raised with the same kind of limitless love God calls forth from each other. We teach, we forgive, we persevere, and we never stop caring no matter how much we are tried.

As Dr. Dominion (1982) expresses it,

Parents have a unique opportunity to make their children feel lovable. . . . They need to feel they are loved not for what they have done or achieved but because they exist. This acceptance of self and others, because they are and not because of what they are worth to us, is a necessary prelude to treating people as persons and not as objects. Love belongs to personhood and much of the yearning in contemporary marriage is to be treated as a person.

Hospitality is the mark of the fully Christian home. This is a hospitality to others who are in need of loving care whether relative or stranger. Some of us remember that the Gospel tells us the person in need is really Christ on our doorstep.

The domestic Church is a sign to our neighborhood, to our places of work of this presence. This is not an option for those of us who claim to believe. Whether we consciously choose it or not, we are a sign. Our children are living evidence of our two-in-one flesh, the love we share. Our children carry the marks of the home out to their friends, the neighbors, and the schools.

There is no hope save in limitless love. We are among those who believe the Lord will give us whatsoever grace we need for this love. I close with a passage from I John that reminds us how we are to love:

This has taught us love—
that he gave up his life for us;
as we, too, ought to give up our lives for our brothers.
If a man who was rich enough in this world's goods
saw that one of his brothers was in need,
but closed his heart to him,
how could the love of God be living in him?
My children,
Our love is not to be just words or mere talk,
but something real and active;
only by this can we be certain
that we are children of the truth.

[I John, 3:16-19]

REFERENCES

DOMINION, J. (1982) Marriage, Faith and Love. New York: Crossroad.
GILBERT, M. (1978) "One only flesh." Theology Digest 26: 3.
Jerusalem Bible (1968) Garden City, NY: Doubleday.
JOHN PAUL II (1981) Original Unity of Man and Woman. Boston: Daughters of St. Paul.
MARTOS, J. (1981) Doors to the Sacred. Garden City, NY: Doubleday.
MULLER, E. (1977) "Husband-wife relationship in St. Paul." Catholic Charismatic 2 (April-May).
PEIFER, C. (1982) "The marriage theme in Hosea." The Bible Today 20 (May).
PILCH, J. (1979) "Marriage in the Lord." The Bible Today 17 (April).

MARRIAGE CONTRACTS

Each Couple Should Develop a Marriage Contract Suitable to Themselves

KRIS JETER
MARVIN B. SUSSMAN

The personal marriage contract is an agreement entered into by individuals for the formation of a new family unit. The personal marriage contract is deeply rooted in tradition, being as old as recorded history. Today the personal marriage contract bears the potential for couples to form equitable dyadic relationships and for governments to legislate new marriage laws in which the state is less involved as a third party representing the "public interest" in what is otherwise a private transaction. All marriages involve a contract, albeit one with many hidden provisions that are unknown to the partners until the marriage sours and one or more of the parties seeks redress for presumed wrongful behavior.

In this chapter we plan to describe briefly some historic usage of contracts, contract provisions, the significance of contracts in equitable dyadic relationships, potential consequences for future marriage and cohabitation, and influence on today's marriage law. Then we will examine modern-day personal marriage contracts, their genesis in the gender revolution and counterculture ideology and practice, and as a consequence of general and widespread usage of contract relationships in various life sectors.

HISTORY OF THE
PERSONAL MARRIAGE CONTRACT

Powerful concerns for individual and societal survival over generational time account for the historical precedence of the personal marriage contract. The precedence of the marriage contract of Judeo-Christian heritage has been interwoven into American judicial decisions that still influence the nature and practice of marriage.

The ancient orthodox Jewish marriage contract, or Ketuba, testified to the legitimacy of the marital relation under Talmudic law. The Ketuba functioned as a memorandum of guarantees, mostly economic, and set forth obligations of husband and wife to one another. It was signed by the groom and two witnesses and kept by the bride, since it represented his legal obligation to her in marriage or in divorce.

The Ketuba established Judeo-Christian bases of traditional marriage, whose tenets—the husband is head of the family and responsible for its support while the wife is responsible for domestic and child-care services (Weitzman, 1974)—have permeated the laws and traditions of most complex societies. The Ketuba negotiated a trade-off of support and protection provided by the male for dependency and compliance by the wife. In terms of contemporary models of dyadic relationships, this can be classified as being a superordinate-subordinate association with the male in control and with heavy responsibilities and commitments to support his family while the female assumes the major tasks of running the household and parenting.

An archive in Dubrovnik, Yugoslavia, contains a complete set of Pacta Matrimonealis in chronological order from 1400 to 1808.[1] The series includes contracts of all individuals who agree to marry. The contract was generally a page in length and written in Latin. It specified information on the parents or legal guardians; binding provisions on the dowry and terms of payment; the exact place, date, and time of consummation of marriage; and social class and place of residence of the bride and groom. There is evidence of asymmetry of dyadic relationships in the contracted marriages, with differentiated roles more binding in the higher social classes.

Such sex differentiation in marriage was subsequently adopted by the ecclesiastical courts in their promulgation of churchly laws of marriage and divorce. The church during its period of ascendence and glory sanctified marriage and made it a once and forever proposition; as late as 1876 passionate debates were still in vogue as to whether marriage was a status or a contract. One author in a marriage as a status plea cited God, Justinian, Gregory VII, the Council of Trent, and Thomas Aquinas as supporters (Fraser, 1876).

American jurists were undoubtedly influenced by these exhortations, because in 1888 the Supreme Court handed down a landmark decision on the nature of marriage that still affects marriage and family practice today.

> It is also to be observed that, whilst marriage is often termed by text writers and in decision of courts a civil contract—generally to indicate that it must be founded upon the agreement of the parties, and does not require religious ceremony for its solemnization—it is something more than a contract. The consent of the parties is of course essential to its existence, but when the contract to marry is executed by the marriage, *a relation between the parties is created which they cannot change.* Other contracts may be modified, restricted, or enlarged, or entirely released upon the consent of the parties. *Not so* with marriage. The relation once formed, the law steps in and holds the parties to various obligations and liabilities. It is an institution in the maintenance of which in its purity the public is deeply interested, for it is the foundation of the family and of society, without which there would be neither civilization nor progress [Maynard vs. Hill, 1888].

Thus stated is the state's vital interest in maintaining the marriage by forbidding dissolution without its consent. A less expressed reason under the rubric of "interests of public policy" was the potential burden to the state to support children and women of marriages terminated at the will of the parties.

Since 1888 and in the period since 1930 and as recently as 1975 in the United States there have been a number of important court decisions that have deviated from the immutability of the marriage contract norm. Specific changes have occurred in antenuptial agreements concerning waiver of dower (Seuss v. Schukat, 1934) and alimony provisions (Florida Supreme Court: 257 So. 2nd 530, 1972). Also, in light of recent court decisions regarding privacy and the right of association, it is unlikely that the state can constitutionally refuse to recognize a component of a marriage contract that provides that parties shall not have children, comarital relationships, or agreements for termination of a marriage after a set period of time unless there is a mutual agreement on renewal (Fleishmann, 1974).

From a comparative perspective these shifts in the United States from the notion of marriage as an inscrutable institution with a compelling state interest to preserve its traditional form have consequences for legal change in other societies. It is not that the United States has extensive influence on the legal systems of other societies, but international associations of lawyers, similar to scientists, have a highly integrated communication system, and the rapid changes in marriage and divorce laws in the United States catalyzed by the gender-role revolution and counterculture ideology and experimentation can have reciprocal influences on societies elsewhere.

PERSONAL MARRIAGE CONTRACTS

The gender-role revolution and the counterculture movement have been powerful catalysts for intensifying public awareness in the sixties and seventies of the diverse social inequities that have been fostered by system and custom. The thrust toward social equality that generated the civil rights and sex-role liberation movements has also engendered the insistence by many couples on deciding the terms by which they are willing to be bound.

Social historians, marriage counselors, and observers of the academic scene testify to the increasing incidence of either written contracts or a contractual approach to married and unmarried relationships. The majority of these stipulate new rules and roles for men, women, and children in an attempt to legitimize a more equalitarian system of relationships. One contractee has written,

"Certainly, while one of our motives was an equalization of existing state laws, another . . . was to publicize the inequities of those laws at the present time."

At another level, contracts may be regarded as the product of an interpersonal process between individuals who are together identifying and working out personal problems and issues; another contractee told us, "Part of the reason for thinking out a contract is to find out what your problems are; it forces you to take charge of your life. Once you have the contract, you don't have to refer back to it. The process is what's important." At this level, the contract functions as a moral or ethical basis for a relationship in terms of reciprocal expectations and responses to expectations.

Some contracts attempt a prenuptial property agreement only, a likely occurrence in remarriage. These contracts on waiver of dower, sometimes called "death" agreements, are legally binding. Some contracts deal almost exclusively with domestic and interpersonal relationships, defining marital expectations very generally; still others set forth specific obligations and tasks, especially household ones. Specification of duties is likely to occur in families where both partners are gainfully employed. The majority of contracts combine both economic and dyadic relationship provisions even though it is still unlikely that the interpersonal provisions will have any legally binding effect.

The objectives of the partners—what purpose is the agreement to serve—influence the particular entry of provision, and the detailing of each one. Is the objective simply to provide ground rules for parity decision making generally or to effect decision making in each area—such as parenting, jobs, and expenditures of funds—using a model of specified obligations, tasks, and responsibilities? Is the intent to provide suggestions for meeting marital expectations or actual instructions on how to behave in dyadic relationships? Finally, is it a long-range plan subject to periodic review, or is it a day-to-day cookbook on how to live in a marital or cohabiting relationship without even trying?

OUTLINE FOR MARRIAGE CONTRACTS

(1) *Process*: Persons planning to wed often feel the great pull of attraction and the ecstasy of a new love; a field ripe for the growth of unchallenged assumptions. The act of the contracting process pro-

vides an opportunity for each person to communicate and negotiate. Before and after each negotiating session the couple may wish to quietly focus inward.

(a) *Centering*: It is recommended that each person sit in a balanced position directly across from the other. Each may breath deeply, behold the other's eyes, and attune to each other by either holding hands or placing the right hand on the heart and the left hand on the partner's right hand.

(b) *Communication*: It is preferable for each to use "I sense," "I think," and "I want" language rather than "you are" language, thus taking responsibility for personal behavior. Awareness of the communication process is important; repeated defensiveness and dependent statements may be indicative of a relationship that could be more mature. Throughout the negotiation sessions each person will want to be aware of any changes in body tension, breath, and eye contact.

(2) *Relevant history:* Each partner will want to relate the history that could have a possible effect on the intended union. Past marriages and the existence of children could affect the legality of a marriage if untold. The health history of the intended and the intended's family is important, especially for couples desiring to procreate.

(3) *Economic provisions*: Over 95 percent of contracts contain economic provisions.

(a) *Assets held prior to marriage*: The contractors may opt to continue to separately hold and manage assets acquired before marriage. Other contractors may opt to merge and jointly manage such assets to give each partner an equal start.

(b) *Property, debts, and living expenses after marriage*: Partners may wish to reject the concept that superior earning power should not increase the burden on the lesser earner. Couples choosing to adopt the practice of keeping resources separate contributing to expenses in amount proportional to income will place neither partner in the dependent position of begging economic favors.

(4) *Name*: The name bespeaks identity. Each partner may wish to retain her or his own birth name. Such a partner would not suffer loss of identity, confusion of professional record and reputation, or embarrassment of bearing the name of an exhusband. Partners may wish to choose a joint or new name consciously.

(5) *Legal domicile*: It is currently presumed that the husband's domicile could be decided jointly. Individuals (such as those in commuting dual-career couples) could choose to maintain separate domiciles.

(6) *Career*: Individuals could agree to attach equal importance to the careers of the wife and the husband. Subprovisions arising from this would concern prospective choice making regarding career opportuni-

ties in other geographical locations. The partners could indicate their preference for and not for joining in career-social obligations that could enhance a career—for instance, the image of the corporate spouse. The role of homemaker would be deemed to be as valuable as outside employment.

(7) *Relationships with others*: Partners may wish to contract guidelines regarding their relationships with others. These may be general relationships, sexual relationships, and relationships with the spouse and other relatives from a previous marriage.

   (a) *General relationships*: The partners may wish to address their preference to present or not to present an inseparable couple front at social functions. Partners may want to affirm the extent and time commitments that each may spend with others, so that individual needs are fulfilled and potential capacities are developed.

   (b) *Sexual relationships:* Some marital partners may want the security and exclusive commitment of sexual monogamy, specifying in the contract penalties to be imposed for failure to live up to the agreement. Other marital partners may indicate that sexual access be subject to the consent of individual participants, thus eliminating the current doctrine that a husband cannot rape his wife. The contracting couple may choose to permit sexual relationships, specifying boundaries, time commitment, and communications.

   (c) *Relationships with spouse and relatives of previous marriage*: Separation or divorce does change day-to-day relationships; however, kin is always kin, and children especially always need parents. The limits of such relationships are established depending on whether or not there are children from the former marriage; the level of hostility or affection experienced during the divorce process; the general conditions of the separation; and quality of ties with kin, especially in-laws. The contracting couple may specify the length of time periods that children of a previous marriage may live with them so that there is less interference in the development of the new dyadic relationship.

(8) *Children*: The contracting couple first indicates a preference to bring or not to bring children into the union. With the choice to bear children, other contract options may be considered.

   (a) Partners may anticipate having children only as a result of mutual and deliberate agreement. Responsibility for birth control will be shared or mutually assigned; abortion at the woman's discretion is occasionally stipulated in case of accidental pregnancy.

   (b) Responsibility for parenting may be outlined with attention to general guidelines for child rearing and social control (discipline) to specific responsibilities. The type of religious training as well as type of education (parochial, state, or private) may be specified.

(c) Contracting parties may elect to indicate that support for the children will be provided in the same proportion to the earnings, even after divorce, irrespective of custody. Other rules for determining support payments, division of assets, and payment of alimony or its waiver could be set.

(d) Provisions for support of the children and a partner when death of a provider occurred: life insurance beneficiaries could be designated.

(9) *Ritual:* The intending partners will want to reflect on and indicate the significance of ritual to their individual lives and to their relationship. The observation of ritual or rites of passage stimulates naturally occurring "highs" in the celebrants. It reunites the couple across the fabric of seasons with past and future generations of families.

(10) *Renewability and change of contract:* Partners may plan a periodic evaluation of the partnership or of any specific issue to be initiated by either partner. The other partner is expected to cooperate. In case of unresolved conflicts, partners may agree to accept arbitration by an objective third party. The contract may hold for a limited time (for example, until birth of the first child) to acknowledge the fluid, changing, "living contract."

(11) *Provisions affecting termination:* The partnership may be terminated by mutual consent, desire of either partner, or breach of a substantial provision. If one partner supports the other through school and the marriage then terminates, the receiving partner is obligated to reimburse the first one for the educational expense. Should one partner have agreed to forgo further education and career opportunities and stay home and care for children and the household, a lump sum for compensation for loss of earning ability for the sake of the marriage could be negotiated.

SUMMARY AND ANALYSIS

The act of developing such a contract is a socialization process. Participants are forced to examine themselves—their quirks and sensitivities—and whether their hangups in relation to prerequisites (often mundane routines) of day-to-day living may spoil a beautiful relationship. This process of negative assessment (realistic evaluation) to reach a positive or negative decision is a trying experience often fraught with self-doubt and feelings of inadequacy. Yet it can be a critical learning situation, one that partially answers "Who am I?"

even with a negative outcome—not to attempt a marriage and the subsequent emotional and legal problems of becoming disentangled.

The time of preparatory work for the personal contract may be the equivalent of the traditional engagement and the actual steps prior to signing a throwback to the arranged marriage, with one major difference. In the personal contract, the parties themselves rather than parents or emissaries "arrange" the marriage. They are actually exploring and experiencing with one another the possibilities of a long-term arrangement.

Contracts are not worth the paper they are printed on unless there is trust, commitment, and a developing flexibility in role relationships. Strict check-off of "minor" provisions, such as "You do the laundry on Tuesday, Thursday, Saturday while I take out the trash," may precipitate more conflict than gender-role change in the direction of equality in the relationship. Contracts may start out with such provisions, but if they do, at some time a value and role shift must occur in the direction of mutual support and exchange. This is exemplified by internalization of behaviors related to the marital role expectations as stated in the written contract. The success of a contract is noted when the contractees no longer refer to the specific provisions. This notion can be viewed as a hypothesis, and its standing as a viable one will result from analysis of how contracts are implemented, renegotiated, and internalized.

The development of a workable contract is no easy task and, while we have no incidence of prevalence figures, the impression is that an increasing number of people of all ages are viewing this procedure as requisite to the formulation or continuation of a marriage-like relationship. If this pattern persists and increases in incidence, and we suspect this will be the case, it will become the first major development in marriage law in modern times to come from the people (clients) themselves. In time, jurists and legislators will take heed and co-opt those contractual elements viewed as new mores of the people.

NOTE

1. Zdravko Sundrica, a Dybrovnik archivist, made documents available and assisted in translation from Latin to English.

REFERENCES

FELDSTEIN, D. (1974) Personal communication, February 11.

FLEISCHMANN, K. (1974) "Marriage by contract: defining the terms of relationships." Family Law Quarterly (Spring): 27-49.

FRASER, W. (1876) "Is marriage a contract?" J. Juris. 20.

Maynard v. Hill (1888) 125 U.S. 190

Seuss v. Schukat (1934) 358 111.27, 34, 192 N.E. 668, 671

WEITZMAN, L. J. (1974) "Legal regulation of marriage: tradition and change." California Law Review 62, 4: 1169-1288.

Homosexual Marriage and Parenthood Should Not Be Allowed

TERESA DONATI MARCIANO

Literature is filled with stories of forbidden love and thwarted marriages, Romeo and Juliet tragedies that apply also to same-sex partners. These show only futility in so-called logical or objective arguments that attempt to suppress unacceptable affection between adults. Moral principles are often so inhumane in their application that they become themselves immoral in their ruthlessness.

I will say directly that any argument concerning moral behavior is subjective. What we call objectivity is simply a cultural definition of the objective. The final premise of a moral argument is always one that people agree to treat as the final one. Where there is disagreement, as with gay love or abortion, the high emotionalism of public argument betrays the claim for objectivity. It is only a political agreement to disagree, a support for pluralism in belief, that keeps subjective moral principles from becoming a basis for civil war. Even with this, however, the rights of dissenters in pluralism are always in danger of being ignored or suppressed.

This chapter addresses public arguments against gay marriage and parenthood, although my research and beliefs are at odds with such arguments against gay people. The academic and libertarian communities must, however, pay attention to those who attack gays lest their arguments go unnoticed, the flaws in their reasoning remain uncorrected, and lest their effects include the power to suppress diversity and dissent. That is why I have written this chapter.

The major public arguments against gay marriage flow into each other, from the model of nature, to biology, to religion, to social control, to family role models for sexual identity and the protection of children.

(1) The argument from nature is that homosexuality is unnatural and therefore intrinsically disordered. It is deviant because it is out of harmony with the purpose of male-female psychological and phys-iological differences. Marriage based on same-sex pairings com-pounds that disharmony. The complementarity of the two sexes for intercourse, reproduction, and mutual support sets the model for proper behavior toward one's own and the opposite sex. Gay marriage makes a mockery of natural bonds, where two sexes procreate and, among selected species, stay together for life.

This argument assumes that sexual dimorphism exists for repro-ductive purposes above all; it subordinates the emotional ties and drives of sexuality to potential pregnancies. It is the old love-is-for-procreation argument that has already been rejected by heterosexual couples, who have made ours a contraceptive age. For those as for all marriages, love is not about children but about itself, valued for its capacity to enhance those who are drawn to each other. Nor is the psychological balance within a loving pair dependent on biological sex. Psychologically healthy individuals have different components of masculine and feminine attributes, culturally defined and labeled but not naturally preordained in any quantity in either sex. Some people, hetero- or homosexual, are so balanced in those attributes as to be androgynous, that is, not fixed in one set of traits, but free to respond more adaptively to others and to the environment (Bem, 1977).

The more basic problem with the argument from nature is that nature has no single set of meanings. What nature is depends on the person making the argument and not on an objectively verifiable truth. The futility of natural arguments must evidently be rediscovered in each generation: John Stuart Mill's essay, "Nature," first published in 1874, could have repudiated for all time the argument that nature is the source of morality (Mill, 1969). He pointed out that if nature is a proper model to imitate, we would kill without remorse. Instead, we do some but not all the things nature does. What we call justice and benevolence are products of resisting the model of an amoral nature.

Applications of the natural model to gay life are extensively discussed by Boswell (1980: 11-16 and *passim*), who shows how culture-bound are ideas of nature. For example, if the nonhuman animal world is the model for sexual pairings, same-sex intercourse would often be attempted by humans, as by animals. One sees that however nature is described, humans get lifted out of nature when their drives are considered: What animals do by nature, and therefore innocently, becomes in the human case sinful and unnatural. The natural, then, is a set of social definitions, and not a derived set of truths about human sexuality that arise from one infallible source.

(2) Biological arguments against gay marriage are the link between natural and religious arguments, for science is set in cultural values, and hypotheses are formed in terms of cultural understandings (see, e.g., Hubbard, 1981). There are two major yet somewhat contradictory arguments in biology regarding gay marriage: first, that there is no reproductive capacity, and it is therefore incomplete and will not survive. Quite aside from the fact of world hunger due to too much reproduction, this biological argument is spurious because gay people are not a species that will die out without children. Gay people exist in every generation, in every age, in just about every culture (though this last is a matter of incomplete and often biased record in the case of primitive cultures). Gay marriage, furthermore, may exist after prior heterosexual marriage and parenthood. Gay is not synonymous with sterile.

Second, there is the sociobiological view, which does not treat gay marriage specifically, but which does see gay people as part of kin networks, where gay kin are "helpers" who protect and provide for their siblings' children; because nieces and nephews carry some of our genes, the genetic survival of gay people lies not in marriage but in helping protect and feed their siblings' children. This simply adds a subordinate role to gay existence, since in our activist and autonomous-adult culture, the doer, not the helper, is the one receiving status rewards. The gay family member is a servant of the group, rather than a creator of its identity or a direct guarantor of its survival. Sociobiology is also caught by a Darwinian variation that Darwin himself drew away from (i.e., that all evolution is adaptive in that it promotes survival through the inheritance of beneficial genetic traits). In sociobiology, homosexuality is treated as a tendency that is genetic and heritable—never-proven and highly questionable assertions (Wilson, 1975, 1979; Ruse, 1978; Sociobiology Study Group, 1978).

The best answer to both arguments is provided by Werner's (1979) cross-cultural examination of male homosexuality. He shows that cultures in varying degrees support or repress homosexual behavior, that this behavior is culturally adaptive where population pressure taxes the resources of a group. In that sense, gay marriages would be adaptive for the group as a whole, permitting same-sex love to be expressed while conserving resources for the young produced in heterosexual pairs. It still does not, however, deal with the fact that in all cultures, gay people are also biological parents. Nor does it consider that Darwin's "fitness to survive" as a biological concern is not a central value for same-sex pairs who love each other and form marital bonds.

(3) Religious arguments against gay marriage in the West are based in Judeo-Christian scriptures (the Bible), which for Christians has Old and New Testament divisions. Judaism, the basis of Christianity (and Islam), maintains in orthodoxy a strict condemnation of gay behavior and, by derivation, gay marriage. First, gay marriage violates the commandment to "be fruitful and multiply." Second, gay men commit the sin of Onan, who was slain by God for spilling his seed on the ground rather than trying to impregnate his dead brother's wife, under the laws of levirate. Third, men are specifically enjoined against homosexuality in Leviticus (18:22): "You must not lie with a man as with a woman." God destroyed those who disobeyed divine moral precepts, first in the great flood, then in Sodom and Gomorrah. The term "sodomy" implies today the sin for which God destroyed that city. Finally, in Judaism, heterosexual marriage is both an obligation and a blessing, to be consummated between a man and a woman who live together and have children to continue the man's name in Israel.

In Christian scripture (the New Testament) Jesus made no specific injunction against homosexuality. His words about marriage, in the four gospels, were expansions of Jewish law, diminishing the legal emphasis and substituting emotional emphasis (i.e., love and inner feelings rather than written prescriptions for behavior). (Modern Christian orthodoxy is, however, as legalistic as orthodox Judaism; the translation of the gospels into rules of behavior is a central part of the history of the Christian churches.) The commandments of Jesus regarding marriage included fidelity of body and spirit to the spouse. But only husbands and wives, not same-sex pairs, were discussed by Jesus. After the gospels and Acts of the Apostles come the Epistles, which are letters explaining the faith, and written mostly by Paul. But there are also seven short letters by James, Peter, John, and Jude. In all of these, where homosexuality is mentioned at all, it is condemned as a pagan practice.

No place in the scriptures, then, alludes to any valid marriage except between women and men, and same-sex love, where mentioned, is declared un-Christian and sinful. The scriptures as the revealed Word of God and therefore the moral basis for Western culture, preclude gay marriage, and make gay practices of all types sinful.

Aside from the fact that important religious figures in Christianity (including great abbots and popes) have been gay (Boswell, 1980), even in Jewish scripture we see that David and Jonathan had a love for each other that was uncommonly deep. After Jonathan was slain in battle alongside his father, King Saul, David commemorated Jonathan in what is called "The Song of the Bow," where he says Jonathan's love was "more wonderful than the love of a woman" (2 Samuel 1:17-27).

In addition, there is no single interpretation of the scriptures, even among those who accept the Bible as inerrant, that is, as literally true. For example, God slew Onan after *many* occasions of coitus interruptus. Just as the Fall is interpreted as the sin of pride, where Adam and Eve wanted to be like God in eating from the Tree of Knowledge, so Onan's pride and selfishness in refusing to beget a child that would bear his brother's name can be interpreted as the reason for his death. It is the same with Sodom, whose sin in latter-day interpretations is not sodomy, but the sin of cruelty to strangers, inhospitality.

The injunctions of scripture are obeyed selectively: If Leviticus is to be obeyed completely, then all men would observe sexual abstinence from their wives during menstruation and for seven "clean" days afterward, no one would wear clothing that contained a mixture of linen and wool, and animals would be burned at altars for the atonement of sin. Rather, the sexual prescriptions and taboos of Jewish scripture show a nation beset by enemies, often wandering and/or at war, needing many children in order to survive.

With Christianity's dominance in the West, the selectivity of scriptures to attack gay love shows even more clearly the weakness of anti-gay religious arguments. Boswell (1980) demonstrates how religion was a convenient additional reason to suppress gay love, rather than the core of such reasons. Religious reasons served political and economic needs as historical changes occurred. Other cultural needs dictated the use of religious reasons against gay people.

That cultural embeddedness of religion is also seen directly in the Epistles: Paul, whose converts were mainly Greeks, declared the old (Jewish) Law abrogated, and a new covenant to be in force. Where he deals with sex at all, he recommends complete sexual abstinence, preferring no marriage to take place, but all living as eunuchs for God. James and Jude were especially active in converting Jews to Christianity in Jerusalem, the seat of Jewish life; their tone, and occasional injunctions about sexual purity, reflects the deeply felt Judaism of their own lives as well as of the Jewish setting. John and Peter also were primarily focused in Israel, and Peter did not support the negation of Jewish law that Paul declared, and that was eventually victorious. In the gospels themselves, however, not only are tolerance and forgiveness preached, not only love and feelings of the heart lauded, but the Law was used to challenge the hypocritical and selective sexual applications made by the people. Mary Magdalene, for example, was saved by Jesus from being stoned to death for adultery. In addition, the fourth gospel (John) is the only gospel written in the first person. There, John calls himself the "beloved disciple." From that special relationship with Jesus that John claimed, gay men have taken heart that the love of men for men was felt by Christ.

Finally, lesbian love, the bonding of women to each other in lifelong commitments, is absent from the scriptures. Leviticus enjoins women not to put on men's clothes, and the commandment to multiply applies to both sexes. Theoretically, if one had children *and* same-sex love between women, no law is violated.

The convenience of religious arguments rather than their unswerving application in all cases is shown by Christians in divorce:

Whereas Jesus never said gay love was wrong, he absolutely forbade divorce. Yet divorce proceeds apace, while gay love continues to be stigmatized as sinful.

(4) Social control arguments against gay life and marriage are illustrated by a passage from Rebecca West's biography of St. Augustine (1977: 174):

> Certainly he confesses to homosexual relationships in a sentence which . . . puts its finger on the real offence of homosexuality, by pointing out that it brings the confusion of passion into the domain where one ought to be able to practise calmly the art of friendship.

The boundedness of socially approved relationships is always challenged by passion, not only in homoerotic but also in heterosexual love. One need only substitute the term "adultery" for "homosexuality" in West's passage to see this. Confusion—the blurring of boundaries in socially prescribed behavior patterns—always threatens the ability of a society to control its members. Lehne (1976) showed that homophobia is above all a device whereby men control other men; and McIntosh (1968:183) shows that gay life (and marriage) violates the "clear-cut, publicized and recognizable threshold between permissible and impermissible behavior." Once people are defined as "deviant," furthermore, they can be segregated and contained (bounded), reaffirming for the rest of society its probity and righteousness.

Same-sex marriage has, however, served the purposes of some cultures, and though actual sexual contact may not be permitted, women have married women and men taken men as wives in other cultures (Oboler, 1980; Ford and Beach, 1951: 130-133). Where inheritance or the absorption of excess spouses is at issue, cultures have incorporated and legitimated the male wife and female husband. The cultural need and its response, rather than any objective definition of deviance, is the key to permissible same-sex marriage.

(5) Blurred sexual identity formation where children are reared by gay parents is the final argument discussed here. Gay parents are held to set confusing models for children, especially in critical early years; it is believed that children in gay-parent households are more likely to be gay than children raised in heterosexual settings, because gay seems normal. Children in gay households are more likely to be

seduced into gay lives or to be sexually molested by unscrupulous partners of gay parents. Children are therefore doubly penalized by living in deviant settings.

The first reply is that gay preference in adult love partners is completely different from the desire to have children, or parental love for them. If gayness were so unnatural in the biological sense, infertility would be a likely correlate of gay preference. Far from that, gay men and women number a significant proportion of people who have children from heterosexual marriages or planned nonmarital conceptions. Gay adult love does not cancel out the desire or love for children, the rewards of parenthood, or its responsibilities.

Sexual molestation, furthermore, is overwhelmingly a phenomenon of heterosexual men against children. The child molester is often a married man with children of his own. Even where an organization such as NAMBLA (National Man-Boy Love Association) exists, the idea of adult-child sexual love is overwhelmingly condemned by the vast majority of gay people of both sexes, who share the view that children are not the lawful or legitimate targets of adult sexual experience. Adults who happen to be gay are as ethical and child-protecting—if not more so, because they are so often denied the opportunity to nurture and enjoy the company of children—as heterosexuals. As gays fight their own victimization, they fight for others who are helpless, such as the children. Children are an allied cause, not a predatory goal, of gay struggles for dignity and recognition. The child-care settings where child molestation scandals exploded in New York City, and then throughout the country in 1984, show heterosexual men molesting children of both sexes; married men, who with their wives run such centers, have been shown to be molesters. Gay people are absent from the indictments.

Children who are raised in gay-parent single or paired households are no more likely to be gay than are children of heterosexual households. The honesty of gay parents, in fact, sets models for sexual honesty and integrity among the children. Indications are also strong that gay parents, knowing the pain and stigma still borne by gays who "come out," strongly support heterosexual preferences in their children. These parents, as most parents, would gladly spare their children any pain that they themselves have experienced. An excellent summary of these findings on gay parenthood and marriage is provided by Scanzoni and Scanzoni (1981: 235-261).

A person cannot be seduced into being gay. The absence of consistent same-sex and opposite-sex models does not produce gay children. Those in widow-headed households, children of divorce and desertion, do not have consistent models and there is little talk of their gay vulnerabilities. Ironically, troubled heterosexual marriages can produce greater sexual identity difficulties since the sexual roles of traditional marriages can be confused with spouse abuse, alcoholism, child beating, and incest. Heterosexual marriage is a troubled institution; to attack gay marriage by presenting a halcyon view of heterosexual marriages compounds a lie.

To say that gay marriages should not exist, then, is to accept a culturally bounded definition, not shared by the total society, and highly selective in finding reasons to condemn such unions. Gay bondings are the sociological equivalents of legal heterosexual marriages. The laws as they currently stand, however, as interpreted by state courts and the Supreme Court, hold a common law understanding of marriage as a bond that may legally be made only between two people of different sex. The law says same-sex marriage cannot be licensed, legally performed, or regarded as legally binding; nor can it give to the pair the legal rights of spouses (Scanzoni and Scanzoni, 1981: 241-246). Legislative change, not court challenges to current legislation, would seem to be the only legal way to undo the fact that the title of this chapter is the common legal reality.

REFERENCES

BEM, S. L. (1977) "Psychological androgyny," in A. G. Sargent (ed.) Beyond Sex Roles. St. Paul, MN: West.
BOSWELL, J. (1980) Christianity, Social Tolerance, and Homosexuality. Chicago: University of Chicago Press.
FORD, C. S. and F. A. BEACH (1951) Patterns of Sexual Behavior. New York: Harper & Row.
HUBBARD, R. (1981) "The emperor doesn't wear any clothes: the impact of feminism on biology," in D. Spender (ed.) Men's Studies Modified. New York: Pergamon.
LEHNE, G. K. (1976) "Homophobia among men," in D. David and R. Brannon (eds.) The Forty-Nine Percent Majority. Reading, MA: Addison-Wesley.
McINTOSH, M. (1968) "The homosexual role." Social Problems 16, 2: 182-192.
MILL, J. S. (1969) Three Essays on Religion. New York: Greenwood.
OBOLER, R. S. (1980) "Is the female husband a man? Woman/woman marriage among the Nandi of Kenya." Ethnology 19 (January): 69-88.
RUSE, M. (1978) "Sociobiology: a philosophical analysis," in A. L. Caplan (ed.) The Sociobiology Debate. New York: Harper & Row.

SCANZONI, L. D. and J. SCANZONI (1981) Men, Women, & Change. New York: McGraw-Hill.

Sociobiology Study Group of Science for the People (1978) "Sociobiology—another biological determinism," in A. L. Caplan (ed.) The Sociobiology Debate. New York: Harper & Row.

WERNER, D. (1979) "A cross-cultural perspective on theory and research on male homosexuality." Journal of Homosexuality 4, 4: 345-362.

WEST, R. (1977) "St. Augustine," in R. West, A Celebration. New York: Viking.

WILSON, E. O. (1979) On Human Nature. Cambridge, MA: Harvard University Press.

———(1975) Sociobiology: The New Synthesis. Cambridge, MA: Harvard University Press.

HOMOSEXUALITY AND THE FAMILY

Homosexuals Should Be Allowed to Marry and Adopt or Rear Children

ANDREA PARROT
MICHAEL J. ELLIS

This chapter will focus on discrimination against gay men and lesbian women. This form of discrimination is still considered acceptable by many. To remain focused on this issue we will not discuss other forms of human oppression. Other forms of discrimination deserve attention in other areas. Discrimination against lesbian women and gay men is an issue that affects everyone, because gay men and lesbian women are everywhere. They are represented in every race, age group, social class, and religious denomination. We will focus on the other issues of human oppression only insofar as they are subsumed under the issue of discrimination against gay men and lesbian women.

DEFINITIONS OF TERMS

According to Webster's New World Dictionary, *discrimination* is a showing of partiality or prejudice in treatment—specifically, action or policies directed against the welfare of minority individuals. The terms *gay men* and *lesbian women* are preferred over *homosexual* because lesbian women and gay men refer to individuals whose sexual orientation and affectional attractions are to a member of the same gender. It also acknowledges nonsexual aspects of an individual's life. People with no sexual experiences whatsoever may still consider themselves gay men or lesbian women. A homosexual is a man or woman who has preferential sexual attraction to people of his or her same sex over a significant period of time (Masters et al., 1982). This heterosexist definition does not address the difference between *sexual* and *affectional* attraction, and defines lesbian women and gay men as one-dimensional sexual beings only. It also implies that gay men and lesbian women choose to be homosexual.

The only definitive thing we can say about homosexuals is that the objects of their sexual interest will be members of their same sex. "Homosexual" (when used as a noun) is a term that does not include any nonsexual aspects of a person's behavior. Some lesbian women and gay men may have partners of the opposite sex and may have had heterosexual experiences. Some may exhibit heterosexual behaviors exclusively.

Homosexual phobia (sometimes called "homophobia") is the ignorance and irrational fear of homosexuality that underlies all discrimination against gays and lesbians. The notion that there is some legitimate medical, moral, or social basis for such discrimination is without foundation. Such beliefs are rooted in homophobia. Homophobes may seek to find the cause of homosexuality. Are the causes medical, moral, social, or a combination thereof? Such questions assume the cause of heterosexuality.

The cause of heterosexuality is not known. Therefore, the appropriate question is, What causes sexual orientation? We can assume that there is no legitimate medical or moral justification for homophobia. In his award-winning sermon "Walls of Ice," in 1974, the Reverend Steven Johnson of the First Unitarian Church of Cleveland, Ohio, stated, "I question our easy cultural assumption that heterosexuality is, by definition, either medically, morally, or humanly healthier and better than homosexuality." Sexual orientation refers only to the gender of one's sexual partner. One's sexual preference indicates very little else about the individual. Therefore, if sexual orientation indicates so little about the individual, any discrimination on the basis of sexual orientation is not only irrational, it is without basis.

Homosexuality deviates from the norm only when heterosexuality is assumed to be the norm. Homosexuality is considered abnormal by many because heterosexuality is the statistical norm. That type of logic would make being male, American, and Caucasian abnormal. The major argument behind the myth that heterosexuality is most natural (implying that other forms of sexual expression are unnatural) is that intercourse is required for reproduction, and without it the race would become extinct. We know that this is not true in the twentieth century, and will probably become less true as medical technology improves.

Although potatoes are more common than rutabagas, both are acceptable vegetables. In the same light, although heterosexual behavior is more common, that fact does not make homosexuality unnatural. Homosexual behavior has been reported to have occurred at many historical points in the development of the human race. It is also very common in many animal species (Kirsch, 1984). Therefore, it is natural (occurring in nature).

RELIGIOUS BASIS FOR HOMOPHOBIA

The homophobic reasoning given by religious fundamentalists is that God loves the person but hates homosexual acts, and homosexual acts are therefore a sin. Some conservative religious groups point to the Bible to support this homophobic notion. They agree that discrimination is wrong, but see themselves discriminating against only abnormal and immoral behaviors practiced "exclusively" by lesbian women and gay men. These acts are oral sex, anal sex, and mutual masturbation. Since these are sexual acts practiced by gay men, lesbian women, and heterosexuals, sexual orientation becomes a nonissue. Differentiating the person from the act (by saying that we love the lesbian woman or gay man only if she or he does not engage in homosexual behaviors) is a homophobic rationale to allow a bigot to appear nondiscriminatory.

In his scholarly historic work, *Christianity, Sexual Tolerance, and Homosexuality*, John Boswell (1980) suggested that prejudice against gay men and lesbian women could not be traced to Christianity. Christianity's opposition to homosexuality was neither specific or consistent. Lack of tolerance toward gays began in the thirteenth century according to Boswell. It occurred at a time when there was a general increase in bigotry and prejudice, particularly against Jews.

In the New Testament Jesus never mentioned homosexuality. He viewed sexual sins in the same way he viewed all sins, in the context of broken relationships. Those who would use the gospel of love as a textbook of ethics would require us to take an "eye for an eye."

UNITED STATES GUARANTEED
LEGAL RIGHTS

The Constitution of the United States, the Bill of Rights, and the Declaration of Independence all provide for the equal rights of all citizens in the United States. Each of these documents guarantees these rights to all citizens, and does not exclude lesbian women or gay men. The Declaration of Independence contains the following passage:

> We hold these Truths to be self-evident, that all Men are created equal, that they are endowed by their Creator with certain unalienable Rights, that among these are Life, Liberty, and the Pursuit of Happiness.

The Fourteenth Amendment to the Constitution of the United States includes the following passage:

> No State shall make or enforce any law which shall abridge the privileges or immunities of citizens of the United States; nor shall any State deprive any person of life, liberty, or property, without due process of law; nor deny any person within its jurisdiction the equal protection of the laws.

Our nation was founded on the principle that personal freedoms are important and legally guaranteed. Sexual/affectional behaviors should be permitted and sanctioned if others are not harmed by them. There is no reference to sexual orientation or affectional preference in these documents that would allow discrimination against those who engage in love relationships with members of their sex. These freedoms are legally and morally guaranteed. It is immoral to prevent a person from entering college, obtaining a job, or securing housing based on their personal sexual or affectional behaviors.

Imposing specific restrictions and requirements on people because of arbitrary personal behavioral criteria such as sexual orientation or affectional preference is discriminatory and is a violation of the principles upon which our nation was founded.

TYPES OF DISCRIMINATION

There are a number of ways in which gay and lesbian Americans experience discrimination in the 1980s. Marriages between lesbian women and between gay men are legally prohibited. Gay men and lesbian women are prevented from adopting. They are also barred from entrance to the armed services and various organizations and occupations. The educational system has frequently denied gay men and lesbian women teaching positions due to a fear that children will be corrupted and recruited to the so-called homosexual way of life. This is an unfounded fear since most people who sexually abuse and assault children are heterosexual men. The media have helped create the image of the gay man as a child molester and fiend. The media have also been discriminatory. Movies such as *Making Love* and *Cruising* present the topic either in an unrealistically positive, Hollywood fashion or as negative and dehumanizing.

The medical community even contributed to the discrimination by classifying homosexuality as a certifiable psychiatric illness until 1973 (when the American Psychiatric Association removed homosexuality from their list of mental illnesses). Even though homosexuality has not been considered an illness since that time, some medical practitioners still refuse treatment or ignore the special medical needs of the gay and lesbian community.

With the advent of acquired immune deficiency syndrome (AIDS, a deadly disease that is most commonly contracted by gay males) the need for research funding to determine its cause and cure became critical. There was very little money contributed to research efforts until heterosexuals began to develop the disease. The lack of funding for AIDS research reflects the notion that gay men and lesbian women are inferior to heterosexuals. Some have suggested that the disease may be retribution by God to punish lesbian women and gay men for their sinful lifestyle.

The legal system selectively enforces laws against certain types of sexual behavior, which are performed by heterosexual as well as homosexual couples (such as oral-genital contact); but this selective enforcement primarily affects lesbian and gay couples. The military organizations of our nation also discriminate against gays and lesbians by denying them employment based on admission of their sexual orientation or affectional preference. The government and many churches further discriminate against gay and lesbian couples by denying them the right to legally or religiously establish and maintain a permanent and legally sanctioned relationship, such as a marriage. In addition, problems arise in regard to inheritance rights and other legal rights that are guaranteed to married couples in the United States.

DISCRIMINATION IN FAMILY ISSUES

There are several ways in which the quality of life for gay men and lesbian women is infringed upon regarding family issues. (1) Lesbian women and gay men are often perceived as a threat to family life. The real threat, however, is the ignorance and prejudice that cause family members to turn their backs on a gay or lesbian family member, destroying the family unit. Lesbian and gay children are often rejected by their families because the family is embarrassed by them. (2) Gay marriages are not legal. (3) Although most gay men and lesbian women do not become parents through traditional means, those that do are often discriminated against in child custody cases. They are also often discriminated against when attempting to become parents through nontraditional means. Because gay men and lesbian women do not usually have children by traditional means, "family planning" is not thought important for them (since family planning usually means postponing conception rather than planning how to have a family).

MARRIAGE

The reasons often given for marriage of heterosexual couples include love, to have children, to attain the rights to make important decisions for the other person (such as life and death decisions in intensive care wards), to pass on inheritance, to be able to own things together (such as houses), to support each other financially, to gain cultural recognition as a couple, and to file joint tax returns (VanGelder, 1984). Most of these reasons are also important to gay and lesbian couples, but society discriminates against lesbian women and gay men by disallowing gay and lesbian marriages.

Tax and insurance regulations discriminate against nonmarried couples. If one member of a married heterosexual couple is working and the other is not, their incomes are pooled and taxed based on two deductions rather than one. The tax savings are significant.

If the nonworking member of a lesbian or gay (unmarried) couple sustains a serious illness and is not covered by insurance, the medical costs could be astronomical. If the couple were married heterosexuals, the working member could cover the nonworking partner under the company's family insurance plan, and much of the medical cost would be borne by the insurance company rather than the non-working partner. If the unmarried lesbian or gay individual is not working, she or he will probably not have the resources to pay high medical bills. The working partner or the government may end up paying the cost.

In the event of an illness requiring hospitalization in the intensive care unit (ICU) of a hospital, the only individuals allowed to visit are members of the immediate family. A gay or lesbian partner may not be permitted ICU visits or to make life and death decisions, because there is no legal bond. In the event that the ICU staff discover that the couple is gay or lesbian, there is always the worry that at least one staff member may be homophobic, and therefore the sick partner may get less than adequate care. The dilemma becomes whether to risk potentially harmful health care in the hope that you will be allowed to make decisions for the sick partner. Explaining your relationship with the hospitalized individual may only make the partner vulnerable to homophobic actions, and you may still be barred from entry in ICU.

Some gay and lesbian couples solve this problem by one adopting the other. That, in itself, is an example of financial discrimination because a marriage license costs very little, while a legal adoption requires hiring an attorney.

PARENTHOOD

It is possible for lesbian women and gay men to become parents through traditional means (by having intercourse with a member of the opposite sex), but for many that is not desirable. Some gay men and lesbian women are already parents as a result of living a heterosexual lifestyle. In many cases, these people lose the custody rights to their children after "coming out." A gay father or lesbian mother is the same person (and same type of parent) after coming out as he or she was before. The courts are often pompous and presumptuous to assume that what is best for a child is primarily based on the sexual orientation of the parent. The quality of parenthood is not affected by the sex of the parent's lover. Rather, quality parenting consists of love, care for the child, quality time spent with the child, ability to provide for the child, and an ability to act in the child's best interest.

Another problem gays and lesbians encounter regarding parenthood is how to become parents through nontraditional means. There are laws prohibiting lesbian and gay individuals or couples from adopting a child in some states. It is still extremely difficult for gay men and lesbian women to adopt children in the states where it is legal. There are many heterosexual couples who want children and who can provide them with a home environment that is culturally more acceptable. Research that negates the notion that children raised by lesbian and gay parents are any less well adjusted than children of straight parents makes this situation frustrating (Lewin, 1981). Another fear is that children raised by gays or lesbians will become gay or lesbian. This is an extremely homophobic fear. Rigorous research conducted by Miller (1979) and others (Green, 1978) indicates that this fear is unfounded. Lesbian and gay children are almost always raised by heterosexual parents who have little or no effect on their sexual or affectional preference.

If these avenues are not open to gays and lesbians, how then do they become parents? Many of the newer methods of becoming parents are not open to lesbian women and gay men because partners of the other gender are necessary (such as *in vitro* fertilization). Sperm banks, although possibly helpful for lesbians, are not helpful for gay men. Surrogate motherhood, although possibly helpful for gay men, is not helpful to lesbians. Even the available methods require that the health care practitioners, attorneys, or surrogate mothers not be homophobic (nondiscriminating against the gay and lesbian clients seeking help), and unwilling to assist the lesbian women and gay men seeking the service.

CONCLUSION

These are forms of discrimination that reflect cultural homo-phobia, and they are not likely to be resolved until homophobia is confronted. The legal system generally reflects societal standards rather than establishing them. Family interactions for gay men and lesbian women are likely to continue to be very difficult due to individual, legal, and cultural homophobia and discrimination.

REFERENCES

BOSWELL, J. (1980) Christianity—Social Tolerance of Homosexuality. Chicago: University of Chicago Press.

GREEN, R. (1978) "Sexual identity of 37 children raised by homosexual or transsexual parents." American Journal of Psychiatry, 135: 692-697.

KIRSCH, J.A.W. (1984) "There are many natural forms of sexual expression," in H. Feldman and A. Parrot (eds.) Human Sexuality: Contemporary Controversies. Beverly Hills, CA: Sage.

LEWIN, E. (1981) "Lesbianism and motherhood: implications for child custody." Human Organization 40, 1: 6-12.

MASTERS, W. H., V. E. JOHNSON, and B. KOLODNY (1982) Human Sexuality. Boston: Little, Brown.

MILLER, B. (1979) "Gay fathers and their children." Family Coordinator 28: 544-551.

VanGELDER, L. (1984) "Marriage as a restricted club." Ms. (February): 59-60.

V. Middle and Old Age

There are two topics in this section—the issue of who should provide care for older persons and the issue of the place of the family in making crucial medical decisions for family members who are unable to make decisions for themselves. The questions revolve around the obligations and rights of the middle generation.

DISCUSSION QUESTIONS

(1) At present adult children are not required to pay for any of the expenses of nursing home care for their frail elderly parents if the parent is unable to. Should this be a family responsibility?

(2) Discuss some problems with the government's taking greater responsibility for care of the frail elderly. Compare these consequences with the government's taking too little responsibility.

(3) Discuss how the proposed insurance plan for long-term care might be different if the family were to take primary responsibility for care of the frail elderly from the way it might work out if the government or private insurance business would take the responsibility.

(4) If the family does not take responsibility for making the decision about removing the life-support system, what kinds of functions should the family have for the very frail elderly?

(5) Under what conditions would you not allow the family members to make this crucial decision if the person involved is unable to do so?

(6) What general principles would you develop for deciding who should make this important family decision?

(7) What is the connection, if any, between who has provided the major care for the elderly person (the government or the family) and who should be involved with making the decision about removing the support system?

CLASS ACTIVITIES

(1) Invite some elderly persons and their children to class. Include some where there is intergenerational home sharing and some where there is not. Have them discuss some problems and some gratifications with their arrangement.

(2) Invite some representatives of social agencies and government bureaus to discuss their programs and how they perceive their functions. What needs do they perceive for more government intervention?

(3) Have members of the class visit various care units in the community for elderly persons, including nursing homes, hospice care, respite facilities, senior centers, nutritional centers for the elderly, day-care centers, and meals on wheels. For each place visited have the students discuss how this facility relates to care of the older person by the family. Does the service facilitate or inhibit family responsibility and intergenerational relations?

(4) Invite a panel of hospital personnel and someone involved in medical ethics from the university to discuss who they think should make the life and death decisions.

(5) Have a family conference with several members of an extended family. Discuss what to do about removing the life-support system.

(6) Have each class member discuss with another class member what they would like to happen to themselves if they were unable to make the decision for themselves about removal of life-support systems. Discuss the conditions for having or not having the family make the decision. Who would they include in this decision? Would they have a living will that would state their preferences, or would they feel better having others make the decision?

(7) What kind of government or family resources should be available to help persons having to make these decisions?

It Is the Primary Responsibility of Adult Children to Care for Their Aged Parents, Even If There Is Some Hardship to the Children and Their Families

JAMES RAMEY
BETTY RAMEY

Most Americans would agree with the title of this chapter. In fact the vast majority—about 85 percent—of elderly parents are currently not in acute or extended care institutions. Many of these elderly people live with a mate or alone, while most of the rest live with their children.

Typically one child takes active responsibility for taking care of the parent in his or her home and the other children or relatives contribute financially. This arrangement usually continues until the aged person becomes so ill or infirm that constant nursing or professional care beyond the financial resources of the family is required. This is the point at which the family is forced to place the elderly patient in either a hospital or a nursing home. The average age at first admission to a nursing home is 85, and the average patient survives only a year after admission.

A major benefit of home care of aged parents is intergenerational continuity. Among the most striking differences between European and American families is our lack of a sense of continuity. Most Europeans can readily trace their families back four or five generations; indeed, most of them are in constant contact with parents, grandparents, and even great grandparents. But maintaining generational continuity has never been a long suit of American culture.

Americans have a 250-year history of family dispersal. First there was the influx of immigrants—not only the founders of our nation but the successive waves of immigrants who followed, from Europe first, then from Africa, Asia, and more recently from South and Central America. Typically, the husband comes first, followed by the nuclear family, most often leaving the extended family behind in the old country. In a country as young as ours, which until a few years ago had a physical frontier beckoning adventurous youngsters ever westward, it is not surprising that families continued to be fragmented even after having been settled in America for many years.

Today we maintain this tradition of fragmentation of the extended family. One out of every five Americans moves out of the county of residence each year, so that many Americans are still physically distant from their parents, let alone their grandparents or great grandparents. Yet there is a deep longing in most of us for a sense of continuity. Witness the astounding success of the TV program *Roots* and the current interest in genealogies.

While some ethnic groups have managed to maintain extended family ties, many have not, so that family lore is lost, and the resulting sense of isolation adds fuel to the existential sense of lack of purpose and continuity. The opportunity and ability to care for an aged parent or grandparent at home helps allievate this sense of isolation.

Home care of the aged occurs in the overwhelming number of cases regardless of the massive governmental bias in favor of some type of institutional care. Despite study after study showing that home care would cost only a fraction of the amount we currently spend on institutional care, Medicare support is available only for acute (hospital) care, not for extended care in a nursing home. Some types of rehabilitative care are available at home, but only for a few narrowly defined conditions. Some state and local financial support is available for institutionalization or home care of the elderly, but not enough to deal with the problem in many situations.

In the United States the desire appears to be almost universal among the elderly not to be a burden on the children. We have so emphasized personal freedom and independence that mainstream families no longer want to share quarters on an intergenerational basis. Children long for the day when they can move out of the parental home and be on their own; even in the home, the current ideal is for each child to have his or her own room. Except in certain ethnic minority families, this pattern has taken root so completely that we have witnessed a complete reversal of the former pattern of intergenerational home sharing. Where once it was common to have grandparents, uncles, aunts, and other married and unmarried relatives sharing a home, we now strive to avoid such sharing. Thus we have destroyed the valuable learning situation that we once enjoyed, wherein each generation learned from understudying several generations of close relatives.

Unfortunately this emphasis on the independence of the young has a built-in backlash—the isolation of the parents after the children depart and their continued isolation in old age. The elderly seem more and more determined to maintain their own homes as this shift becomes more pronounced. They say with almost one voice, "I don't want to be a burden on my children." The spread of the Social Security system to almost all senior citizens has helped foster as well as support this effort on the part of elderly parents to maintain their own households.

This, together with the desire to maintain independence, accounts for the many elderly people who go it alone after their partner (usually the husband) dies. In this intermediate stage the parent stays independent in his or her own home even if their adult children pay the bills, help with maintenance, take the parent shopping and to the doctor, and help with crises. This strategy helps preserve parental dignity and independence from institutions but without home sharing with the children.

Children can supply emotional support and often provide financial support as well to such a parent, but sooner or later the need for physical assistance proves the Achilles heel of the elderly parent living alone. Osteoporosis may cause a back or hip fracture that makes living alone impossible; or blindness, lameness, or some other problem of old age may make living alone too hazardous to continue.

Many elderly people fall through the cracks: They are either not sick enough or poor enough to qualify for social services, or else they simply cannot afford high-priced private services, so they must move in with their children. In a situation of this type the children are often relieved, because the home they have been very willing to provide must now be accepted. It is usually very much easier to keep an eye on mom or dad in one's own home than to have to call or drop in on her or him several times a week to make sure she or he is in reasonable shape and is eating regularly, and to take care of her or his shopping needs.

It is important for all of us that the vast majority of children are willing to accept this responsibility, regardless of the mental, emotional, physical, and financial strain, since our many levels of government seem less and less able to provide support.

Social Security appears to be running out of money, and already the government has begun to curtail benefits, first cutting back cost-of-living increases from twice a year to once a year, then pushing back the retirement age, stripping many elderly people of their disability, and steadily increasing both the percentage and the amount on which Social Security taxes must be paid, thus making Social Security the fastest-growing tax in our nation's history.

Medicare has also been slashed. It was already inadequate, because it covered only acute care, with a couple of trivial exceptions. The portion of the medical bill that must be paid before Medicare becomes responsible has been raised, as has Part B, which is deducted from the elderly person's Social Security check each month. Anyone who visits a doctor knows that the amount Medicare allows for various expenses is nowhere near adequate. Further reductions are contemplated, not to mention those already being imposed on hospitals, providing penalties for expenses above the average and encouraging minimal treatment. Medicaid is also inadequate and being cut further.

Research studies comparing home and institutional care of the aged invariably indicate that the available funds would be spread more equitably if they were dispersed to families instead of being used to support huge medical and extended-care institutions. As long ago as 1976, it cost $18,000 per year to care for an elderly person in a nursing home. Today the cost is probably twice that much, yet only a few hundred dollars a month can often make the difference between allowing children to care for their aged parent at home and placing that parent in a nursing home.

Parent-sitting expense, home nursing expense, drugs and doctor bills, loss of income due to staying home to care for the parent—all these things can be so expensive that the child is forced to let the parent go into a nursing home despite the desire to keep the parent at home. Sometimes the mere one-time cost of special ramps, special railings in the bathroom, and similar aids could spell the difference in being able to keep the parent at home despite having to be away at work during the day.

Unfortunately, we have built up a tremendous health care infrastructure that militates against such a reasonable approach. Even though the presently available facilities are less than adequate to handle the load, and the population is aging rapidly, those whose careers and income depend on institutional care of the elderly are not about to allow redistribution of the available funds for care of the elderly in a manner that leaves them a smaller rather than a larger share of the pie.

Most people feel that placing an elderly parent in an institution constitutes "early burial," which in fact is a correct perception, since the average individual lives only about a year after entering the nursing home. The reasons for this are clear. Most elderly parents are placed in the nursing home as a last resort, at about age 85, with a steep trajectory downward already clearly evident in their physical and/or mental abilities.

An elderly person living with the family is constantly stimulated, whereas in the nursing home boredom is the rule. The staff has little time to devote to stimulating clients, and many are of an age such that they provide minimal stimulation to one another. Nor would we expect strangers to provide the degree of stimulation that one would get from participation in the family. Consequently, it should come as no surprise that the elderly parent who lives with his or her children survives longer and stays healthier because he or she maintains interest in the activities of the family.

Many vital interests are interfered with by the nursing home setting and routines. One of these, sexual outlet, is considered by some people to be one of the direct causes of loss of interest in staying alive. I recall a 91-year-old man and an 89-year-old woman who were reduced to kissing in the elevator because they were punished by being forced to go without a meal if they were even caught holding hands. This old lady also suffered the indignity of having her hands tied at night to keep her from masturbating. No one would want their parent to suffer such indignities, and the catalog goes on and on. It is therefore not surprising that adult children go to such great lengths to keep their parents out of nursing homes.

At the same time, lifestyle changes have made home sharing more difficult. Gone is the day of the front porch, large rooms, and a large family in residence. The average American family has only 1.7 children today and, thus, has no need for a large house. Furthermore one out of five children live in a single-parent home, and the percentage is growing. Many people live in apartments or co-ops or condos, where the possibilities for expansion are limited. Thus there is no separate place for grandma, who must be shoehorned into the existing space. Nevertheless, most families somehow manage to find space, even though no one is comfortable with the situation. One of the things the government could do to help would be to provide or guarantee low-interest loans to build an extra room on the family home for grandma, or defray the cost of making the existing space safe for her.

The fact that American families have so dramatically shrunk in size also means that, instead of five or six children getting together to shoulder the load of caring for an aged parent, we are rapidly approaching a time when the responsibility must be assumed by only one child.

It is imperative that the government seriously consider various means to facilitate home care of the aged. Obviously in a single-parent home, for example, the parent must go out to work and is in no position to stay home to take care of an aged parent. Yet the desire remains and, with a little financial help, can be fulfilled.

The difficulty of maintaining home ownership—particularly in the face of rising taxes, fuel costs, and so on—is forcing many middle-aged persons from their homes. If these people received a small governmental supplement to help defray the cost of taking care of their elderly parents, they would be better able to keep their homes.

Our parents never looked at us when we were children and said, What will be the return on our investment in these kids? But we nevertheless owe them and should be willing to accept primary responsibility for their care even at the expense of hardship to us and our own children.

Government and Social Agencies Should Provide the Major Care of Older Persons, with the Family Providing Supplementary Care at Most .

MARGARET FELDMAN
HAROLD FELDMAN

In this article we are focusing on the frail elderly, those who are unable to live independently because of failing physical or mental health. Their condition is long-term and chronic. In Western tradition individuals are assumed to have primary responsibility for saving money to provide for their old age. When these savings are not adequate, the two possible secondary resources are the family and the government.

There is a nostalgic picture of the extended family caring for its own without any governmental intervention at all. For some families this is adequate and very satisfying, but for others it is very difficult or impossible. It is the thesis of this essay that, although there are other possible models, the appropriate secondary source of responsibility for today is the government.

The idea of filial responsibility goes back as far as Aristotle, who described how anyone who wanted to hold office in Athens was required to answer "whether he treats his parents well" (Constitution of the Athenians, 55.3). But Shorr (1968) writes that the idea that the community is not responsible until children have made their maximum effort has developed since medieval times, primarily in the rules provided by the Elizabethan Poor Laws. These ideas of filial responsibility and personal liability for whatever befalls us have made children and their parents feel guilty when they have to call upon the government for assistance.

All of the features of our present policies toward the aging, according to Estes (1979: 233), "tend to segregate the aged, often with the poor, as a special class within society." Estes calls for universalistic (governmental) solutions given as a right because of the recognition that the frail elderly are not responsible for their situation. The victims are not to be blamed. The challenge is to develop creative ways to meet universal needs so as to reduce stigma and get away from blaming people for their condition. At the same time, we must channel scarce resources where they are most needed. Today's means-tested programs make the assumption of incompetence.

TODAY, MANY INDIVIDUALS ARE UNABLE TO PAY FOR LONG-TERM CARE

Because of improved public health measures and medical advances, a larger and larger share of the population is surviving to old age. In 1900 only 4 percent of the total population was over 65, while in 1980 the percentage was 11 percent. The age group over 85 is increasing at the fastest rate and is now 22 times its absolute size at the turn of the century (Allen and Brotman, 1981). Most of those living into these older ages are living fully and enjoying their lives, but some number, because of surviving into the older ages when chronic conditions are more frequent, are at risk of high health care costs and a need for assistance.

The high cost of medical care today to society and to individuals has made it impossible for many to prepare financially for their own medical care. In 1985 the per capita cost of medical care for those 65 and over is estimated to be $4,643, of which $1,632 will be private pay or private insurance. The costs for those 65 and over is 2½ times the cost of medical care for those 19 to 64 (Allen and Brotman, 1981). Even with Medicare, one study (Wilensky, 1983) showed that those

> with only Medicare coverage (and no supplementary insurance) incur substantial out-of-pocket expenses, which may account for their comparatively low levels of health service utilization. The poor elderly with private insurance do not appear to be similarly deprived of health services.

There is a high cost for the insurance, however.

The proportion of the elderly spending some time in a nursing home has gone up 150 percent since 1963. Seven percent of the 75 to 84 age group and 20 percent of the 85 and over age group are in a nursing home on any one day (Allan and Brotman, 1981: 88). A 1982 study of nursing home costs showed that even then the yearly costs averaged from $7,000 in some states to a high of $16,000 in the highest-cost states (Holahan et al., 1982: 25). Costs today are perhaps double, and within any one city may be much higher. Families step in to provide care in order to postpone nursing-home placement.

Medicaid rules require spend-down of a person's resources before any governmental help with nursing home costs can be received. To become a welfare recipient is shattering to a person's self-esteem.

FAMILIES CANNOT CARRY THE BURDEN OF PROVIDING NEEDED CARE

There are a number of reasons the family cannot carry the total burden for the frail elderly who cannot be responsible for themselves.

(1) Some older persons have no living immediate family members available. According to Allan and Brotman (1981) approximately 10 percent of those over 65 have never married. Twenty percent of

women aged 65 and over never had a child. Of those with a child, about 25 percent had no contact within the last month. In addition there are those who have outlived their children and their spouses. Ten percent are divorced, and 74 percent of women and 30 percent of men over 65 have no spouse to care for them in case of illness or frailty. For older women, especially, the government needs to take an active part.

(2) Never before have so many women been employed out of the home. About 42 percent of women age 55-64 and 48 percent of women 45 to 54 were in the labor force in 1980. While projections to the year 2000 show the rate for 55-64 remaining more or less constant, the rate for the 45-54 age group is projected to go up to 64 percent (Federal Council on Aging, 1981). These age groups of women are the traditional home-care givers for the elderly, and without their availability as caregivers, there is a severe loss in family capability. The facts of divorce, widowhood, and small families have made it imperative for women to get a job when they are past childbearing years, even if they did not work earlier. For a woman who has gone back to work after her children are raised, the necessity to stop work to care for a parent may be a very difficult choice, since dropping out may make it impossible for her to reenter the labor force later because of age discrimination. Furthermore, if she drops out she will lose health insurance benefits, which are exceedingly important.

(3) Some families have negative adult parent-child attitudes. A study by Feldman and Feldman (1984) found that, although the percentages were not high, some persons expressed a denial of filial responsibility. For example, one item in this scale was, "Each generation should live their own life without being tied to the other." Some of the parent-child relationships were characterized by the authors as being overly differentiated; that is, each was dealing with the adult development problem of finding a separate identity. Resolving this identity problem would be hampered by the two generations having to live together. They also found that those with conservative political attitudes were less willing to accept responsibility for care of an older parent.

Sussman (1965) found that 40 percent of persons said they would not accept older persons in their home. Brody (1984), in a three-generation study, found that the oldest group were less willing to have their children care for them than were the children in the middle generation, and these in turn were less willing than the younger.

Perhaps being closer to the event forces the person to view the event more realistically.

(4) Caring for a frail elderly parent creates strains in the family. Troll (1981) in a decade review article found that several studies about parent-child relationships during aging reported special strains created for the care-giving middle-aged children, especially women, when they provided care for their elderly parents. A study by Cicirelli (1983) found that 34 percent of adult children reported substantial strain when caring for elderly parents.

An unintended consequence of the increased number of divorces and remarriages is that the reconstituted families now include a larger number of elderly parents, so that those responsible for an elderly parent may now include persons who are further removed, creating the likelihood of greater resentment.

This strain may be resulting in increased violence in the family directed toward the frail elderly. The number of abused parents is showing a marked increase, so that one estimate is that 10 percent of elderly parents in the community may be abused.

(5) Some families do not have the economic resources to take care of an elderly parent, and some do not have the physical space. Taking on the burden can have deleterious effects on family finances and integration.

(6) The large increase in the numbers of surviving oldsters of 85 and over has meant that increasing numbers of adult children, some even of retirement age themselves, are involved in advocacy for the 20 percent of this age who are in nursing homes or the equivalent number estimated to be maintained in the community who are equally frail (Weissart and Scanlon, 1982). For some of these adult children the strain of caring for an older parent has been very great indeed.

GOVERNMENT MUST SHARE A LARGER PART OF THE RISK OF FRAILTY

The possibility of becoming old and frail can be determined on an actuarial basis, but the particular individuals and families who will be affected cannot be predicted. Needing assistance is a risk for which we should be able to acquire insurance. Social Security and Medicare can be thought of as insurance systems (although many think of them as a retirement and health benefit program). In these programs, those who are employed pay into the system to provide retirement income and health care for those who have completed their work years. Although the payments into the system are not saved for the individual who pays them, the effect is the same.

Government should accept responsibility for long-term care needed by the frail elderly for the following reasons.

(1) It is impossible for people to buy insurance that covers the condition of frailty in old age—long term care. Private insurers are unwilling to provide this insurance since they fear negative selection—only purchased by those who are likely to need it. Government has access to the total 65 and over population, which is the only pool large enough to share the risk.

(2) The only program now existing to take care of those who have exhausted their resources is Medicaid, a means-tested program. Accepting Medicaid is demeaning for middle-class persons, who feel they are accepting welfare. Furthermore, if resources of a couple are spent down for the first one to become ill, the spouse may be faced with poverty for the last years of life.

(3) Providing government support facilitates better family relations between parents and adult children. A study by Smith and Bengtson (1979) found that the relationship between frail elderly parents and adult children improved when the parent went to a nursing home. A strained parent-child relationship had existed in the home, because the parent felt like a burden and the child found the care a strain. After placement in a nursing home the child was able to take a more positive role as advocate and friendly visitor.

(4) Unless the government addresses the problems of the frail elderly, there is potential for the breakdown of the social fabric and of capitalism itself (Katznelson, 1983). The imperatives of the marketplace lead to a lack of concern for those who fall by the wayside and are no longer able to participate in income-producing activities. In order to maintain people in the labor force, the government needs to facilitate care giving of both children and older adults. If the working population is not able to provide the care for their elders they feel obligated to provide, there may be a breakdown in social integration between and among the generations or an exodus from the labor market as workers, particularly women, find they cannot both work

for pay and provide care. Either of these outcomes is negative and may lead to disaffection with the system.

Women who give up jobs to care for parents may themselves in turn become dependent on others. The strain of economic aid and personal care can lead to breakdown in families, thus necessitating expensive mental health services. And if children in a family are denied the resources necessary for them to prepare to be productive workers because the resources are going to care for elderly members, there will be a loss in the potential creativity within society necessary to provide for orderly growth.

A NEW MINIMUM SOCIAL POLICY IS NEEDED

The present mixed system of governmental and family responsibility has been defined by Katznelson (1983) as a "minimum" necessary to maintain the productivity of capitalism.

> The minimum is in part genuinely a minimum by intention that connotes widely shared meanings and understandings about the appropriate dimensions and character of government interventions in the market. Although largely the result of past group and class struggles, the minimum at a given moment is no longer the subject of struggle [p. 318].

Social Security and later Medicare and Medicaid are examples.

The extra medical and social supports needed by the frail elderly are not now considered part of the minimum. The inadequacies of the present system have been documented in this chapter. Only when other resources are exhausted does the government become the insurer of last resort with Medicaid and welfare. This is the present minimum. Families have stepped in and provided care and economic assistance with no compensation as their filial responsibility. A poll commissioned for the National Council on Aging (Louis Harris and Associates, 1981) found that 90 percent of the respondents thought families who provided care should receive a tax break. This showed that people think the risk is partly the goverment's.

The question is whether the time has come to declare a new minimum that the government should provide in order to share the risk more broadly. The appropriate model may be a new title to the Social Security Act, Title XXI, which would provide for long-term care for the frail elderly in the home or an institution as an insured right.

A PROPOSAL

In these years of cuts to already lean social programs, it appears that this is not a time when a new program such as Title XXI could be added to the Social Security Act, despite the need. A "window of opportunity" may exist, however, because the huge federal budget deficit has forced the administration to open discussion about all the entitlements. This might be the time to consider ways to use the present tax system to retarget funds to the frail elderly. Nelson (1983) has suggested the possibility of reallocation of some of the present tax expenditures (losses in revenue due to deductions, credits, and exemptions). One such possibility is withdrawing the double exemption now allowed for each person 65 and older. Revenue created by bringing this income back to taxable status could be earmarked to provide a monthly insurance payment to all those who are evaluated to be unable to care for themselves alone in their homes. Payment would equal each individual's share of the money raised by dropping the second deduction and should be about equal to what is paid into the fund by 20 persons over 65. This figure is arrived at by taking the known statistic that about 5 percent of those over 65 are in an institution at any one time and that there is estimated to be another 5 percent of equal frailty who are cared for at home (Weissert and Scanlon, 1982). So, on the average, about 5 percent of those over 65 would be eligible at any one time to share what was paid in by the total.

Using the figures provided by Nelson for 1980, we find that nearly $2.5 billion was lost to the government from the double exemption. The population of the United States over 65 that year was some 25.5 million. Dividing the money by 5 percent of the people—those predicted to be frail at home—we come to an expected amount somewhat under $2000 per year for each. Taking account of administrative costs, we could expect an insurance payment of about $150 per month.

This program would provide insurance at a low cost to spread the risk among the total 65 and over population. There would be no cost to those not paying taxes, and the amount paid by taxpayers at the low end of the scale or the high end would be small in consideration of the amount of insurance they would obtain. The money would be paid to the individual. The ability to use the money as the individual pleased in paying for care would add to a feeling of control over one's life, which is cited as an important measure in preventing elder abuse.

Although the amount would be small, it might make the difference between being able to pay a family member or other care giver, and/or the respite or day care necessary to make home care giving low-stress enough to continue.

This insurance would meet goals of efficiency and equity, but would surely not meet the goal of adequacy for all. However, it would go a long way for many to supplement what is already available and would be a recognition of a new minimum.

SUMMARY

Although there are potential dangers from the government's doing too much, it is unlikely that such a level of governmental support will ever be reached. In the meantime, it is our thesis that the government should be accepting a much larger part of the risk of becoming old and frail in today's world.

We have shown that, because of greater longevity and higher medical costs, many middle-class people are unable to save for long-term care if they should need it. For a number of reasons, the family cannot do more than it now does, and even the care now provided by families places a great strain on some. There are fewer traditional care givers in the home because of women's high labor-force participation rate and because many older people have no living relatives.

Care for the dependent members of society in a humane way, acceptable to families, is essential to maintain the social contract and to allow workers to participate in the economic system. Assistance to families who care for frail elderly today is a meager minimum. The financial and care burden can be predicted in an actuarial sense, but the particular individuals who will be affected cannot be predicted. It therefore fits the model of an insurable phenomenon with the necessity for a shared risk. This essay makes the point that the proper population pool to share the risk is the total 65 and over population. Only the government can sponsor a program that will include this total population.

Given the federal budget situation at the present time, it is very unlikely that a new entitlement could be initiated, such as a Title XXI to the Social Security Act, which would indicate governmental acceptance of the risk of frailty. We have suggested a new look at the ways government can meet the needs of the frail elderly and have proposed an idea suggested by Nelson (1983) that the double income tax exemption those 65 and over be withdrawn, and the amount of taxes produced by this withdrawal become an insurance fund to provide payments to the frail elderly. Payments would be a lump sum based on physical need, not age or economic position. Since the funds would be those now lost to the government by the present deduction, there would be no additional cost to the government. Instead, a present universal benefit (to those who pay taxes) would become a targeted program to those with special need at no additional cost. Not Affirmative Action but Infirmity Action!

REFERENCES

ALLAN, C. and H. BROTMAN (1981) "Chartbook on aging in America," in The 1981 White House Conference on Aging.

BRODY, E. (1984) "What should adult children do for elderly parents? Opinions and preferences of three generations of women." Journal of Gerontology 39, 6: 736-746.

CICIRELLI, V. G. (1983) "Adult children and their elderly parents," in T. H. Brubaker (ed.) Family Relationships in Later Life. Beverly Hills, CA: Sage.

ESTES, C. L. (1979) The Aging Enterprise. San Francisco: Jossey-Bass.

Federal Council on the Aging (1981) The Need for Long Term Care: Information and Issues. Washington, DC: Department of Health and Human Services.

FELDMAN, H. and M. FELDMAN (1984) "The filial crisis: research and social policy implications," in V. Rogers (ed.) Adult Development through Relationships. New York: Praeger.

Louis Harris and Associates (1981) Aging in the Eighties: A National Poll. Washington, DC: Author.

HOLAHAN, J., J. COHEN, and W. SCANLON (1982) Nursing Home Costs and Reimbursement Policy: Evidence from the 1977 National Nursing Home Survey. Washington, DC: The Urban Institute.

KATZNELSON, I. (1983) "A radical departure? Social welfare and the election," in T. Ferguson and J. Rogers (eds.) The Hidden Election: Politics and Economics in the 1980 Election. New York: Pantheon.

Louis Harris and Associates (1981) Aging in the Eighties: A National Poll. Washington, DC: Author.

NELSON, G. M. (1983) "Tax expenditures for the elderly." The Gerontologist 23, 5.

SCHORR, A. L. (1968) Explorations in Social Policy. New York: Basic Books.

SMITH, K. F. and V. L. GENGTSON (1979) "Positive consequences of institution-alization: solidarity between elderly parents and their middle aged children." The Gerontologist 19: 438-447.

SUSSMAN, M. B. (1965) "Relations of adult children with their parents in the United States," in E. Shanas and G. Streib (eds.) Social Structure and the Family: Generational Relations. Englewood Cliffs, NJ: Prentice-Hall.

TROLL, L. (1981) "The family of later life: a decade review." Journal of Marriage and Family Relations 33: 263-290.

WEISSERT, W. and W. SCANLON (1982) Determinants of Institutionalization of the Aged. Washington, DC: The Urban Institute.

WILENSKY, G. R. (1983) Statement before the Special Committee on Aging, U.S. Senate, April 13.

Even If a Deformed Baby or a Person in a Long-Term Coma or with a Terminal Illness Is Unable to Make a Decision for Him- or Herself to Remove Life-Support Systems, the Family Has No Right to Make the Decision

SYLVIA CLAVAN

The statement that the family has no right to make a proxy decision about using or terminating life-support treatment for a member who cannot speak for him- or herself may seem audacious to many. There are evolving signs, however, that what one may consider audacious today will be normative in the future.

In simpler technological times in medicine, a physician's decision to treat or to no longer treat was rarely questioned. The ability to prolong life via machinery, coming as it did with growing assertion about autonomy and individual rights, complicated and limited the medical profession's decision-making authority. Families were increasingly called upon to share that decision making for an incompetent relation. This view of the family as best-qualified protector of the individual remained impregnable except for occasional objections. Those objections and others are being heard more frequently as changes in family life, changes in social thought, and escalating health care costs further complicate decision making for an incompetent patient.

BACKGROUND

Medical technology can prolong life.[1] It is commonly accepted that new findings, new methods, and invention in medicine and public health keep us living longer than our forefathers. Part of our modern body of medical knowledge includes methods, both simple and elaborate, that aid, support, or supplant a vital body function that is seriously impaired. These methods are usually referred to as "life-support systems." They may be as simple as mouth-to-mouth resuscitation, or as sophisticated as artificial pacemakers, but their purpose remains the same.

Most of us are in awe of the abilities and potential of modern medical technology. Less thought is probably given to the ethical questions that the new technology raises. In general, these have to do with (1) the decision to initiate a life-support method, (2) the problem of weaning a patient from such support, (3) the decision to continue life-support care, and (4) the decision to terminate such care when death is likely to follow. It is this last problem that concerns us here.

Autonomy, self-determination, and informed consent. In order to understand the family's role in making a medical decision for a family member, it is important to know something about the relationship of the idea of autonomy and informed consent. The evolution of the notion of the right of individuals to fashion their own lives can be traced back in time to the era of feudalism, a period that saw very little consideration of individual rights. From that point in time, the principle of human and individual rights gained increased support until it became a vital part of English common law and later, American common law. It was not until 1947, however, that the principle began to be seen as having application to decision making in medical treatment. At that time, at the trials of World War II criminals at Nuremberg the consent requirement in research using human subjects was first articulated. The document, known as the Nuremberg Code, stated the necessity for "voluntariness" on the part of human subjects. The need for consent of the individual as a subject was soon extended to apply also in cases of treatment. Consent to medical and surgical intervention was always required in medical treatment. The new dimensional was that consent must be informed.

The doctrine of informed consent was not introduced into U.S. case law until 1957 (Salgo v. Stanford University, 317 p. 2d 170, Calif. 1st Dist. Ct. App.). The doctrine of informed consent is an attempt to protect patient's rights to self-determination, and requires that a physician inform patients of risks and benefits of proposed treatment in obtaining consent. From that day to this, the issue of informed consent has been clouded in controversial questions. Not the least of these is the question of informed consent when the patient cannot competently give consent.

When incompetency is determined (no simple feat legally, ethically, or philosophically), the next step is to obtain informed consent from a legally acceptable surrogate. Persons giving proxy consent to medical procedures on behalf of incompetent patients are guided by two primary standards: substituted judgment and best interests. The President's Commission for the Study of Ethical Problems in Medicine and Biomedical and Behavioral Research (1982a) notes that the substituted judgment standard "requires that the surrogate attempt to replicate faithfully the decision that the incapacitated person would make if he or she were able to make a choice."

The commission states further that "decision-making guided by the best/interests standard requires a surrogate to do what, from an objective standpoint, appears to promote a patient's good without reference to the patient's actual or supposed preferences." The report opts for using the principle of substituted judgment "since it promotes the underlying values of self-determination and well-being better than the best interests standard does."

The report goes on to outline preferred procedures for selecting a surrogate to make decisions for the incapacitated patient. It suggests that in emergency situations, health care professionals are the proper decision makers. In nonemergency situations, however, the report states that "the proper assumption is that the family, defined to include closest relatives and intimate friends, should make health care decisions for the incapacitated patient."

It is interesting to note that the recommendation for selecting a surrogate decision maker takes a dual stand. First, it supports the widely held and traditional view that the family of the incompetent patient is in the best position to make a decision for her/him. On the other hand, the recommendation's broad definition of family seems to take into account contemporary variations in family life. The report elaborates on this point by noting that "many of those with most knowledge and concern for the patient may not be his or her actual relatives." It states further that, "The presumption that the family is the principal decision-maker may be challenged for any number of reasons: decisional incapacity of family members, unresolvable disagreement among competent adult members of the family about the correct decision, evidence of physical or psychological abuse or neglect of the patient by the family, evidence of bias against the patient's interest due to conflicting interests, or evidence that the family intends to disregard the patient's advance directive or the patient's undistorted, stable values and preferences." Let us look at some of the factors that question the traditional acceptance of the family as the appropriate proxy decision maker for an incompetent relative.

CHALLENGES TO THE FAMILY'S RIGHT AS SURROGATE DECISION MAKER

The above comments provide a brief explanation of how the idea of need for a proxy decision maker in some medical matters evolved. One can also infer from them, given the historical era, the logic of assuming the family as the preferred source for a surrogate for an incompetent relative. The literature, court decisions, and public opinion attest to the common acceptance of that preference (see, e.g., Shannon and Maufra, 1982; Beauchamp and Childress, 1979; President's Commission, 1982b).[2]

Objections to looking to the family for a substitute to give informed consent in medical treatment can loosely be categorized under the headings of (a) traditional objections, (b) the transition, and (c) evolving objections. The challenges mentioned in the commission's report noted above highlight the most frequently mentioned traditional objections to the family in the role of surrogate decision maker.

TRADITIONAL OBJECTIONS

Decisional incapacity of family members. Physicians commonly hold the view that lay persons are in no position to make serious medical decisions about treatment because of their lack of technical knowledge. It is also argued in an epistomological and philosophical sense that there can rarely be a completely "informed" consent. In everyday life, however, the problem of needing a treatment decision from a member of the family who is unable to make such a decision does arise. The following case, from a case history at St. Francis Hospital, Honolulu (Beauchamp and Childress, 1979: 275-276), illustrates this point.

A 40-year-old widow who had been on maintenance hemodialysis for ten years was told that she now needed a kidney transplant in order to survive. Her 35-year-old brother was proven to be an excellent donor prospect. However, he was mentally retarded and had been institutionalized since age eight. He was so severely retarded that he could not comprehend any of the risks of acting as donor. Doctors projected an 85 percent chance of survival for the patient, given her retarded brother's kidney. Others in the family felt that the donor should be this brother.

Disagreement among family members about correct decision. Individuals may be members of one family, but those ties do not necessarily unite them in thought. A family may not be able to resolve conflicting opinions about what treatment decision is best for an incompetent relation. The following is a case in point (Veach, 1977: 43-45).

An 80-year-old widow with a poor health background was admitted to Beth Israel Hospital, New York City, in a medical emergency. Her condition was diagnosed as "diabetic and arteriosclerotic gangrene, with infection, and with extensive gangrene of the right foot and heel." Amputation, either above the ankle or above the knee was recommended by attending physicians, with an admonition that if deterioration were permitted to progress, death would follow. The patient said she wanted to live, but wanted no part of any amputation.

A hospital psychiatrist reported that the woman was not capable of understanding the nature of consent to operate. The physicians turned to her family to obtain permission.

The widow had three sons. Two of them (one a lawyer) were willing to approve the surgical procedure. The third, a practicing physician, refused to approve on the grounds that his mother might not be able to tolerate surgery. Attending physicians turned to the court next, where a guardian was appointed. The guardian's report stated

a) that the woman was in fact unable to render informed consent, b) even so, she is aware of her body, and wants no amputation, c) that since her consciousness of pain is diminished by her condition, that d) intervention of the court is not indicated [Veach, 1977: 45].

Evidence of abuse and/or neglect of the patient by the family. A long-held picture of family life has been one of love and harmony. This perception has persisted in the face of a growing body of evidence that shows a darker side of family interaction. Studies reveal a significant amount of what is broadly described as family violence. Violence in the family encompasses a wide range of acts from psychological abuse to overt, physical abuse between husbands and wives, and parents and children. In recent years a growing number of studies show that abuse of elderly parents is also occurring (Atchley, 1983: 118). As a rule, abuse is directed at a vulnerable member of the family (e.g., children and wives). A sick, incompetent family member also fits the picture of vulnerability. Can a family be depended upon, given the phenomenon of family violence, to give reliable substitute judgment or a best-interests consent for their incapacitated relative?

Conflicting interests/disregard of patient's known preferences. The fact that individuals, whether related by blood or not, experience conflict of interest is supported from the time of written ancient history and literature. The risk of its presence cannot be estimated, but in selecting a relative to act as a surrogate for an incompetent family member, the risk must be considered.

The above are the most frequently voiced objections to the traditional presumption that a family member can best make a proxy decision about medical care for one who is unable to take part in the decision. The problem becomes acute when a proxy decision must be made to forgo life-sustaining treatment. Two recent celebrated cases reflect current social concern about the problem: the case of Karen Ann Quinlan in the mid-seventies, and that of Baby Jane Doe in 1983.

A PERIOD OF TRANSITION

The two cases just mentioned could be said to mark a period of transition with respect to the thinking about substitute or proxy consent for an incompetent patient. In both cases the courts had to question the right of parents to give or withhold consent for life-support procedures for a child who was not able to take part in the decision making.

Twenty-two-year-old Karen Ann Quinlan was brought into Newton Memorial Hospital in New Jersey in an unconscious state on the night of April 15, 1975. After several days of examination, she was declared to be in a chronic vegetative state, but not legally brain dead. She was put on a respirator to assist her damaged breathing ability. Karen's father, Joseph, petitioned the court to be named guardian of the "person and property" of his daughter. He asked that the letters of guardianship, if granted, give him power to authorize discontinuance of the life-support system allegedly keeping Karen alive. The court granted him guardianship of his daughter's limited property, but not of her person. A court officer was appointed to that function.

The case was appealed to the Supreme Court of New Jersey, and Justice C. H. Hughes handed down a decision giving Joseph Quinlan guardianship of his comatose daughter (In re Quinlan, 1976). The lengthy written decision showed struggle with several complex questions, among them, the right of Joseph Quinlan to make a life/death decision for his daughter. The judge stated that the lower court was convinced of Joseph Quinlan's high character, but felt that "the obligation to concur in the medical care and treatment of his daughter would be a source of anguish to him and would distort his 'decision-making processes.' " Justice Hughes did not agree with the lower court's view, and he granted Quinlan full guardianship.[3]

The case of Baby Jane Doe is a more current but equally complex case. Among the several important issues it raises is the right of the parents to deny life-saving meaures to a severely impaired child. Baby Jane was born October 11, 1983, with multiple congenital defects.

Doctors concluded that she would be paralyzed, severely retarded, and in pain for the remainder of her life. They estimated this to be about two years without corrective surgery. With surgery, longevity was estimated to be about 20 years. Baby Jane's parents decided that hers would not be a life worth living, and decided on conservative medical measures (nutrition and hygiene) as appropriate treatment for their child.

A Vermont lawyer, a right-to-life activist, sued to force an operation. A lower court ruled in his favor, but an appellate court reversed the order to operate on grounds that the parents' choice was a reasonable one. The federal government then intervened by suing for the baby's medical records to determine whether refusal of spinal surgery constituted discrimination on the basis of handicap. The New York Federal District Court ruled against the government's request (Conley, 1984; Time, 1983, 1984).

Both of these cases have broad legal and ethical implications, but both also reflect a transition, a move away from the strongly held traditional value of the rights of family members—in these cases the parents—to make the decision about life-support treatment for another family member.

Increasing court intervention in medical-ethical cases such as these and similar ones reveals a growing ambiguity about family as the best source of protection for incompetent individuals. Other evolving social factors that increase this concern result in decreasing the family's primary position as surrogate spokesperson for any one of its members.

EVOLVING OBJECTIONS

The traditional view of the family as protector of the individual is based on the prevailing assumption of a nuclear family unit composed of mother, father, and children. Current statistics show a different reality about contemporary family organization: It is projected that half of first marriages taking place today will end in divorce. Further, it is estimated that 41 percent of all people now at marriageable age will experience divorce at some time. The other side of the coin is that marriage and remarriage rates are at a record high. Children involved in divorce now number more than 1 million a year (Blumstein and Schwartz, 1983).

A recent study suggests continuing changes for future family organization, Masnick and Bane (1980) found consistent trends in analysis of life-course patterns that allowed them to project future trends. They write that from 1975-1990, they expect that there will be (a) more total households, (b) fewer married couples than now in those households, (c) fewer with children at home, and (d) more single or previously married men and women living alone or with children. The authors predict that people will spend fewer years in conventional families than in the past, and that most will have a variety of family experiences. Masnick and Bane also note that maintaining cross-household family ties depends on factors such as geography, available time, and personal preference. With respect to the last, they point to the increasing importance of friendship, neighborhoods, and organizations as sources of social support and personal ties.

These changes now taking place in family life and those projected for the future minimize the view of family as a long-term, harmonious unit. The evidence is not all in yet, but it could be argued that nontraditional family patterns diminish the traditional assumption that kin will know what is best for a patient, or what that patient might want for herself or himself.

On the other hand, where nontraditional family patterns may generate more formal, objective surrogate decisions, traditional families are frequently hampered by overinvolvement. Not enough attention is paid to the psychological dilemma of a family member asked to make a surrogate life-or-death decision for a dying relation. As an example, the judge in Quinlan's case acknowledged Joseph Quinlan's "anguish" in coming to a decision to "pull the plug."

Another point that suggests a new turn in evolving objections to the family as surrogate decision maker needs mentioning. There is some evidence suggesting that the highly valued concept of autonomy may itself be questioned. For instance, Richard O'Neil (1983), in a paper exploring the question of determining proxy consent, classifies cases of incompetent persons into six distinct types. In some instances, autonomy becomes secondary to a standard the author describes as a "rational choice test," or "what would the patient choose if his/her choice were rational?"

A last, and what may prove to be a crucial, factor in removing family from its primary role in giving substitute informed consent is the economic factor. The meteoric escalation of health care costs is generating an atmosphere of cost-efficiency in the delivery of health care services today. A variety of plans—such as free-standing surgicenters, birthing centers, diagnostic centers, and emergency centers—are all examples of current cost-consciousness in medical care. Added to this list, and predicted to have significant impact, is the government's new plan for reimbursing hospitals for Medicare and Medicaid patients.

Beginning in July 1984, hospitals will be reimbursed a set fee for a given diagnosis for a patient. If the hospital can care for the patient for less, it will make money. If the necessary procedures cost more, they will lose money. Critics of the diagnosis-related group (DRG) plan say that the overwhelming effect of this payment method will be to encourage hospitals to get patients out of beds as quickly as possible with as-yet-unknown consequences for the patient. One hospital administrator suggests developing an "economy class" of health care (Feldman, 1984: 169). Whatever the final outcome of these cost-efficiency measures may be, the costs of extraordinary life-sustaining procedures are sure to receive new scrutiny. Another health care administrator puts the situation in these words:

> With the explosion of new medical technologies—treatments that can cost hundreds of thousands—just how much health care can we afford to promise everyone? Is everyone entitled to a Cadillac or is there a limit [Feldman, 1984: 169]?

Traditional objections to families' giving consent for extraordinary medical treatment for incompetent family members form a strong argument against the right of the family in that role. Evolving objections add strength to the stand. Audacious as it may now see, the family's rights in these matters may very soon give way completely to the combined interests of physicians, hospital administrators, and the courts.

NOTES

1. The material in this section and the one that immediately follows is drawn in part from Gray (1978), Lebacqz and Levine (1978), and Katz (1978).

2. In a survey of physicians and the public taken by the President's Commission, 57 percent of those surveyed said that they preferred to have a family member make important decisions about their medical care if they, themselves, were too sick to do so. The next preference (3 percent) was for the doctor to make the decisions in these circumstances.

3. There is an ironic aftermath to this particular case. National attention was given to Joseph Quinlan's order to "pull the plug." At the time of this writing, and contrary to all expectations, Karen Ann remains alive, in a vegetative state, and without the aid of a respirator.

REFERENCES

ATCHLEY, R. C. (1983) Aging: Continuity and Change. Belmont, CA: Wadsworth.
BEAUCHAMP, T. and J. CHILDRESS (1979) Principles of Biomedical Ethics. New York: Oxford University Press.
BLUMSTEIN, P. and P. SCHWARTZ (1983) American Couples. New York: William Morrow.
CONLEY, J. J. (1984) "Baby Jane Doe: the ethical issues." America (February 11): 84-89.
FELDMAN, L. (1984) "Only the strong survive." Philadelphia Magazine (June): 169.
GRAY, B. (1978) "Informed consent in human research (social aspects)," pp. 751-754 in W. T. Reich (ed.) Encyclopedia of Bioethics. New York: Free Press.
In re Quinlan (1976) 70 N.J. 10,355 A. 2d 647
KATZ, J. (1978) "Informed consent in the therapeutic relationship," pp. 770-778 in W. T.Reich (ed.) Encyclopedia of Bioethics. New York: Free Press.
LEBACQZ, K. and R. J. LEVINE (1978) "Informed consent in human research (ethical and legal aspects)," pp. 754-762 in W. T. Reich (ed.) Encyclopedia of Bioethics. New York: Free Press.
MASNICK, G. and M. J. BANE (1980) The Nation's Families. Boston: Auburn House.
O'NEIL, R. (1983) "Determining proxy consent." Journal of Medicine and Philosophy 8: 389-403.
President's Commission for the Study of Ethical Problems in Medicine and Biomedical and Behavioral Research (1982a) Making Health Care Decisions, vol. 1. Washington, DC: Government Printing Office.
———(1982b) Making Health Care Decisions, vol. 2. Washington, DC: Government Printing Office.
SHANNON, T. A. and J. A. MANFRA [eds.] (1982) Law and Bioethics. Ramsey, NJ: Paulist Press.
Time (1984) "Death agonies." January 9: 44.
———(1983) "Whose lives are they anyway?" November 14: 107.
VEACH, R. M. (1977) Case Studies in Medical Ethics. Cambridge, MA: Harvard University Press.

The Family Has the Right to Make the Decision to Remove Life-Support Systems If the Affected Individual Is Unable to Do So

DAVID A. SCHULZ

The question of who has the right to remove life-support systems from an incompetent individual is one that must be reconsidered from time to time in light of advancing knowledge, medical technology, and our changing attitudes toward death. In the past, there have been many patterns of dying. In most of them the dying individual, the individual's family, and various members of the larger community have participated in some form of ritualized definition of death as a religio-cultural event. With the advent of brain death and the spectre of a prolonged coma, our understanding of life and death has been called into question. Nevertheless, human death can never be merely a biological event. It is in large measure what we make of it, and what we make of it has consequences for the way in which we live as well as die.

While there are some benefits to be derived from placing the primary responsibility for terminating life support in the hands of physicians, the hospital's ethics committee, or the courts, the social and personal costs of such alternatives are, in my opinion, prohibitive. Certainly the direct intrusion of the federal government (as currently desired in the Baby Jane Doe rule of the Department of Health and Human Services) is costly, ineffective, and ill conceived.

Families come in many forms. The primary social function of most of these family forms is the replacement of society's members. The primary interpersonal function of any form is the nurturance of its members. In each case, however, the family's responsibility to terminate life support derives from its compassionate concern for the well-being of its members, the practical principle that those who must bear the major burden of a decision should have the right to make it, the patient's need for continuing social support even in a comatose state, and our collective and individual need to learn how to die. No expertise is adequate to the task of defining death, though all sorts of experts can make their contributions.

ILLUSTRATIVE CASES

Although it is true that some Americans still die surrounded by family and friends, many writers and critics (e.g., Becker, 1977a, 1977b) have pointed out that we have characteristically tried to deny death. The scientific/technological/legal battle to save lives is but the most visible aspect of this cultural denial. In this battle, all too often the technical concerns of disciplines and professions override the cultural effort to cope with death as a significant human event. A few examples can illustrate the major issues involved.

Karen Quinlan. In 1975, 21-year-old Karen Quinlan suddenly lapsed into a coma at a party she was attending.[1] The early suspicion was that she was suffering from some adverse drug reaction brought on by social drinking. She was rushed to the hospital, where she was put on a life-support system to assist her eating and breathing. She became comatose. There was no reasonable hope that she would ever regain even a limited degree of cognitive life. Her parents asked the physician to take her off the respirator. He refused to do so without a court order relieving him of liability. Her father went to court and, after considerable debate, the court granted the parents permission to take Karen off the respirator provided that both the responsible attending physician and the newly established hospital ethics committee agreed.

Karen was taken off the respirator, but to everyone's amazement she did not die. She survives to this day in a vegetative state sustained by feeding through a nasogastric tube. Part of the cost of her care is being borne by Medicare. Her parents refuse to petition the court to allow them to remove the tube. "She's still our daughter," says Joseph Quinlan, 58, who visits her daily. "We're not going to turn our back on her." Even though the Quinlans are active in the right-to-die movement and listen with sympathy to the debate over withdrawing feeding tubes, they would never remove Karen's. "It's her nourishment," says her father. "We'll never remove the tube" (USA Today, March 27, 1984: 1).

There are about 10,000 comatose persons in the United States at present and several thousand more critically ill who may soon become so. To sustain each one on a life-support system costs several hundred thousand dollars a year, though it is unlikely that most will live that long.

Joseph Saekewicz. Karen Quinlan has been a major media event over the past eight years, but Joseph Saekewicz's claim to fame is largely through the legal precedent his death established (Baron, 1983: 17). Saekewicz, 67, had an IQ of 10. He was living in a home for the retarded without contact with next of kin, and in 1977 he came down with leukemia. At first, the superintendent of the school wanted to treat his leukemia, then decided not to do so. The best that could be hoped for was thirteen months of prolonged life, which would likely be uncomfortable because of severe side effects from treatment. A considerably more comfortable death within a much shorter period of time was likely to occur without treatment.

The superintendent went to court to deny treatment to Saekewicz and the court ruled that he could do so. It contended that if Saekewicz were competent, he would have made the same decision. In this case, the Massachusetts court reserved the right to terminate care without the consultation of next of kin or an ethics committee.

Such questions of life and death seem to us to require the process of detached but passionate investigation and decision that form the ideal on which the judicial branch of government was created. Achieving this ideal is our responsibility and that of the lower court, and is not to be entrusted to any other group purporting to represent the "morality and conscience of our society", no matter how highly motivated or impressively constituted [Baron, 1983: 18].

While the court clearly attempts to establish its prerogative over and against groups like the Moral Majority, it is interesting to observe that it may think of itself as closer to the conscience of our society than families.[2]

Infant Doe. Infants born with gross deformities or incurable diseases are allowed to die every day in the course of normal medical practice. Commonly, the matter has been negotiated informally between the parents, attending physicians, and concerned others close to the family. Several such cases have made the news lately because of the increasing concern of right-to-life groups (Fleishman and Murray, 1983; Pless, 1983).

In 1982 a baby boy was born in an Indiana hospital with a severe blockage of the esophagus (Pless, 1983; Baron, 1983). Infant Doe was also diagnosed as a Down's syndrome baby with a strong prognosis for mental retardation. The parents, in consultation with the attending physician, decided not to permit surgery to remove the blockage of the esophagus and allow the baby to die of starvation. A member of the hospital staff reported the incident and the media became involved. "These people loved the baby," one county official is quoted as saying, "It was not an act of anything but absolute love, given the child's medical condition" (Baron, 1983: 35).

But other medical authorities disagreed. They contended—but could not prove—that this particular baby was a relatively uncomplicated case of Down's syndrome and could have expected to live a reasonably normal life. They concluded that Down's syndrome, in and of itself, is not a justification for not treating an otherwise correctible life-threatening condition in a newborn child. "Societal demands and political currents make it impossible to return to the old way of allowing parents and doctors to decide without review by some other party" (Pless, 1983: 663).

On October 11, in Port Washington, New York, Infant Jane Doe was born with multiple neural tube defects including spina bifida, microcephaly, and hydrocephaly (Fleishman and Murray, 1983: 6). After consulation with a Roman Catholic priest and attending physicians, the parent opted for conservative medical treatment rather than surgery. An attorney who lived in Vermont learned of the case, got a court order appointing a guardian *ad litem* for the infant. This guardian, in turn, sought to have surgery performed.

The trial court ruled in favor of surgery. The appeals court overturned the lower court's decision stating,

> It would serve no useful purpose at this stage to recite the unusual and sometimes offensive activities and proceedings of those who have sought at various stages in the interests of Baby Jane Doe, to displace parental responsibility for and management of her medical care [Fleishman and Murray, 1983: 6].

The Port Jefferson case prompted the federal Department of Health and Human Services to enact its Baby Jane Doe hotline rule, which encourages anyone learning of suspicious practices in the care of incompetent patients to notify the agency. It will then send a squad of investigators to the hospital to determine if malpractice has occurred. Of the over 1500 cases thus far investigated, only 22 have pertained to nontreatment decisions for live infants and 13 additional reports concerned possible malpractice in cases where the infant had already died (Pless, 1983: 6).

These few examples do not exhaust the issues now being hotly contested in the courts. They do, however, point out some of the points at issue between advocates of the hospital's, the court's, and the family's rights to decide. Even the right of competent patients to refuse treatment is being challenged. A great deal of money is involved not only in the care of the incompetent patients, but in the possible awards to be gained through litigation in malpractice cases. The cost of malpractice insurance is soaring. It is very evident that death is not merely a biological event, but a social decision with far-reaching implications.

THE FAMILY SHOULD DECIDE

The decision to turn off the life-support system cannot reasonably be made independent of professional advice, some awareness of the social services that are available, and some degree of sensitivity to the societal demands and political currents of our times. Whoever decides must do so in the context of such environmental constraints. A family without resources living in a society that does not provide Medicare or its equivalent cannot effectively decide to keep a comatose member alive for a long period of time. It can, however, refuse treatment. Whether a family does this or not should be a function of the expert advice it receives as well as its own perception of the likely consequences of its action.

Nevertheless, within these inevitable constraints, it should be the responsibility of the family to turn off the life-support system in the case of an incompetent member. The family's right to do this derives first of all from its compassionate identification with the patient. If anyone can determine a comatose patient's wishes in regard to treatment, surely it must be those who have loved that patient and have known as much as can be known about this many-faceted life. The patient is less likely to be treated as an experiment or a mere object if the family is responsible for this aspect of medical care. Physicians widely respect the wishes of the family in regard to the terminal care of an incompetent patient, but feel that it is their responsibility to decide about the termination of care. They would not be as likely to assume this were the patient competent. Because of the family's intimate knowledge of the patient, it should decide whether or not to terminate life support—with the advice of the physician and any other pertinent expert taken into consideration. Physicians must remain in the service of the family, not the other way around.

A second justification for the family's assumption of this responsibility derives from the practical principle that those who must bear the major burden of a decision should have the right to make it. While it is true that society supports the family and sometimes provides services that the family cannot afford, it does not follow that assuming the major financial costs is bearing the major part of the burden. Since it is unlikely that anyone cares for the patient as much as the family cares, it is unlikely that anyone will suffer as much in the caring for or the loss of the patient. It may suit the moral principles of a Vermont attorney to appoint a guardian *ad litem* for Baby Jane Doe, but what costs does this attorney bear after the surgery has been performed? Is he willing to watch over the child for her lifetime—or even pay to provide adequate service for her continued care? Who has the right to ask her family to exhaust its resources in her maintenance? Only the family should decide what it means to love this incompetent patient under these circumstances.

The final justification for the family's deciding to turn off the life-support system is more difficult to articulate. It may well be the most important justification of all, however. It has to do with the fact that death is, to a considerable extent, what we collectively and individually make of it (DeVries, 1981). We have already noted the critics who say we are making less and less of it to our harm. The family's compassionate identification with the dying not only provides support for the dying; it also becomes the primary means by which other family members learn how to die. Only through such compassionate identification with the dying can our personal and cultural symbolization of death be adequately refurbished.

Death by disciplined experts tends to be a death with minimal social significance. We no longer even recognize what the doctor or lawyer calls death in many instances.[3] What in the Middle Ages had been a formal ceremony of familial leave-taking has been reduced in modern times in some instances to the turning off of a switch. When death is reduced to a Uniform Determination of Death Act, the physicians, the attorneys, the organ bank technicians, and the hospital administrators may benefit—their technical discourse may achieve a degree of clarity useful within some limited situations—but the culture is debased. We do not notice the debasement as long as the number of persons who die incompetent under such circumstances is small. But when the expert definition of death dominates, it undermines the continued creation of a sustaining cultural ritual for dying, and we all lose. Death is denied in our times in part because physicians cannot accommodate it to their heroic defense of life. Whatever else death through a disciplinary perspective might be, it is most likely to be objectified. As such, the death of a beloved becomes the death of an alien other, an experiment in the prolongation of life, or merely the biochemical transformation of an object having no interior experience worth taking into consideration.

The family should be the proper context for the discussion of such matters. If it lacks adequate information on the subject, it should be educated, not ignored. It is the proper context within which to learn how to die. The family as a natural symbol of immortality enables the dying to see themselves perpetuated in the faces of their children, and the living can participate in the death of another before their own hour comes around. Death often takes on its deepest significance when it takes a beloved before it takes us. We often experience the value of life most intensely under such circumstances, and can directly understand the inevitability of suffering and loss. Our understanding of love is thereby enriched. Death is thus preeminently a social event in which the deepest dimensions of our personal lives intertwine with religio-cultural symbols of its significance. Without the personal involvement, the symbols lose their power and death its significance (Etzioni, 1976: chap. 5).

We can, of course, participate more readily in the death of a beloved if that person is conscious and competent in the face of death. But, in the case of an incompetent, participation is still possible and is far more likely to occur if the family is responsible for the decision to terminate life support than if others do so by means of some standard operating procedures.

And what about those who do not have families? The Joseph Saekewiczes of the world will still have to rely on the good graces of others who are not related to them. These others sometimes serve well as substitutes for family, but clearly not everyone cares. In writing a living will, we might want to indicate who our family might be if this is not obvious. Who do we want to entrust with the decision to turn off our life-support system if we ourselves cannot make the decision?[4]

Some write living wills because they want to spare those who love them the burden of this decision by providing the physician with evidence of their intentions in their own behalf. But in doing so, we again reduce the significance of love as well as death. Death, as well as life, is sacred. Sometimes the decision to allow a beloved to die is indeed a loving act.

The decision not to do so may also be an act of love, especially if the family continues to care for its comatose member. We do not know what persons such as Karen Quinlan experience. They cannot tell us. The objective probes we might wish to make into their interior worlds cannot feel for them. As a society we may have to declare formally that we cannot afford to keep 10,000 or 100,000 comatose patients alive for a prolonged period of time, in which case we limit the options of families who might wish to sustain them. But, whatever the social constraints we might place upon the decision, the primary responsibility for making the decision should be the family's.

NOTES

1. For an account of this incident, see Baron (1983: 15).
2. Remember the Clarence Herbert case in California in 1981, in which two physicians were charged with murder because they removed the support from a comatose patient at the request of the next of kin. The lower court declared the physicians guilty, but the appeals court overturned the lower court and held that withholding treatment was not an act of murder (Steinbeck, 1983).
3. The Uniform Determination of Death Act declares that death has occurred when an individual sustains either (1) "irreversible cessation of circulatory and respiratory functions" or (2) "irreversible cessations of functions of the entire brain including the brain stem."
4. Living wills are legal in fifteen states. Delaware is one of two states that allows for the specification of a proxy to determine when the care of a comatose patient should be terminated.

REFERENCES

BARON, C. (1983) "Medicine and human rights; emerging substantive standards and procedural protection for medical decision making within the American family." Family Law Quarterly (Spring).
BECKER, E. (1977a) The Denial of Death. New York: Free Press.
———(1977b) Escape from Evil. New York: Free Press.
DeVRIES, R. G. (1981) "Birth and death: social construction at the poles of existence." Social Forces 59 (June): 1084-1091.
ETZIONI, A. (1976) The Active Society. New York: Free Press.
FLEISHMAN, A. and T. H. MURRAY (1983) "Ethic committee for infant Doe?" Hastings Center Report 13: 5-9.
PLESS, J. E. (1983) "The story of Baby Doe." New England Journal of Medicine 309 (September): 663 ff.
STEINBECK, B. (1983) "The removal of Mr. Herbert's feeding tube." Hastings Center Report 13: 19-20.

SOME INTEGRATIVE QUESTIONS

(1) What is the connection between the ways persons deal with their premarital relations and their postmarital lives?

(2) Discuss the advantages and disadvantages of other than traditional approaches to marriage.

(3) Discuss parenthood in traditional and nontraditional family forms. Which might be better for children and which for the married couple?

(4) Discuss the place of the government in regulating marriage and parenthood. Examine the Family Protection Act as an example.

(5) How might having marriage contracts help resolve some of the issues raised in this book? For which issues are they less applicable?

(6) How do different family theories relate to a stand you take on some issue?

(7) Examine several texts in marriage and family studies to determine their positions on several issues.

(8) Develop several criteria for integrative questions and then make up two good examples.

(9) Consider a utopian society and indicate how marriage and families would exist in it. What functions would they serve?

(10) Redesign your textbook so that it would deal more directly with controversial issues, keeping Perry's three stages of intellectual and ethical development in mind.

ABOUT THE AUTHORS

DOUGLAS A. ABBOTT is Assistant Professor in the Department of Human Development and the Family at the University of Nebraska—Lincoln. He received his master's degree in child development and family relations at Brigham Young University and his Ph.D. in child and family development at the University of Georgia. His research interests and publications are in the area of parent-child relations.

LYNN ATWATER is currently Associate Professor in the Department of Sociology/Anthropology at Seton Hall University. Her research interests focus on sexuality, family, and gender roles, with particular emphasis on noninstitutionalized relationships. She has researched and published a book on extramarital involvements, and is currently studying adult sibling relations.

ANDREA BALIS is a freelance writer living in New York City. She is the author of a number of books and plays, including *What Are You Using?* a guide to contraception for teenagers. She has a B.A. in philosophy from the University of Pennsylvania and an M.F.A. from New York University. She serves on the board of the New York State affiliate of the National Abortion Rights Action League, and works with other feminist political organizations as well.

DAVID M. BECKER is the Editor of *Family Policy Insights* and Associate Editor of *Family Protection Report*, newsletters published by the Free Congress Research and Education Foundation in Washington, D.C. The author of *Backgrounds of the Members of the National Advisory Committee of the White House Conference on Families,* he has written on such topics as the sexual exploitation of children, significant women's issues legislation enacted since 1970, public policy for building family strengths, and sources for profamily information and activism. He was educated at Lawrence University and the Simon Greenleaf School of Law.

CARLFRED B. BRODERICK is currently Professor of Sociology, Director of the Marriage and Family Therapy Training Program, and Director of the Human Relations Center at the University of Southern California. He graduated with an A.B. in social relations from Harvard University and a Ph.D. in child development and family relations from Cornell University and took postgraduate work in marriage and family counseling at the University of Minnesota. He directed a major research project on the normal development of heterosexual interest in childhood and youth in the 1960s, and his monograph on the subject has been translated into several foreign languages. He is past president of the National Council on Family Relations and past editor for two terms of the *Journal of Marriage and the Family.* He has also published eight books.

MARIE COLES CALDWELL, Associate Professor at the State University College at Buffalo, New York, has a master's degree from Smith College School for Social Work and a Ph.D. in social work from the University of Pittsburgh. She also has a master's from the Graduate School of Public Health, University of Pittsburgh. Having practiced in both psychiatric and medical settings, she now teaches human behavior in the social environment and field studies in the Department of Criminal Justice and Social Work and has research interests in the areas of the family, health, and aging.

SYLVIA CLAVAN is Associate Professor of Sociology at Saint Joseph's University, Philadelphia. She holds a Ph.D. in sociology from Temple University. Her research interests center primarily on family sociology and the sociology of medicine. She has published numerous articles and book reviews in those areas in such journals as *Journal of Marriage and the Family, The Gerontologist, Ethics in Science and Medicine,* and *Contemporary Sociology.* She is currently preparing a research monograph on an organizational model for delivery of long-term care to the disabled elderly in the Commonwealth of Pennsylvania.

ANNA L. COLE is currently a marital and family therapist in private practice in Ames, Iowa. Cole received her master of science degree in family studies, specializing in marital and family therapy, at Iowa State University. In addition to maintaining her own private practice, Cole is a frequent consultant for local mental and physical health agencies in Iowa. Her research and writing have focused primarily on marital quality and marriage and family enrichment. Her current research interests include the reciprocal effects of ecological illnesses on marital and family functioning, developing coping strategies for dealing with health disabilities, the importance of support systems in the healing process, anger and conflict processes and patterns, and strategies for upgrading family and marital functioning.

CHARLES LEE COLE is currently Associate Professor at Iowa State University in the Department of Family Environment. Cole has a master of arts degree from Texas Christian University in sociology and psychology, and a Ph.D. in family sociology and social psychology from Iowa State University. He has done postdoctoral work in marital and family therapy and clinical sociology. He has been in practice as a marital and family therapist for more than ten years. He has been principal investigator of several research projects studying marital adjustment and family wellness. His current research focuses on marital quality and family functioning in the middle years.

RICHARD MARSHALL DUNHAM is currently on the faculty of the Psychology Department at Florida State University. He received his doctorate at Duke University, specializing in the study of personality development and culture within the clinical psychology department. For several years he served as Chief Psychologist at the Dorothea Dix Hospital in Raleigh, NC. He was also a psychologist with the Astronaut Training Office of NASA. His research and publications include work in the area of family policy, stress and the family, the effects of family lifestyle on the development of young people, and the effects of cultural background on individual development. He also maintains a private clinical practice in Tallahassee. He is married to Jeannie Kidwell.

MICHAEL J. ELLIS is a member of the board of directors of the Human Relations Training Program at Cornell University. He earned his master's degree from Hofstra University. He has served Cornell University as a Student Development Specialist since 1975. His research interests include homosexuality, heterosexism, and homophobia. He is also a Director in Cornell University's Department of Unions and Activities.

J. ROSS ESHLEMAN is currently Professor at Wayne State University in the Department of Sociology. Eshleman has a master's and Ph.D. in sociology from the Ohio State University. He is author of *The Family*, an introduction to a sociology of the family currently in its fourth edition, and coauthor of a second edition of *Sociology: An Introduction*. He has had two Fulbright lectureships to the Philippines and has conducted research on ideal family size and acceptable measures of fertility control in that country.

HAROLD FELDMAN is currently Professor Emeritus at Cornell University in the Department of Human Development and Family Studies. He has a master's degree in social work from the University of Minnesota and a Ph.D. in clinical and social psychology from the University of Michigan. He has been principal investigator of many research projects, including studies on the development of the husband-wife relationship, the welfare woman's employment and her family, the filial obligation, and parents' rights. His major research focus has been on people who have "made it," and he has summarized this research in a monograph.

MARGARET FELDMAN is Professor Emerita at Ithaca College in the Department of Psychology. She has a master's degree from Case Western Reserve University in social work and a Ph.D. from Cornell. Her interests have been in life-span psychology and policy as it relates to families. Her publications have been in the areas of adolescent pregnancy and passages of all, but especially the middle-aged woman, through the stages of the family life cycle. Most recently her interest has been in family responsibility for the care of the elderly and the policy issues surrounding this issue.

MERYL FINGRUTD is currently teaching at Queens College, City University of New York, and working on a National Science Foundation grant studying women's reform organizations in nineteenth-century New York State. She recently received her Ph.D. in sociology from SUNY, Stony Brook, and is now living the life of a single in New York City.

NED L. GAYLIN is currently Professor and Director of the Specialization in Marriage and Family Therapy in the Department of Family and Community Development at the University of Maryland, College

Park. He received his B.A. and Ph.D. degrees from the University of Chicago, with a specialization in child and family clinical psychology. He is married, has four children, and considers himself a family advocate. He maintains an active interest in the individual within the family and in issues and research regarding the centrality of the family to the quality of life.

MATTI K. GERSHENFELD received her bachelor's and master's degrees from University of Pennsylvania and her doctorate from Temple University. She took postdoctoral training at the University of Pennsylvania's School of Medicine, Department of Psychiatry, Division of Family Study. She is an Adjunct Professor at Temple University in the Department of Psychoeducational Processes, and is also a member of the graduate faculty of Pennsylvania State University—Ogontz. She is President of the Couples Learning Center, an educational nonprofit corporation that conducts innovative programs in the area of the family, and is the author of eleven books, including *Groups: Theory and Experience*.

VIRGINIA A. HEFFERNAN is currently a theology student at Washington Theological Union, a Roman Catholic seminary. She has a master's degree in sociology from Catholic University. Her focus has been on the impact of religion and spirituality on marriage and sexuality. She is especially interested in the connection between scriptural reflection and behavior. She has been married for more than thirty years and has five young adult children and two grandchildren. Her published articles include "One in the Flesh, One in the Spirit," which *Marriage Encounter* magazine kept in reprint for several years.

SHARON K. HOUSEKNECHT is currently Associate Professor of Sociology at the Ohio State University. In addition to the career/family patterns of professional women, her current research and writing focus on voluntary/involuntary childlessness; fertility socialization; economic stress in the family; and the family as a mediator of social values. She has published numerous papers on these topics in *Handbook on Marriage and the Family*, *Social Problems*, *Sociological Quarterly*, *Sociology and Social Research*, *Journal of Marriage and the Family*, *Journal of Family Issues*, and other journals.

KRIS JETER is an Associate with Beacon Associates Ltd., a research, training, editing, and program evaluation firm. She has held teaching positions at Murray State University, North Carolina A&T University, and Howard University, and visiting professorships at Delaware State College and the University of Delaware. She is a human development teacher and trainer, and analytic book review editor of the *Journal of Marriage and Family Review*. She is the author or coauthor of 25 publications in the areas of family, human growth, marriage, myths, and archtypical and humanistic psychology.

JEANNIE S. KIDWELL is currently on the faculty of the Department of Child and Family Studies at the University of Tennessee, Knoxville. She received her doctorate at Purdue University, specializing in the study of the family. She teaches human development from adolescence to old age, as well as courses on family dynamics, marriage and intimacy, and interpersonal relationships. Her research and publications include work on the effects of birth order on individual development and the normative stresses and strains of growing up on the adolescent and the family. She is currently completing work toward clinical certification in marriage and family therapy. She is married to Richard Dunham.

DAVID MACE is Professor Emeritus of Family Sociology at the Bowman Gray School of Medicine, Wake Forest University, Winston-Salem, NC. He is a Past President of the National Council on Family Relations; and he and his wife VERA MACE were formerly Executive Directors of the American Association for Marriage and Family Therapy, and Founders and Presidents of the Association of Couples for Marriage Enrichment. Between them, the Maces have published more than thirty books on sex, marriage, and the family.

TERESA DONATI MARCIANO is currently Professor of Sociology at Fairleigh Dickinson University (Teaneck campus). She received her M.A. and Ph.D. from Columbia University. Her current work in the areas of sex roles and sexual diversity include studies of family power and fertility, women's professional lives, and interdisciplinary approaches to the study of the ways in which cultures do or do not support diverse ways of expressing sexual preferences.

CONNAUGHT MARSHNER is Chair of the National Pro-Family Coalition, a Washington, D.C.-based umbrella organization providing information on legislation and public policy to local, state, and national pro-family grass-roots organizations. She was founding editor of *Family Protection Report*, the monthly monitor of the pro-family movement, and founding director of the Child and Family Protection Institute of the Free Congress Research and Education Foundation, a public policy research organization. Currently she is Executive Vice-President of the Free Congress Research and Education Foundation. She has been active for a number of years in organizing the pro-family movement throughout the country, and led the conservative delegation to the 1980 White House Conference on Families. Trained as a teacher, she is author of *Blackboard Tyranny* and coauthor of *Future 21: Directions for America in the 21st Century.*

PHILIP R. NEWMAN is a social psychologist who is an author and consultant in Columbus, Ohio. He has a Ph.D. in social psychology from the University of Michigan. He has coauthored several books with his wife, Barbara M. Newman, including *Development Through Life: A Psychosocial Approach, Understanding Adulthood,* and *Living: The Process of Adjustment.* He was Director of the Human Behavior Curriculum Project of the American Psychological Association and Chief Content Consultant for the Agency for Instructional Television in the production of *On the Level,* an educational television series concerned with adolescent development. He is primarily interested in life-span development and the enhancement of normal developmental processes. He works at home, manages the household, and has educated his three children at home.

ANDREA PARROT is a faculty member in the Department of Human Service Studies at Cornell University, where she earned her Ph.D. She is the coeditor of *Human Sexuality: Contempory Controversies* and is a reviewer for Wadsworth and Little, Brown publishers. She has been teaching human sexuality and health courses, graduate and undergraduate, since 1980. Her research interests include acquaintance rape and acquiring sexual knowledge. She is also the Director of the Kinsey Summer Institutes.

JAYNANN M. PAYNE, formerly National Director of the Center of Family Studies for the Freemen Institute, has a bachelor's degree in English from the Brigham Young University and has taught continuing education classes for fifteen years. She has addressed the Utah White House Conference on Families and the American Family Forums I and II. She organized and addressed three national conferences on the family, was an elected delegate to the I.W.Y. Women's Conference, and was State Chair of the Task Force on Teenage Pregnancy for the Utah Association of Women. She has written monographs, including *Life Support Systems for Youth, Creative Dating—Promoting Healthy Gender Relationships,* and *Teach a Child to Be a Winner.* She prepared twelve seminars for the Center of Family Studies. She is the wife of Dean W. Payne, mother of 12 children, and grandmother of 23 grandchildren. She has written books and articles on women's issues and family issues. Her focus has been coping with stressful family relationships, teen problems, and changing parental and marital roles.

BETTY RAMEY is currently Chief Executive Officer and "Hot Line" host of radio station WRKL, which has won more than 150 awards for excellence, including the Columbia-Dupont Award and the Edward R. Murrow Award. She is Past President of the New York Associated Press and was host of the NBC network TV series *Through the Enchanted Gate.* She is a former faculty member of Bank Street College, the Museum of Modern Art, and St. Thomas Aquinas College. She studied painting and sculpture at Cooper Union, Beaux Arts, and Columbia University and is an exhibiting artist and participating author of a number of books on art education. She is a member of the Groves Conference on Marriage and the Family and has presented at numerous professional conferences around the world. She held a Fulbright to India in 1980 and has been especially concerned with the social role of mass media and the resocialization of women for careers and career advancement.

JAMES RAMEY is currently Chief Executive Officer of H. F. Enterprises and Senior Research Associate at the Center for Policy Research. He was a Kellogg Scholar at Columbia University, where he received his doctorate in 1958 and was certified by the American College of Sexologists in 1979. He has been both an information science and medical professor, a college dean, and an executive director of a medical research institute. He has held national office in several professional associations and has been principal investigator on a number of foundation and federally funded research projects, on such topics as aging, alternative lifestyles, forensic medicine, blood studies, and biomedical communication. He has authored several books, including *Using TV to Teach Medicine, Mechanization of the Library and Information Center, Intimate Friendships,* and (co-authored) *Talking with Your Child About Sex,* as well as more than 100 professional articles and book chapters.

ROGER H. RUBIN is Associate Professor and Acting Chairperson of Family and Community Development at the University of Maryland, College Park. He received his Ph.D. in child development and family relationships from Pennsylvania State University. He has published in the areas of Black family life, interpersonal lifestyles, and income maintenance programs. Currently, he is doing research on divorce. He has been elected and appointed to numerous positions in professional family life organizations at the national, state, and local levels.

DAVID A. SCHULZ is currently Professor at the University of Delaware in the College of Urban Affairs and Public Policy, with joint appointments in the Departments of Individual and Family Studies and Sociology. Schulz has a master's of divinity from Virginia Theological Seminary and a Ph.D. in sociology from Washington University, St. Louis. He has studied low-income Black families and the elderly and is currently interested in household energy use. The major focus of his work is an interest in alternative lifestyles and the possibilities of intentional change.

WALTER R. SCHUMM is currently Associate Professor at Kansas State University in the Department of Family and Child Development. He has a bachelor's degree in physics from the College of William and Mary, a master's degree in family and child development from Kansas State University, and a Ph.D. in family studies from Purdue University. He has authored over fifty journal articles and book chapters with primary research interests in marital interaction, research methodology, parent-adolescent communication, family violence, and premarital counseling. He is married and the father of two preschool children.

LAURA S. SMART is currently Assistant Professor at Northern Illinois University in the Department of Human and Family Resources. She has a master's degree in human development and family studies from Pennsylvania State University and a Ph.D. in family studies from the University of Connecticut. She has published articles on various aspects of divorce and has written textbooks on family relationships and adolescent development.

ADRIAN SOLOMON is Professor in the Department of Criminal Justice and Social Work at the State University College at Buffalo, New York. He has a Ph.D. from the Department of Human Development and Family Studies, Cornell University, and an M.S.W. from the University of Syracuse. His experience includes clinical practice, administration, and university teaching. He currently teaches social work research and interpersonal relations. His research interests include interpersonal communication and conflict resolution.

PETER J. STEIN is Associate Profesor of Sociology at William Paterson College and holds a Ph.D. in sociology from Princeton University. He is the author of five books, including most recently *Single Life: Unmarried Adults in Social Context* (1981) and *Sociology* (second edition, 1985, with Beth Hess and Elizabeth Markson). He has appeared on ABC, CBS, and NBC-TV as a commentator on single life.

MARVIN B. SUSSMAN is currently the Unidel Professor of Human Behavior, College of Human Resources, University of Delaware. He holds joint appointments in the Department of Sociology and the College of Urban Affairs and Public Policy. He is a fellow of many professional organizations, including the Sociological Research Association, and has been awarded the 1980 Ernest W. Burgess Award of the National Council on Family Relations, a lifelong membership for services to the Groves Conference on Marriage and the Family in 1981, and election to the prestigious academy of Groves for scholarly contributions to the field in 1983. In addition to being editor of *Marriage & Family Review,* he served as coeditor of the *Journal of Marriage and Family Therapy* and is an advisory editorial board member of the *Journal of Family History*. He has authored, coauthored, edited, or coedited over 250 books, chapters, and articles dealing with the family, community, rehabilitation, organizations, sociology of medicine, and aging.

GAIL ANN THOEN is currently a postdoctoral fellow in the Department of Psychiatry at the University of Minnesota Hospital, where she is on sabbatical leave from her professional duties in the Department of Social Behavioral Sciences. She has a Ph.D. in family studies and is a licensed consulting psychologist in private practice, specializing in fertility counseling. Her research, clinical, and teaching activities have focused on understanding the intra- and interpersonal interface between alternative lifestyles and compromising society.

MARY JANE S. VAN METER is Assistant Professor at Wayne State University in the Department of Family and Consumer Resources. She holds undergraduate and graduate degrees in home economics and a Ph.D. in human ecology from Michigan State University. She has conducted research on married college women and at the present time is Principal Investigator of the Parents and Children Together (PACT) project, a family-based service program with families of abuse and neglect.

JAMES WALTERS, Professor and Head, Department of Child and Family Development, the University of Georgia, is Past President of the National Council on Family Relations, former Editor of *The Family Coordinator* and *Family Relations*, and coauthor of *Relationships in Marriage and the Family* and more than sixty other professional publications. A recipient of the Osborne Award, presented annually to the Outstanding Teacher of the Year in Family Relations by the National Council on Family Relations, he was named a Distinguished Alumnus of Florida State University in 1980. In 1984 he received the Josiah Meigs Award for Distinguished Teaching at the University of Georgia.

ROBERT N. WHITEHURST is Professor of Sociology at the University of Windsor, Ontario. He holds master's and Ph.D. degrees from Purdue University and is involved in research on changing relationships involving intimacy, sexuality, and marriage. One of his research interests has been the study of nontraditional forms of relationships; currently he is studying changing role perceptions of the sexes, involving such disparate problems as asking for sex from the female viewpoint and the perceived readiness of males to adapt to househusband roles.